Truth Seekers

Truth Seekers

*Voices of Peace and Nonviolence
from Gandhi to Pope Francis*

Edited with introductions
and commentary by

David Cortright

ORBIS BOOKS
Maryknoll, New York 10545

ORBIS BOOKS
Maryknoll, New York 10545

Founded in 1970, Orbis Books endeavors to publish works that enlighten the mind, nourish the spirit, and challenge the conscience. The publishing arm of the Maryknoll Fathers and Brothers, Orbis seeks to explore the global dimensions of the Christian faith and mission, to invite dialogue with diverse cultures and religious traditions, and to serve the cause of reconciliation and peace. The books published reflect the views of their authors and do not represent the official position of the Maryknoll Society. To learn more about Maryknoll and Orbis Books, please visit our website at www.orbisbooks.com.

Copyright © 2020 by David Cortright

Published by Orbis Books, Box 302, Maryknoll, NY 10545-0302.

All rights reserved.

The acknowledgments on pages xvi–xviii represent an extension of this copyright page.

No part of this publication may be reproduced or transmitted in any form or by any means, electronic or mechanical, including photocopying, recording, or any information storage or retrieval system, without prior permission in writing from the publisher.

Queries regarding rights and permissions should be addressed to: Orbis Books, P.O. Box 302, Maryknoll, NY 10545-0302.

Manufactured in the United States of America

Library of Congress Cataloging-in-Publication Data

Names: Cortright, David, 1946– editor.
Title: Truth seekers : voices of peace and nonviolence from Gandhi to Pope Francis / edited with introductions and commentary by David Cortright.
Description: Maryknoll : Orbis Books, 2020. | Includes bibliographical references and index. | Summary: "Readings on the theory and practice of nonviolence, from Gandhi, King, and other contemporary voices (including Pope Francis, Nelson Mandela, and many more)" — Provided by publisher.
Identifiers: LCCN 2019031324 (print) | LCCN 2019031325 (ebook) | ISBN 9781626983564 (paperback) | ISBN 9781608338214 (ebook)
Subjects: LCSH: Pacifists—Biography. | Peace. | Nonviolence.
Classification: LCC JZ5540 .T78 2020 (print) | LCC JZ5540 (ebook) | DDC 303.6/10922—dc23
LC record available at https://lccn.loc.gov/2019031324
LC ebook record available at https://lccn.loc.gov/2019031325

Contents

Introduction: The Resistance ix

1. **Gandhi the Pioneer** 1
   The Meaning of Nonviolence 4
   A Power over War 7
   Non-Harm 10
   Defining Satyagraha 12
   For the Strong 16
   Religion and Political Action 17
   Living for Truth 21

2. **Martin Luther King Jr.:**
   The American Gandhi 22
   Loving Our Enemies 24
   The Six Elements of Nonviolence 31
   Ends and Means 34
   "Letter from a Birmingham Jail" 36
   On Power 45
   "Beyond Vietnam": A Time to Break Silence 47

3. **Pacifism and Nonviolent Action** 54
   Cesar Chavez (1927–1993) 56
   Impressions of Gandhi 57
   Homage to Dr. King 60
   Dolores Huerta 63
   Dorothy Day (1897–1980) 66
   For a Vital Religion 66
   Conversion to Catholicism 68
   In Solidarity with Workers 69
   Pacifism Against War 71

A. J. Muste (1985–1967) 75
   Nonviolence in an Aggressive World 75
   On the Gandhi Movement 79
   Ending War 82
Albert Camus (1913–1960) 85

4. Women's Voices 89
Barbara Deming (1917–1984) 91
   "On Revolution and Equilibrium" 93
   "On the Necessity to Liberate Minds" 101
bell hooks 107
Sara Ruddick (1935–2011) 114

5. Strategy and Nonviolent Action 120
Gene Sharp (1928–2018) 122
   The Strategy of Nonviolent Action 123
   Tactics and Methods 126
   Power and Obedience 128
   Undermining Pillars of Power 130
   Facing Repression 132
Erica Chenoweth and Maria J. Stephan 135
   Why Civil Resistance Works 136
   Proving Dr. King Right 138

6. Africa Rising 146
Nelson Mandela (1918–2013) 147
   Message to the Satyagraha *Centenary
      Conference, New Delhi* 150
   Global Peace 151
   Upon Accepting the Africa Peace Award 152
   Upon Accepting the Nobel Peace Prize 154
Desmond Tutu 157
   No Peace without Justice 158
   Christians as Peacemakers 159
   The Costs of Our Calling 160
Wangari Maathai (1940–2011) 162
   Development, Democracy, and Peace 165

Contents • vii

7. The Struggle for Palestine and Israel 168
    Jean Zaru 169
    Mubarak Awad................................... 174
    Youth Against Settlements 181
    Julia Chaitin.................................... 187
    Ilan Baruch..................................... 192
    Soldiers of Yesh G'vul 194

8. Religious Sources of Peacemaking............. 198
    Abraham Joshua Heschel (1907–1972)..............200
    Lynn Gottlieb 203
        The Practice of Shalom 204
        Interpreting a Torah of Nonviolence............206
        Quotes from Scripture 207
    Leonardo Boff...................................207
    Jim Wallis...................................... 213
    William J. Barber II............................. 216
    Pope Francis................................... 219
        Nonviolence: A Style of Politics for Peace........ 221
    John Paul II (1920–2005) 226
    Maulana Wahiduddin Khan 229
        Islam Is Peace................................ 231
        War and Peace 232
        Climate of Peace 234
    Abdul Ghaffar Khan (1890–1988)................. 235
        Violence or Nonviolence 237
        The Servants of God..........................238
        With Gandhi 239
        On Revolution............................... 241

Conclusion...243

Index..247

Introduction
The Resistance

In an age of fake news and alternative facts, with the rise of reactionary populism in the United States and other countries, it is more urgent than ever that we cling firmly to truth. Democracy depends upon free access to information, reasoned debate, and the negotiation and reconciliation of differences to achieve agreement. These approaches are sorely lacking in official Washington today, where political discourse is shaped more by ideology than evidence, warped by irrational fears and prejudice toward immigrants and those of a different color, religion, or national origin. Although people today are more educated than ever and through the Internet have access to vast stores of information, genuine understanding remains elusive. We are inundated with misinformation, as political leaders spout lies that are meant to obfuscate and confuse rather than shed light.[1]

In this era of increasing polarization, we have become more narrow-minded and intolerant of others. Facebook and social media platforms permit the spread of anonymous and unverified claims that distort our thinking. They enable us to create self-defined bubbles and echo chambers that affirm preexisting convictions and shield us from inconvenient facts. Our knowledge becomes particular rather than comprehensive, technical rather than scientific. Our biases and preconceptions are reinforced,

---

[1] Glenn Kessler, Salvador Rizzo, and Meg Kelly, "President Trump Made More Than 10,000 False or Misleading Claims," *Washington Post*, April 29, 2019.

and our minds are closed to evidence that might challenge our assumptions. In this new reality, the quest for truth becomes more indispensable than ever, and is necessary for our survival.

Gandhi made the search for truth the central focus of his life and core principle of his philosophy of active nonviolence. He titled his autobiography *The Story of My Experiments with Truth*. The very purpose of life, he said, is to pursue truth. Those who are religious believe that God is truth. Reason is the attempt to understand truth through intelligence and logical analysis. As no one can have complete knowledge of all reality, different interpretations of truth always exist and may lead to conflict. Our perceptions of what is true are shaped by patterns of power and authority and by the socioeconomic and cultural context in which we live. Learning how to resolve inevitable differences without violence is the enduring challenge of human society and is the central focus of peace studies.

Oppression and human suffering are based on ignorance and denial of truth. The shibboleths that undergird injustice and violence are many: people of a different race are less human, domination over others is for their benefit, war is the answer to terrorism, and so on. In rejecting these deceits, we speak truth to power, as the Quakers say, but always through nonviolent means and humble recognition of the limits of human understanding. Because we can never know absolute truth, we have no authority to impose our moral values on another by physical force. Only through nonviolent means, through the contestation of ideas and the demonstration of moral commitment, can we come closer to the truth, striving constantly toward higher synthesis and greater understanding.

The readings in this volume examine the dilemmas of searching for truth and using nonviolent means to overcome violence and oppression. Each author addresses particular issues and challenges, but all arrive at a common conclusion about the importance of nonviolence as the means for achieving change. Martin Luther King Jr. applied Gandhian methods in the struggle against racial segregation in the United States and said that "nonviolent resistance is the most potent weapon available to oppressed people in the struggle for freedom."[2] Writer and activist Barbara Deming wrote in the 1960s of the need for more forceful nonviolent defiance of war and oppression. She used the image of two hands: one firmly resisting injustice, the other calmly reassuring and refusing to harm the adversary, creating the possibility for accommodation and escape from the condition of mutual enmity.[3] Feminist writer bell hooks connected the struggle against sexism to the larger goal of ending violence and all forms of domination, "reorganizing society so that the self-development of people can take precedence over imperialism, economic expansion, and material desires."[4] Pope Francis has linked violence to the marginalization of the poor and the exploitation of the environment. He calls us to be in solidarity with the *miserando*, the lowly who are "mired in desperate and degrading poverty, with no way out, while others . . . [are] vainly showing off their supposed superiority and leaving behind so much waste that, if it were the case everywhere, would destroy the planet."[5] Help for the poor, John Paul II tell us, comes from the rights of labor and "nonviolent commitments of people" refusing to accept oppression and lies. In these and all the writings in this volume, we see a consistent commitment to seeking truth and overcoming injustice, and achieving change through peaceful means.

Some may think it naïve to produce a work on nonviolence and pacifism at a time of xenophobic nationalism and right-wing politics, in a world threatened by civil war, terrorism, and

---

[2] Martin Luther King Jr., "My Trip to the Land of Gandhi," in *A Testament of Hope: The Essential Writings and Speeches of Martin Luther King Jr.*, ed. James M. Washington (San Francisco: Harper & Row, 1986), 25.

[3] Barbara Deming, "On Revolution and Equilibrium," in *Revolution and Equilibrium* (New York: Grossman Publishers, 1971), 203–4.

[4] bell hooks, *Feminist Theory: From Margin to Center*, 2nd ed. (Cambridge, MA: South End Press, 2000), 26.

[5] Pope Francis, *Laudato Si: On Care for Our Common Home*, Encyclical Letter (Huntington, IN: Our Sunday Visitor Publishing Division, 2015), 62–63, ¶91.

nuclear proliferation. Civil conflicts and wars (the latter defined as a conflict with a thousand or more deaths per year) remain widespread, the bloodiest in Syria and Afghanistan.[6] Terrorist attacks continue to take thousands of lives annually.[7] Nuclear dangers exist in North Korea and have grown in Pakistan and India. Tensions with Russia and Iran have worsened as Washington tears up nuclear agreements and rebuilds its nuclear arsenal. No wonder Pope Francis spoke of "piecemeal" world war.[8] Yet it is precisely in such times of increased insecurity and danger that the quest for peace and nonviolence becomes all the more urgent. For inspiration we can turn to the masters of the past, and the most significant voices of today, as we seek to defend the essential truths of nonviolence and peace.

Part of the war we seek to end is happening here at home in our streets, schools, and places of worship, where gun violence destroys thousands of lives a year. The students of Marjory Stoneman Douglas High School in Parkland, Florida, suffered this violence firsthand. In response, they began the March for Our Lives and issued an impassioned plea for action against gun violence. They see themselves as standing on the shoulders of those who resisted war before. Matt Deitsch, class of 2016, wrote this:

> Organizing put an end to the war in Vietnam. Young people organized to stop their friends from coming back in body bags. Today, the war is on our soil, with our weapons, taking our lives. It will take young people organizing to end this war too.

---

[6] Therése Peterssen and Kristine Eck, "Organized Violence, 1989–2017," *Journal of Peace Research* 55, no. 4 (July 2018): 535–47.

[7] National Consortium for the Study of Terrorism and Responses to Terrorism. *Annex of Statistical Information: Country Reports on Terrorism 2016*. Final report prepared for the U.S. Department of State (College Park, MD: START, 2017), https://www.state.gov.

[8] BBC News, "Pope Francis Warns on 'Piecemeal World War III,'" September 13, 2014, http://www.bbc.com.

These students bring an urgent new voice and social standing to the movement against violence.[9] They reinforce the campaigns of Black Lives Matter and other groups against police abuse and the killing of unarmed people of color.

In the United States and other countries, social resistance to the policies of bigotry and ignorance has increased.[10] Moments of political crisis can become times of social mobilization. The Women's March at the time of Trump's inauguration was an unprecedented moment of protest, as more than 4 million people across the country, seven hundred thousand in Washington, DC, spoke out for human decency. It was the largest single day of protest in American history.[11] Organizations working for social justice, women's rights, the environment, and peace have experienced a surge of membership and support. These movements have many agendas but they share a common commitment to preventing violence, upholding truth, and protecting the vulnerable.

Those of us who participate in this resistance are following in the footsteps of Gandhi, King, and so many others. Our success depends on maintaining nonviolent discipline and acting in the spirit of love that is appropriate to our purpose, seeking to attract ever larger numbers to the cause of defending human freedom and dignity. My hope is that the reflections and insights contained in these readings will encourage continued commitment toward that end.

---

[9] Matt Deitsch, "Mobilizing Countrywide and the Future of the Movement: April and Beyond," in *Glimmer of Hope: How Tragedy Sparked a Movement*, by the Founders of March for Our Lives (New York: Razorbill Dutton, 2018), 204.

[10] David S. Meyer and Sidney Tarrow, eds., *The Resistance: The Dawn of the Anti-Trump Opposition Movement* (New York: Oxford University Press, 2018).

[11] Conor Friedersdorf, "The Significance of Millions in the Streets," *The Atlantic*, January 23, 2017, https://www.theatlantic.com.

An Outline of the Book

In this volume I present excerpts from the writings of some of the world's most significant nonviolent leaders and strategists. The selection of readings is eclectic and idiosyncratic, reflecting my interest in nonviolence not only as a set of moral commitments but as a guide to effective action for change. The volume is intended for engaged scholars who seek insights on nonviolence from primary sources, and active practitioners who hope to learn from lived experience.

My interest in nonviolence stems from a lifetime of activism for peace, beginning with opposition to the Vietnam War as an active-duty soldier and continuing over the decades in numerous campaigns against war and nuclear weapons, and today in supporting implementation of the peace agreement in Colombia. I have participated over the years in many peace and disarmament movements, and also in campaigns for the environment, human rights, and racial justice.

My perspectives on nonviolence are informed by writers past and present, many of them excerpted here, both thinkers and doers: Mohandas Gandhi, Martin Luther King Jr., Barbara Deming, Cesar Chavez, Dorothy Day, A. J. Muste, Desmond Tutu, Leonardo Boff, Abdul Ghaffar Khan, and many others. Some led historic nonviolent campaigns for social justice. Others are scholars and analysts, including Erica Chenoweth and Maria J. Stephan with their cutting-edge empirical research, and Gene Sharp with his study of nonviolent methods and strategy. The final section of the volume includes religious perspectives from Judaism, Christianity, and Islam.

My purpose in offering these selections is to examine both the principles and practices of nonviolence. I have a scholarly interest in peace research, but that curiosity is shaped by a desire to apply the acquired knowledge in practical movements for change. In this sense, scholarship and practice are interrelated and mutually reinforcing. Theory guides practice, and practice informs theory. Knowledge and social action are in constant dialectic to forge new meaning and a deeper understanding of why and how nonviolence works.

The readings reflect the evolution of knowledge through distinct historical experiences and cultural contexts. They show refinement and expansion over the years in how we understand peace and the principles of nonviolence. The concept of peace has broadened to incorporate issues related to economic and social justice, and more recently issues of gender, governance, and the environment.

The works range from early pieces by Gandhi more than a hundred years ago to important writings of today. They are classic not only in their enduring value but in their relevance for now. The authors are from nearly every continent and draw lessons from an array of historical experiences and movements for change: the freedom struggle of India, the civil rights movement in the United States, the global campaign against apartheid in South Africa, the struggle for human rights in Latin America, and the movement to free Palestine. The readings address the theory and practice of nonviolence, the methods and strategy of social action, and the religious roots of nonviolence in Judaism, Christianity, and Islam.

A special word about gendered language. Many of the writings cited here were authored before the recent shift in English language usage, long overdue, toward gender-neutral pronouns and nouns. Most of the authors, including Deming, use "man" to represent humankind, a usage that is no longer acceptable to many readers. In the early phases of excerpting and editing these writings, I attempted to change the noun and pronoun usage of Gandhi, King, Muste, and others to gender-neutral forms, but the resulting edited text was awkward and difficult to read, and in some cases lost the eloquence and majesty of important writings, such as King's "Letter from a Birmingham Jail." To preserve the meaning of the authors and the authenticity of their work, therefore, I have retained the language usage of the originals in the excerpts.

xvi • *Introduction*

Acknowledgments

I gratefully acknowledge the following sources for permission to publish the excerpts included in this volume:

The Writers House, New York, for permission to publish excerpts from the work of Dr. Martin Luther King Jr., including "Loving Our Enemies," a portion of Martin Luther King Jr., *Stride Toward Freedom Stride Toward Freedom: The Montgomery Story* (New York: Harper & Row, 1958), "Letter from a Birmingham Jail," "Beyond Vietnam," and other speeches.

University of Minnesota Press, for permission to publish an excerpt from Jacques E. Levy, *Cesar Chavez: Autobiography of La Causa* (Minneapolis: University of Minnesota Press, 2007).

University of New Mexico Press, for permission to publish an excerpt from *A Dolores Huerta Reader*, edited with an introduction by Mario T. Garcia (Albuquerque: University of New Mexico Press, 2008).

Orbis Books, for permission to publish excerpts from *Dorothy Day, Selected Writings*, ed. Robert Ellsberg (Maryknoll, New York: Orbis Books, 1983, 1992).

Harper Collins, for permission to publish excerpts from A.J. Muste, *Nonviolence in an Aggressive World* (New York: Harper & Brothers, 1940).

Simon and Schuster, for permission to publish excerpts from *The Essays of A.J. Muste*, ed. Nat Hentoff (New York: A Clarion Book, Simon and Schuster, 1967).

Beacon Press, for permission to publish excerpts from Sara Ruddick, *Maternal Thinking, With a New Preface: Toward a Politics of Peace* (Boston: Beacon Press, 1995).

Porter Sargent Publishers and Gene Sharp, for permission to publish excerpts from Gene Sharp, *Waging Nonviolent Struggle: 20th Century Practice and 21st Century Potential* (Boston: Extending Horizons Books, Porter Sargent Publishers, 2005).

Erica Chenoweth and Maria J. Stephan, for permission to publish excerpts from "Why Civil Resistance Works: The Strategic Logic of Nonviolent Conflict," *International Security* 33, no. 1 (2008); and "How the World Is Proving Martin Luther King Jr. Right about Nonviolence," Monkey Cage, *Washington Post*, January 18, 2016, https://www.washingtonpost.com/news/monkey-cage/wp/2016/01/18/how-the-world-is-proving-mlk-right-about-nonviolence/?utm_term=.f7a9f7b3f811.

Nelson Mandela Foundation, for permission to publish excerpts from the speeches of Nelson Mandela at http://www.mandela.gov.za/mandela_speeches/.

The Nobel Peace Prize, for permission to publish excerpts from the "Address by President Nelson Mandela on Upon Accepting the Nobel Peace Prize Award," December 10, 1993, https://www.nobelprize.org/prizes/peace/1993/mandela/26130-nelson-mandela-nobel-lecture-1993/.

Idea Architects, for permission to publish excerpts from Desmond Tutu, *The Rainbow People of God: The Making of a Peaceful Revolution*, ed. John Allen (New York: Doubleday, 1994).

The Nobel Peace Prize, for permission to publish excerpts from Wangari Maathai, "Nobel Lecture," Oslo, Norway, December 10, 2004, http://www.nobelprize.org/nobel_prizes/peace/laureates/2004/maathai-lecture-text.html.

Fortress Press, for permission to publish excerpts from Jean Zaru, *Occupied with Nonviolence: A Palestinian Woman Speaks* (Minneapolis: Fortress Press, 2008).

Mubarak Awad, for permission to publish excerpts from "Nonviolent Resistance: A Strategy for the Occupied Territories," *Journal of Palestinian Studies* 13, no. 4 (Summer 1984); and his interview in Waleed Shahid, "Lessons in Nonviolent Palestinian Resistance rrom the First Intifada: An Interview with Mubarak Awad," *In These Times*, October 26, 2015.

Youth Against Settlements in Hebron, Palestine, for permission to reprint their official statement.

Julia Chaitin, for permission to publish excerpts from "Darkness in Qassam-Land," *Washington Post*, December 31, 2008, http://www.washingtonpost.com/wp-dyn/content/article/2008/12/30/AR2008123002661.html; and "Studying and Living Conflict: Working for Peace," *Peace and Conflict: Journal of Peace Psychology* 20, no. 2 (2014).

Ilan Baruch, for permission to publish excerpts from "What Netanyahu Should Learn from the Fall of Apartheid," July 10, 2013, *Haaretz*, http://www.haaretz.com/misc/article-print-page/.premium-1.535069?trailingPath=2.169%2C2.216%2C2.218%2C.

PLS Clear, for permission to publish excerpts from *Refusnik!: Israel's Soldiers of Conscience*, compiled and edited by Peretz Kidron (London: Zed Books, 2004).

Octagon Books, for permission to publish excerpts from Abraham Joshua Heschel, *God in Search of Man: A Philosophy of Judaism* (New York: Octagon Books, 1972).

Ken Sehested and the Baptist Peace Fellowship, for permission to publish excerpts from *Peace Primer II: Quotes from Jewish Christian Islamic Scripture & Tradition*, eds. Lynn Gottlieb, Rabia Terri Harris, Ken Sehested (Charlotte, NC: Baptist Peace Fellowship of North America, 2012), http://www.bpfna.org/sm_files/ePeacePrimer.pdf.

New Society Publishers, for permission to publish excerpts from Leonardo Boff, "Active Nonviolence: The Political and Moral Power of the Poor," in *Relentless Persistence: Nonviolent Action in Latin America*, eds. Philip McManus and Gerald Schlabach (Philadelphia: New Society Publishers, 1991).

Beacon Press, for permission to publish excerpts from Reverend Dr. William J. Barber II, with Jonathan Wilson-Hartgrove, *The Third Reconstruction: How a Moral Movement is Overcoming the Politics of Division and Fear* (Boston: Beacon Press, 2016).

Jim Wallis, for permission to publish excerpts from *The Soul of Politics: A Practical and Prophetic Vision for Change* (New York: The New Press, Orbis Books, 1994).

The Vatican, for permissions to publish excerpts from *Message of His Holiness Pope Francis for the Celebration of the Fiftieth World Day of Peace; Nonviolence: A Style of Politics for Peace*

January 1, 2017, https://w2.vatican.va/content/francesco/en/messages/peace/documents/papa-francesco_20161208_messaggio-l-giornata-mondiale-pace-2017.html; and John Paul II, Holy Father, *Centesimus Annus*, Encyclical Letter … on the Hundreth Anniversary of *Rerum Novarum*, The Vatican, Rome, May 1, 1991, paragraphs 22, 23, 25, 51, 52, http://w2.vatican.va/content/john-paul-ii/en/encyclicals/documents/hf_jp-ii_enc_01051991_centesimus-annus.html#%241I.

Goodword Books, for permission to publish excerpts from Maulana Wahiduddin, *Islam and World Peace* (Chennai, India: Goodword Books, 2015).

Orient Pocket Books, for permission to publish excerpts from *An Autobiography of Badshah Kahn as narrated to K.B. Narang, My Life and Struggle* (Delhi: Hind Pocket Books/ Orient Paperbacks, 1969).

1

Gandhi the Pioneer

The study of nonviolence in the modern era begins with Mohandas K. Gandhi (1869–1948). He was the first to turn the practices of noncooperation and civil disobedience into a coherent philosophy and strategy for achieving political change on a mass scale. Prior history included many examples of nonviolent action, as Sharp documented,[1] but Gandhi more than anyone before him applied the concepts and methods of nonviolence systematically and demonstrated their effectiveness for achieving political change. He developed a revolutionary new form of social transformation that resisted racial restrictions against Asians in South Africa and achieved political independence for India. The movement he helped to lead brought down the mighty British Raj without firing a shot. His words and actions established a philosophy and model of social change that have been applied with increasing frequency and success all over the world.

Gandhi was not a scholar or eloquent orator. He wrote prolifically as a campaigner for justice (one hundred volumes in his collected works), but he never produced a comprehensive coherent work on the theory and practice of nonviolent action. Many of the excerpts included here were written for the journals

---

[1] Gene Sharp, *The Politics of Nonviolent Action*, 3 vols. (Boston: Porter Sargent, 1973).

Gandhi founded or edited to guide his action campaigns: *Indian Opinion*, founded in 1903 in Johannesburg; *Young India*, which Gandhi edited in India from 1919 to 1933; and *Harijan*, founded in India in 1933. Gandhi's early book *Satyagraha in South Africa* is perhaps the best in explaining the ideas and describing the action campaigns that shaped his pioneering method of nonviolent struggle. His autobiography is a difficult work that addresses his personal moral struggles with sexuality, meat-eating and other "sins," but it also includes some accounts of his early campaigns. A number of excellent anthologies of Gandhi's works have been produced over the years, the best of which are Raghavan Iyer's *The Essential Writings of Mahatma Gandhi* and Louis Fischer's *The Essential Gandhi: An Anthology of His Writings on His Life, Work, and Ideas*.[2]

Gandhi's commitment to pacifism and nonviolence was rooted in religious belief. He was greatly influenced by the Hindu philosophy of detachment from material wants and was shaped especially by the Jain tradition of the Gujarat region where he was born and raised. Jains believe in noninjury and follow a strict code of vegetarianism and pacifism. Gandhi studied Islam and Christianity as well and was deeply moved by the teachings of the Gospels, particularly the Sermon on the Mount and Jesus's commandment to love all, including enemies. Gandhi believed in the essential unity of all the great religious traditions, seeing them as different paths leading to the same loving and merciful God.

Gandhi wrote often of his basic philosophy, which he called *satyagraha*. The word combines the Hindi words for *satya*, truth, and *graha*, grasping or forcefulness. *Satyagraha* is the act of grasping and affirming the truth. It is "truth-force," or "soul-force," a method for fighting against injustice and oppression while remaining true to moral and religious principles.

---

[2] *The Essential Writings of Mahatma Gandhi*, edited by Raghavan Iyer (Delhi: Oxford University Press, 1990); *The Essential Gandhi: An Anthology of His Writings on His Life, Work, and Ideas*, ed. Louis Fischer (New York: Vintage Books, 1962).

Gandhi wanted a word that would convey the active and assertive dimensions of nonviolence, the need for engaged struggle to uphold truth and resist oppression. His method provided a way to fight against injustice without relying on violence and enflaming the passions of hatred and revenge that so often result from armed conflict. At a deeper level, *satyagraha* is a means of seeking and testing truth. It is a form of philosophical inquiry conducted through social struggle—the testing of different conceptions of truth through the interplay of contending social forces, achieving a synthesis of diverse interpretations through social interaction and negotiation.

Gandhi emphasized the importance of sacrifice and suffering as essential features of the nonviolent action method. Suffering is a way to dramatize the grievances of the oppressed. It also has social psychological effects. It seeks to pierce the conscience of the adversary and generate a sympathetic response from bystanders. Unearned suffering can overcome the indifference and complacency of third parties, he believed, helping to shift loyalties away from the oppressive regime toward the cause of the nonviolent challengers. It is not enough to appeal to reason, said Gandhi. "You must move the heart also."[3]

Because of this emphasis on the importance of sacrifice, Gandhi insisted upon courage and personal bravery among those who participate in the struggle. One must be prepared to accept suffering to achieve significant change. Those who wield power do not give it up lightly. Concessions from the powerful have to be won through what Frederick Douglass called "earnest struggle."[4] Nonviolent campaigns that seek significant policy

---

[3] Mohandas Gandhi, *All Men Are Brothers*, ed. Krishna Kripalani (New York: Continuum, 1980), 118.

[4] Frederick Douglass, "West India Emancipation" (1857), in *Two Speeches by Frederick Douglass; One on West India Emancipation Delivered at Canandaigua, Aug. 4th, and the Other on the Dred Scott Decision, Delivered in New York, on the Occasion of the Anniversary of the American Abolition Society, May 1857* (Rochester, NY: C. P. Dewey, 1857). Cited in John J. Ansbro, *Martin Luther King Jr.: The Making of a Mind* (Maryknoll, NY: Orbis Books, 1994), 162.

change usually face repression from their adversaries.⁵ It takes courage to stand up against such repression without weapons. Nonviolent campaigns are a kind of warfare, Gandhi often said, but they are fought without weapons. There is suffering, but it falls almost entirely on the side of the victims of oppression. This is difficult to accept, but it is often the price that must be paid to achieve justice. It takes a very special kind of personal fortitude to accept suffering and abuse without fighting back or venting hatred toward the opponent. Gandhi was fearless in his willingness to sacrifice for justice and truth, and he expected no less from his followers.

In this chapter I present core passages from Gandhi's writings on the religious, philosophical, and political dimensions of nonviolence. The excerpts address the essential principles Gandhi emphasized often in his public writings and remarks.

The Meaning of Nonviolence

Gandhi recognized "the hold that the doctrine of the sword has on the majority of mankind," and he felt it necessary to keep repeating what he called the core principles of nonviolence.⁶ This excerpt from *Young India* summarizes well the moral and pragmatic benefits of the nonviolent method:

> I am not a visionary. I claim to be a practical idealist. The religion of nonviolence is not meant merely for the *rishis*⁷ and saints. It is meant for the common people as well. Nonviolence is the law of our species as violence is the law of the brute. The spirit lies dormant in the brute and he knows no law but that of physical might. The dignity of

---

⁵ Erica Chenoweth and Maria J. Stephan, *Why Civil Resistance Works: The Strategic Logic of Nonviolent Conflict* (New York: Columbia University Press, 2011), 51.

⁶ "The Doctrine of the Sword," *Young India*, August 11, 1920, in Iyer, *Essential Writings of Mahatma Gandhi*, 237.

⁷ A *rishi* in Hinduism is considered an inspired poet, seer, or sage who is able to realize ultimate truths and eternal knowledge.

man requires obedience to a higher law—to the strength of the spirit.

I have therefore ventured to place before India the ancient law of self-sacrifice. For *satyagraha* and its offshoots, noncooperation and civil resistance, are nothing but new names for the law of suffering. The *rishis*, who discovered the law of nonviolence in the midst of violence, were greater geniuses than Newton. They were themselves greater warriors than Wellington. Having themselves known the use of arms, they realized their uselessness and taught a weary world that its salvation lay not through violence but through nonviolence.

Nonviolence in its dynamic condition means conscious suffering. It does not mean meek submission to the will of the evildoer, but it means the putting of one's whole soul against the will of the tyrant. Working under this law of our being, it is possible for a single individual to defy the whole might of an unjust empire. . . .

I am not pleading for India to practice nonviolence because it is weak. I want her to practice nonviolence being conscious of her strength and power. No training in arms is required for realization of her strength. We seem to need it because we seem to think that we are but a lump of flesh. I want India to recognize that she has a soul that cannot perish and that can rise triumphant above every physical weakness and defy the physical combination of a whole world. What is the meaning of Rama, a mere human being, with a host of monkeys, pitting himself against the insolent strength of ten-headed Ravanna surrounded in supposing safety by the raging waters on all sides of Lanka?[8] Does it not mean the conquest of physical might by spiritual strength? However, being a practical person, I do not wait till India recognizes the practicality of the spiritual life in the political world. India considers herself to be powerless and paralyzed before the machine

---

[8] Based on the story of the *Ramayana*, an ancient Indian epic poem.

guns, the tanks, and the airplanes of the English. And she takes up noncooperation out of her weakness. It must still serve the same purpose, namely, bring her delivery from the crushing weight of British injustice if a sufficient number of people practice it.

I isolate this noncooperation from Sinn Feinism,[9] for, it is so conceived as to be incapable of being offered side by side with violence. But I invite even the school of violence to give this peaceful noncooperation a trial. It will not fail through its inherent weakness. It may fail because of poverty of response. Then will be the time for real danger. The high-souled people, who are unable to suffer national humiliation any longer, will want to vent their wrath. They will take to violence. So far as I know, they must perish without delivering themselves or their country from the wrong. If India takes up the doctrine of the sword, she may gain momentary victory. Then India will cease to be the pride of my heart. I am wedded to India because I owe my all to her. I believe absolutely that she has a mission for the world. She is not to copy Europe blindly. India's acceptance of the doctrine of the sword will be the hour of my trial. I hope I shall not be found wanting. My religion has no geographical limits. If I have a living faith in it, it will transcend my love for India herself. My life is dedicated to service of India through the religion of nonviolence which I believe to be the root of Hinduism.[10]

They say, "Means are after all [just] means." I would say, "means are after all everything." As the means, so the end. Violent means will give violent *Swaraj* (freedom). . . . There is no wall of separation between means and end. . . . I have been endeavoring to keep the country to means that are purely peaceful and legitimate.[11]

---

[9] A reference to the Irish Republican revolutionary movement, which was engaged in armed struggle at the time.

[10] "The Doctrine of the Sword," *Young India*, August 11, 1920, in Iyer, *Essential Writings of Mahatma Gandhi*, 237–39.

[11] *Young India*, July 17, 1924; in Fischer, *Essential Gandhi*, 199.

... If we take care of the means we are bound to reach the end sooner or later.[12]

A Power over War

In the following excerpt, Gandhi continues the argument for nonviolence and reflects upon efforts to outlaw war in the aftermath of World War I.

Nonviolence is the greatest force man has been endowed with. Truth is the only goal he has. For God is none other than Truth. But Truth cannot be, never will be, reached except through nonviolence.

That which distinguishes man from all other animals is his capacity to be nonviolent. And he fulfills his mission only to the extent that he is nonviolent and no more. He has no doubt many other gifts. But if they do not subserve the main purpose—the development of the spirit of nonviolence in him—they but drag him down lower than the brute, a status from which he has only just emerged.

The cry for peace will be a cry in the wilderness, so long as the spirit of nonviolence does not dominate millions of men and women.

An armed conflict between nations horrifies us. But the economic war is no better than an armed conflict. This is like a surgical operation. An economic war is prolonged torture. And its ravages are no less terrible than those depicted in the literature on war properly so-called. We think nothing of the other because we are used to its deadly effects.

Many of us in India shudder to see blood spilled. Many of us resent cow-slaughter, but we think nothing of the slow torture through which by our greed we put our people and cattle. But because we are used to this lingering death, we think no more about it.

---

[12] M. K. Gandhi, *From Yeravda Mandir* (Ahmedabad: Navajivan Press, 1937), chs. 3, 13.

The movement against war is sound. I pray for its success. But I cannot help the gnawing fear that the movement will fail, if it does not touch the root of all evil—man's greed.

Will America, England, and the other great nations of the West continue to exploit the so-called weaker or uncivilized races and hope to attain peace that the whole world is pining for? Or will Americans continue to prey upon one another, have commercial rivalries, and yet expect to dictate peace to the world?

Not till the spirit is changed can the form be altered. The form is merely an expression of the spirit within. We may succeed in seemingly altering the form but the alteration will be a mere make-believe if the spirit within remains unalterable. A whited sepulchre still conceals beneath it the rotting flesh and bone.

Far be it from me to discount or underrate the great effort that is being made in the West to kill the war spirit. Mine is merely a word of caution as from a fellow seeker who has been striving in his own humble manner after the same thing, maybe in a different way, no doubt on a much smaller scale. But if the experiment demonstrably succeeds on the smaller field, and, if those who are working on the larger field have not overtaken me, it will at least pave the way for a smaller experiment on a large field.

I observe in the limited field in which I find myself that unless I can reach the hearts of men and women, I am able to do nothing. I observe further that so long as the spirit of hate persists in some shape or other, it is impossible to establish peace or to gain our freedom by peaceful effort. We cannot love one another, if we hate Englishman. You cannot love the Japanese and hate Englishman. We must either let the Law of Love rule us through and through or not at all. Love among ourselves based on hatred of others breaks down under the slightest pressure. The fact is such love is never real love. It is an armed peace. And so it will be in this great movement in the West against war. War will only be stopped when the conscience of humankind has become sufficiently elevated to recognize the undisputed supremacy of the Law of Love in all the walks of life. Some say this will never come to pass. I shall retain the faith till the end of my earthly existence that it shall come to pass.[13]

Violence on the part of the masses will never remove the disease. Anyway, up to now experience shows that the success of violence has been short-lived. It has led to greater violence. What has been tried hitherto has been a variety of violence and artificial checks dependent mainly upon the will of the violent. At the crucial moment these checks have naturally broken down. It seems to me, therefore, that sooner or later, the European masses have to take to nonviolence if they are to find their deliverance. That there is no hope of their taking to it in a body and at once does not baffle me. A few thousand years are but a speck in the vast time circle. Someone has to make a beginning with a faith that will not flinch. I doubt not that the masses, even of Europe, will respond, but what is more emergent in point of time is not so much a large experiment in nonviolence as a precise grasp of the meaning of deliverance.

From what will the masses be delivered? It will not do to have a vague generalization and to answer "from exploitation and degradation." Is not the answer to this that they want to occupy the status that capital does today? If so, it can be attained only by violence. But if they want to shun the evils of capital, in other words, if they would revise the viewpoint of capital, they would strive to attain a more just distribution of the products of labor. This immediately takes us to contentment and simplicity, voluntarily adopted. Under the new outlook multiplicity of material wants will not be the aim of life; the aim will be rather their restriction consistently with comfort. We shall cease to think of getting what we can, but we shall decline to receive what all cannot get.

---

[13] "Nonviolence—The Greatest Force," *The Hindu*, November 8, 1926, in Iyer, *Essential Writings of Mahatma Gandhi*, 240–42.

It occurs to me that it ought not to be difficult to make a successful appeal to the masses of Europe in terms of economics, and a fairly successful working of such an experiment must lead to immense and unconscious spiritual results. I do not believe that the spiritual law works on a field of its own. On the contrary, it expresses itself only through the ordinary activities of life. It thus affects the economic, social, and the political fields. If the masses of Europe can be persuaded to adopt the view I have suggested, it will be found that violence will be wholly unnecessary to attain the aim and they can easily come to their own by following out the obvious corollaries of nonviolence.[14]

Non-Harm

At the core of Gandhi's philosophy of nonviolence is the principle of *ahimsa*, or non-harm. This passage from a 1917 article captures the concept well:

Literally speaking, *ahimsa* means non-killing. But to me it has a world of meaning and takes me into realms much higher, infinitely higher, than the realm to which I would go, if I merely understood by *ahimsa* non-killing. *Ahimsa* really means that you may not offend anybody, you may not harbor an uncharitable thought even in connection with one who may consider himself to be your enemy. Pray notice the guarded nature of this thought; I do not say "whom you consider to be your enemy," but "who may consider himself to be your enemy." For one who follows the doctrine of *ahimsa*, there is no room for an enemy; one denies the existence of an enemy. But there are people who consider themselves to be our enemies, and we cannot help that circumstance. So, it is held that we may not harbor an evil thought even

---

[14] "What of the West," *Young India*, September 3, 1925, in Iyer, *Essential Writings of Mahatma Gandhi*, 106–7.

in connection with such persons. If we return blow for blow, we depart from the doctrine of *ahimsa*. But I go further. If we resent a friend's action or the so-called enemy's action, we still fall short of this doctrine. But when I say we should not resent, I do not say that we should acquiesce; but by resenting I mean wishing that some harm should be done to the enemy, or that he should be put out of the way, not even by any action of ours, but by the action of somebody else, or, say, by Divine agency. If we harbor even this thought, we depart from this doctrine of *ahimsa*. Those who join the Ashram have to literally accept that meaning. That does not mean that we practice that doctrine in its entirety. Far from it.

It is an ideal which we have to reach, and it is an ideal to be reached even at this very moment, if we are capable of doing so. But it is not a proposition in geometry to be learned by heart: it is not even like solving difficult problems in higher mathematics; it is infinitely more difficult than solving those problems. Many of you have burnt the midnight oil in solving those problems. If you want to follow out this doctrine, you will have to do much more than burn the midnight oil. You'll have to pass many a sleepless night, and go through many a mental torture and agony before you can reach, before you can even be within measurable distance of this goal. It is the goal, and nothing less than that, you and I have to reach if we want to understand what a religious life means. I will not say much more on this doctrine than this: that a person who believes in the efficacy of this doctrine finds in the ultimate stage, when he is about to reach the goal, not that he wants the whole world at his feet, but it must be so. If you express your love—*ahimsa*—in such a manner that it impresses itself indelibly upon your so-called enemy, he must return that love. Another thought which comes out of this is that, under this rule, there is no room for organized assassinations, and there is no room for murders even openly committed, and there is no room for any violence even for the sake of your country, and even for guarding the honor of precious ones that may be under your charge. After all, that would be a poor defense of honor.

This doctrine of *ahimsa* tells us that we may guard the honor of those who are under our charge by delivering ourselves into the hands of the man who would commit the sacrilege. And that requires far greater physical and mental courage than the delivering of blows. You may have some degree of physical power—I do not say courage—and you may use that power. But after that is expended, what happens? The other man is filled with wrath and indignation, and you have made him more angry by matching your violence against his; and when he has done you to death, the rest of the violence is delivered against your charge. But if you do not retaliate, but stand your ground, between your charge and the opponent, simply receiving the blows without retaliating, what happens? I give you my promise that the whole of the violence will be expended on you, and your charge will be left unscathed. Under this plan of life, there is no conception of patriotism which justifies such wars as you witness today in Europe.[15]

Defining *Satyagraha*

Gandhi's commitment to the principles of love and non-harm were at the core of his action method for fighting injustice. In the following passage, also from 1917, he dispels the notion that nonviolence is passive and gives precise definition to the term *satyagraha*, differentiating it from passivity and armed violence.

> The force denoted by the term "passive resistance" . . . is not very accurately described either by the original English phrase or by its Hindi rendering. Its correct description is "satyagraha." *Satyagraha* was born in South Africa in 1908.

---

[15] "Speech on '*Ashram* Vows' at the YMCA, Madras," *Indian Review*, February 1916, in Iyer, *Essential Writings of Mahatma Gandhi*, 284–86.

There was no word in any Indian language then denoting the power which our compatriots in South Africa invoked for the redress of their grievances. There was an English equivalent, namely, "passive resistance," and we carried on with it. However, the need for a word to describe this unique power came to be increasingly felt, and it was decided to award a prize to anyone who could think of an appropriate term. A Gujarati-speaking gentleman submitted the word "*satyagraha*," and it was adjudged the best.

"Passive resistance" conveyed the idea of the Suffragette Movement in England. Burning of houses by these women was called "passive resistance" and so also their fasting in prison. All such acts might very well be "passive resistance" but they were not "*satyagraha*." It is said of "passive resistance" that it is the weapon of the weak, but the power which is the subject of this article can be used only by the strong. This power is not "passive" resistance; indeed it calls for intense activity. The movement in South Africa was not passive but active. The Indians of South Africa believed that Truth was their object, that Truth ever triumphs, and that with this definition of purpose they persistently held on to Truth. They put up with all the suffering that this persistence implied. With the conviction that Truth is not to be renounced even unto death, they shed the fear of death. In the cause of Truth, the prison was a palace to them and its doors the gateway to freedom.

Satyagraha is not physical force. A *satyagrahi*[16] does not inflict pain on the adversary; he does not seek his destruction. A *satyagrahi* never resorts to firearms. In the use of *satyagraha* there is no ill-will whatever.

Satyagraha is pure soul-force. Truth is the very substance of the soul. This is why this force is called *satyagraha*. The soul is informed with knowledge. In it burns the flame of love. If someone gives us pain through ignorance, we shall win him through love. "Nonviolence is the supreme

---

[16] One who performs *satyagraha*.

dharma" is the proof of this power of love. Nonviolence is a dormant state. In the waking state, it is love. Ruled by love, the world goes on. In English there is a saying, "Might is Right." Then there is the doctrine of the survival of the fittest. Both these ideas are contradictory to the above principle. Neither is wholly true. If ill-will were the chief motive force, the world would have been destroyed long ago; and neither would I have had the opportunity to write this article nor would the hopes of the readers be fulfilled. We are alive solely because of love. We are all ourselves the proof of this. Deluded by modern Western civilization, we have forgotten our ancient civilization and worship the might of arms.

We forget the principle of nonviolence, which is the essence of all religions. The doctrine of arms stands for irreligion. It is due to the sway of that doctrine that a sanguinary war is raging in Europe.

In India also we find the worship of arms. We see it even in that great work of Tulsidas.[17] But it is seen in all the books that soul-force is the supreme power.

Rama stands for the soul and Ravana for the non-soul. The immense physical might of Ravana is as nothing compared to the soul force of Rama. Ravana's ten heads are as straw to Rama. Rama is a *yogi*, he has conquered self and pride. He is "placid equally in affluence and adversity," he has "neither attachment, nor greed nor the intoxication of status." This represents the ultimate in *satyagraha*. The banner of *satyagraha* can fly in the Indian sky and it is our duty to raise it. If we take recourse to *satyagraha*, we can conquer our conquerors the English, make them bow before our tremendous soul-force, and the issue will be of benefit to the whole world.

It is certain that India cannot rival Britain or Europe in force of arms. The British worship the war-god and they can all of them become, as they are becoming, bearers of arms.

---

[17] Goswami Tulsidas (1532–1623) was a Hindu poet-saint, reformer, and philosopher who wrote popular books.

... A *satyagrahi* does not fear for his body, does not give up what is Truth; the word "defeat" is not to be found in his dictionary, he does not wish for the destruction of his antagonist, he does not vent anger on him; but has only compassion for him.

A *satyagrahi* does not wait for others, but throws himself into the fray, relying entirely on his own resources. He trusts that when the time comes, others will do likewise. His practice is his precept. Like air, *satyagraha* is all-pervading. It is infectious, which means that all people—big and small, men and women—can become *satyagrahis*. No one is kept out from the army of *satyagrahis*. A *satyagrahi* cannot perpetuate tyranny on anyone; he is not subdued through application of physical force; he does not strike at anyone. Just as anyone can resort to *satyagraha*, it can be resorted to in almost any situation.

People demand historical evidence in support of *satyagraha*. History is for the most part a record of armed activities. Natural activities find very little mention in it. Only uncommon activities strike us with wonder. *Satyagraha* has been used always and in all situations. The father and the son, the man and wife are perpetually resorting to *satyagraha*, one towards the other. When a father gets angry and punishes the son, the son does not hit back with a weapon, he conquers his father's anger by submitting to him. The son refuses to be subdued by the unjust rule of his father but he puts up with the punishment that he may incur through disobeying the unjust father. We can similarly free ourselves of the unjust rule of the Government by defying the unjust rule and accepting the punishments that go with it. We do not bear malice towards the Government. When we set its fears at rest, when we do not desire to make armed assaults on the administrators, nor to unseat them from power, but only to get rid of their injustice, they will at once be subdued to our will.

The question is asked why we should call any rule unjust. In saying so, we ourselves assume the function of a judge.

It is true. But in this world, we always have to act as judges for ourselves. That is why the *satyagrahi* does not strike the adversary with arms. If he has Truth on his side, he will win, and if his thought is faulty, he will suffer the consequences of the fault.[18]

For the Strong

In these two short writings, Gandhi describes the power of *satyagraha*.

Of the many accomplishments that passive resisters have to possess, tenacity is by no means the least important. They may find their ranks becoming daily thinned under a hot fire. True passive resisters must still stand their ground. They may be reviled by their own and they must cling to their faith as a child clings to its mother's breast. They may be misunderstood, and they must be content to labor under misrepresentation. They may be put to inconceivable personal inconvenience and they must suffer it patiently and cheerfully. . . . They cannot—must not—lose faith in themselves or in their mission because they may be a minority. Indeed, all reform has been brought about by the action of minorities in all countries and under all climes. Majorities simply follow minorities.[19]

Even the most despotic government cannot stand except for the consent of the governed which . . . is often forcibly procured. . . . Immediately the subject ceases to fear the despotic force, the power is gone.[20]

If a father does injustice it is the duty of his children to leave the parental roof. If the headmaster of a school con-

---

[18] "*Satyagraha*—Not Passive Resistance," in Iyer, *Essential Writings of Mahatma Gandhi*, 308–11.

[19] From *India Opinion*, July 2, 1910, in Fischer, *Essential Gandhi*, 92–93.

[20] From *Young India*, June 16 and June 30, 1920; in Fischer, *Essential Gandhi*, 154–55.

ducts his institution on an immoral basis the pupils must leave the school. If the chairman of a corporation is corrupt the members thereof must wash their hands clean of his corruption by withdrawing from it, even so if a government does a grave injustice the subject must withdraw cooperation wholly or partially, sufficiently to wean the ruler from wickedness. In each case conceived of by me there is an element of suffering whether mental or physical. Without such suffering it is not possible to attain freedom.

Courage is the key to the power of nonviolence, Gandhi often emphasized.

I do believe that where there is a choice only between cowardice and violence, I would advise violence. . . . But I believe that nonviolence is infinitely superior to violence, forgiveness is more manly than punishment. . . . Strength does not come from physical capacity. It comes from an indomitable will.[21]

Religion and Political Action

Gandhi was called "mahatma," which means "great soul," and was considered a saint by many. He consciously adopted the persona of a religious ascetic, which enabled him to reach the unlettered Indian masses and communicate to them his philosophy of nonviolence and call for defiance of British rule. He was uncomfortable with the title of "mahatma," however, and wrestled with the challenge of combining saintly beliefs with the decidedly unholy business of achieving political change.

The critic regrets to see me as a politician, whereas he expected me to be a saint. Now I think that the word "saint" should be ruled out of present life. It is too sacred a word to be lightly applied to anybody, much less to one like myself

---

[21] *Young India,* August 11, 1920; in Fischer, *Essential Gandhi,* 156–57.

who claims only to be a humble searcher after truth, knows his limitations, makes mistakes, never hesitates to admit them when he makes them, and frankly confesses that he, like a scientist, is making experiments about some of "the eternal verities" of life, but cannot even claim to be a scientist because he can show no tangible proof of scientific accuracy in his methods or such tangible results of his experiments as modern science demands. But though by disclaiming sainthood I disappoint the critic's expectations, I would have him to give up his regrets by answering him that the politician in me has never dominated a single decision of mine, and if I seem to take part in politics, it is only because politics encircle us today like the coil of a snake from which one cannot get out, no matter how much one tries. I wish therefore to wrestle with the snake, as I have been doing, with more or less success, consciously since 1894, unconsciously, as I have now discovered, ever since reaching the years of discretion.

Quite selfishly, as I wish to live in peace in the midst of a bellowing storm howling round me, I have been experimenting with myself and my friends by introducing religion into politics. Let me explain what I mean by religion. It is not the Hindu religion, which I certainly prize above all other religions, but the religion which transcends Hinduism, which changes one's very nature, which binds one indissolubly to the truth within and which ever purifies. It is the permanent element in human nature which counts no cost too great in order to find full expression and which leaves the soul utterly restless until it has found itself, known its Maker, and appreciated the true correspondence between the Maker and itself.

. . . My critic deplores direct action. For, he says, "It does not work for unity." I join issue with him. Never has anything been done on this earth without direct action. I rejected the word "passive resistance," because of its insufficiency and

Gandhi the Pioneer • 19

> its being interpreted as a weapon of the weak. It was direct action in South Africa which told and told so effectively that it converted General Smuts[22] to sanity. He was in 1906 the most relentless opponent of Indian aspirations. In 1914 he took pride in doing tardy justice by removing from the statute book of the Union a disgraceful measure. . . .
>
> I am not a "statesman in the garb of a saint." But since Truth is the highest wisdom, sometimes my acts appear to be consistent with the highest statesmanship. But I hope I have no policy in me save the policy of Truth and Nonviolence.[23]

Gandhi was influenced most by Hinduism, but he was also shaped by Christianity and the teachings of Jesus, as he explains in these passages:

> I met a good Christian from Manchester in a vegetarian boarding house. He talked to me about Christianity. . . . He said, . . . "Do please read the Bible." I accepted his advice, and he got me a copy. . . . I began reading it, but I could not possibly read through the Old Testament. I read the book of Genesis, and the chapters that followed invariably sent me to sleep. But just for the sake of being able to say that I had read it, I plodded through the other books with much difficulty and without the least interest or understanding. I disliked reading the book of Numbers.
>
> But the New Testament produced a different impression, especially the Sermon on the Mount which went straight to my heart. I compared it with the *Gita*. The verses, "But I say unto you, that ye resist not evil: but whosoever shall smite thee on thy right cheek, turn to him the

---

[22] Jan Christian Smuts, a prominent political leader in South Africa, was the colonial secretary in Transvaal at the time of Gandhi's campaign for equal rights of Indian immigrant workers.

[23] *Young India*, January 20, 1927; in Iyer, *Essential Writings of Mahatma Gandhi*, 45–46; and in Fischer, *Essential Gandhi*, 199.

other also. And if any man take away thy coat let him have the cloak too," delighted me beyond measure and put me in mind of Shamal Bhatt's "For a bowl of water, give a goodly meal," etc.[24] My young mind tried to unify the teaching of the *Gita*, *The Light of Asia*,[25] and the Sermon on the Mount. That renunciation was the highest form of religion appealed to me greatly.[26]

The message of Jesus, as I understand it, is contained in his Sermon on the Mount unadulterated and taken as a whole, and even in connection with the Sermon on the Mount, my own humble interpretation of the message is in many respects different from the orthodox. The message, to my mind, has suffered distortion in the West. . . . I can tell you that in my humble opinion, much of what passes as Christianity is a negation of the Sermon on the Mount.[27]

Tolstoy once said that if we would but get off the backs of our neighbors the world would be quite all right without any further help from us. And if we can only serve our immediate neighbors by ceasing to prey upon them, the circle of unities thus grouped in the right fashion will ever grow in circumference till at last it is coterminous with that of the whole world. More than that it is not given to any person to try to achieve.[28]

The golden rule of conduct . . . is mutual toleration, seeing that we will never all think alike and that we shall always see Truth in fragment and from different angles of vision. Conscience is not the same thing for all. Whilst, therefore, it is a good thing for individual conduct, imposition of that

---

[24] Shamal Bhatt was an eighteenth-century Gurarati narrative poet.

[25] A poetic account of the life and philosophy of Buddha by Sir Edwin Arnold that greatly influenced Gandhi.

[26] Mohandas K. Gandhi, *An Autobiography: The Story of My Experiments with Truth*, trans. Mahadev Desai (Boston: Beacon, 1957), 69.

[27] From *Young India*, December 8, 1927, in Iyer, *Essential Writings of Mahatma Gandhi*, 145–46.

[28] "Neither a Saint nor a Politician," *Young India*, May 12, 1920, in Iyer, *Essential Writings of Mahatma Gandhi*, 48.

conduct upon all will be an insufferable interference with everybody else's freedom of conscience. . . . [Mutual toleration] can be inculcated among and practiced by all, irrespective of their status and training.[29]

Living for Truth

Gandhi confounded those who wanted to place him on a pedestal. He denied any claim to be a philosopher or the author of any new theory of history or life. "My life is my message," he often said. He reserved the right to change his mind based upon experience and new information, but he always remained true to the core principles of nonviolence.

> There is no such thing as "Gandhism" and I do not want to leave any sect after me. I do not claim to have originated any new principle or doctrine. I have simply tried in my own way to apply the eternal truths to our daily life and problems. . . . The opinions I have formed and the conclusions I have arrived at are not final, I may change them tomorrow. . . . All I have done is to try experiments [in Truth and Nonviolence] on as vast a scale as I could. . . . I have sometimes erred and learnt by my errors. . . . By instinct I have been truthful but not nonviolent. . . . [It] was in the course of my pursuits of truth that I discovered nonviolence. . . .
>
> Well, all my philosophy, if it may be called by that pretentious name, is contained in what I have said. But you will not call it "Gandhism," there is no "ism" about it. . . . Those who believe in the simple truths I have laid down can propagate them only by living them.[30]

---

[29] *Young India*, September 23, 1926, in Fischer, *Essential Gandhi*, 213.
[30] D. G. Tendulkar, *Mahatma: The Life of Mohandas Karamchand Gandhi*, 4:66–67, quoted in Fischer, *Essential Gandhi*, 320.

2

Martin Luther King Jr.
The American Gandhi

Gandhi's achievements in resisting racial restrictions on Asian immigrants in South Africa and achieving political independence for India had an enormous impact on world opinion, nowhere more so than among African Americans. As Gandhi's campaigns began to receive press coverage in the 1920s and 1930s, African Americans took notice and began to see his strategy of mass nonviolent disobedience as a method that might be used in the struggle against segregation in the United States. In the Gandhian movement African Americans witnessed people of color effectively resisting colonialism and racial oppression. Many longed for a similar trajectory of struggle in the United States. The prominent African American intellectual W. E. B. Du Bois described Gandhi's noncooperation strategy as a potential means of liberating black Americans. The *Chicago Defender*, a leading black newspaper, asked in a 1932 editorial, "Will a Gandhi Arise?," to lead the African American community toward freedom?[1]

For many, Martin Luther King Jr. (1929–1968) was that American Gandhi, the person who applied the Gandhian method

---

[1] Quoted in Sudarshan Kapur, "Prelude to Martin Luther King Jr.: The Images of Gandhi and the Indian Independence Movement, 1921–1934," *Gandhi Marg* 14, no. 3 (October–December 1992): 427–30.

to the struggle against racial segregation and demonstrated its effectiveness in achieving political change. The success of the civil rights movement and King's eloquence in advocating for nonviolence transformed American political culture. The movement for racial justice became a central part of the American historical narrative. It emerged as a model for strategic success that spread to other movements for justice and inspired struggles for freedom around the world. From South Africa to Northern Ireland to Latin America and beyond, champions for human rights echoed King's words and found new ways to resist oppression by applying the methods of mass noncooperation. King helped to bring Gandhi's ideas and methods to the United States and the world.

King knew of Gandhi from news stories and the black press, but it was not until King's university days that he studied the nonviolent philosophy in depth. In 1950 while a student at Crozer Seminary in Pennsylvania, King attended a lecture on Gandhi by Mordecai Johnson, president of Howard University. He found the presentation "profound and electrifying" and began to examine Gandhi's ideas and accomplishments intensively.[2] Like many others he was greatly impressed by the victory of the Indian independence movement and the peaceful manner in which the struggle was waged. The ability of Gandhi to achieve political freedom without the bitterness and hatred that often result from armed rebellion was particularly impressive. Gandhi had found a means of achieving revolution without violence. He demonstrated the power of collective disobedience and mass noncooperation in struggling against oppression. He did so by applying religious principles drawn from Eastern religions but also from Islam and Christianity. All of this appealed enormously to King and other African Americans.

Gandhi helped King synthesize the gospel message of love with the need for active resistance to segregation. The love ethic of Jesus affects not only interactions among individuals and

---

[2] Martin Luther King Jr., *Stride toward Freedom: The Montgomery Story* (New York: Harper & Row, 1958), 96.

families, King argued, but also relationships within society and between social groups. Love has a social dimension, he showed, and can be a force for change. King combined the Christian message of love with the Gandhian principle of non-harm, forging a synthesis that helped build a broad social movement for racial freedom.

In adapting Gandhi's methods to the struggle against segregation in the United States, King demonstrated the broad relevance of nonviolent action. He elaborated upon the Gandhian method and provided a deeper philosophical foundation for some of Gandhi's principles and practices. He was more realistic than Gandhi about when and how to use negotiation, and more pragmatic in applying the methods of noncooperation. King was less ambivalent about the use of coercive pressure than Gandhi. He understood that it takes power to achieve meaningful change—"constructive nonviolent power," he called it—and he showed in some of his campaigns how to wield that power. He understood as Gandhi did that reason alone is not enough to bring about change and that we must be prepared to sacrifice for the cause. Like Gandhi, King emphasized the need for courage and bravery among those who seek to achieve nonviolent change.

The selections below include some of King's essential writings on the meaning of love, the philosophy and strategy of nonviolent resistance, the link between ends and means, and the basis for resisting militarism and aggressive war. These excerpts are drawn mostly from sermons and speeches but also from his "Letter from a Birmingham Jail." King is revealed in these writings as both prophetic and eloquent, a leader of historic campaigns for racial freedom and a passionate voice for social justice and peace.

Loving Our Enemies

As an ordained minister Dr. King naturally focused on gospel themes in his sermons and speeches. The most challenging message of the gospel is Jesus's command to love our enemies. King explores the meaning of this teaching in this extended excerpt from his famous sermon "Loving Your Enemies." King explains why and how it is possible to love our enemies and explores the deeper meaning of nonviolence and reconciliation for social progress and human well-being.

> Probably no admonition of Jesus has been more difficult to follow than the command to "love your enemies." Some men have sincerely felt that its actual practice is not possible. It is easy, they say, to love those who love you, but how can one love those who openly and insidiously seek to defeat you? Others, like the philosopher Nietzsche, contend that Jesus' exhortation to love one's enemies is testimony to the fact that the Christian ethic is designed for the weak and cowardly, and not for the strong and courageous. Jesus, they say, was an impractical idealist.
>
> In spite of these insistent questions and the persistent objections, this command of Jesus challenges us with new urgency. Upheaval after upheaval has reminded us that modern man is traveling along a road called hate, in a journey that will bring us to destruction and damnation. Far from being the pious injunction of a Utopian dreamer, the command to love one's enemy is an absolute necessity for our survival. Love even for enemies is the key to the solution of the problems of our world. Jesus is not an impractical idealist; he is a practical realist. . . .
>
> Let us be practical and ask the question, *How do we love our enemies?*
>
> First, we must develop and maintain the capacity to forgive. He who is devoid of the power to forgive is devoid of the power of love. It is impossible even to begin the act of loving one's enemies without the prior acceptance of the necessity, over and over again, of forgiving those who inflict evil and injury upon us. It is also necessary to realize that the forgiving act must always be initiated by the person who has been wronged, the victim of some great hurt, the

recipient of some tortuous injustice, the absorber of some terrible act of oppression. The wrongdoer may request forgiveness. He may come to himself, and, like the prodigal son, move up some dusty road, his heart palpitating with the desire for forgiveness. But only the injured neighbor, the loving father back home, can really pour out the warm waters of forgiveness.

Forgiveness does not mean ignoring what has been done or putting a false label on an evil act. It means, rather, that the evil act no longer remains as a barrier to the relationship. Forgiveness is a catalyst creating the atmosphere necessary for a fresh start and a new beginning. It is the lifting of a burden or the canceling of a debt. The words, "I will forgive you, but I'll never forget what you've done," never explain the real nature of forgiveness. Certainly one can never forget, if that means erasing it totally from his mind. But when we forgive, we forget in the sense that the evil deed is no longer a mental block impeding a new relationship. Likewise, we can never say, "I will forgive you, but I won't have anything further to do with you." Forgiveness means reconciliation, a coming together again. Without this, no man can love his enemies. The degree to which we are able to forgive determines the degree to which we are able to love our enemies.

Second, we must recognize that the evil deed of the enemy-neighbor, the thing that hurts, never quite expresses all that he is. An element of goodness may be found even in our worst enemy. Each of us is something of a schizophrenic personality, tragically divided against ourselves. A persistent civil war rages within all of our lives. Something within us causes us to lament with Ovid, the Latin poet, "I see and approve the better things, but follow worse," or to agree with Plato that human personality is like a charioteer having two headstrong horses, each wanting to go in a different direction, or to repeat with the Apostle Paul, "the good that I would I do not; but the evil which I would not, that I do."

This simply means that there is some good in the worst of us and some evil in the best of us. When we discover this, we are less prone to hate our enemies. When we look beneath the surface, beneath the impulsive evil deed, we see within our enemy-neighbor a measure of goodness and know that the viciousness and evilness of his acts are not quite representative of all that he is. We see him in a new light. We recognize that his hate grows out of fear, pride, ignorance, prejudice, and misunderstanding, but in spite of this, we know God's image is ineffably etched in his being. Then we love our enemies by realizing that they are not totally bad and that they are not beyond the reach of God's redemptive love.

Third, we must not seek to defeat or humiliate the enemy but to win his friendship and understanding. At times we are able to humiliate our worst enemy. Inevitably, his weak moments come and we are able to thrust in his side the spear of defeat. But this we must not do. Every word and deed must contribute to an understanding with the enemy and release those vast reservoirs of goodwill which have been blocked by impenetrable walls of hate.

The meaning of love is not to be confused with some sentimental outpouring. Love is something much deeper than emotional bosh. Perhaps the Greek language can clear our confusion at this point. In the Greek New Testament are three words for love. The word *eros* is a sort of aesthetic or romantic love. In the Platonic dialogues *eros* is a journey of the soul for the realm of the divine. The second word is *philia*, a reciprocal love and the intimate affection and friendship between friends. We love those whom we like, and we love because we are loved. The third word is *agape*, understanding and creative, redemptive goodwill for all men. An overflowing love which seeks nothing in return, *agape* is the love of God operating in the human heart. At this level, we love men not because we like them, nor because their ways appeal to us, nor even because they possess some kind of divine spark; we love every man because God loves him. At this level, we love the person who does an evil deed, although we hate the deed that he does.

Now we can see what Jesus meant when he said, "Love your enemies." We should be happy that he did not say, "Like your enemies." It is almost impossible to like some people. "Like" is a sentimental and affectionate word. How can we be affectionate toward a person whose avowed aim is to crush our very being and place innumerable stumbling blocks in our path? How can we like a person who is threatening our children and bombing our homes? This is impossible. But Jesus recognized that *love* is greater than *like*. When Jesus bids us to love our enemies, he is speaking neither of *eros* nor *philia*; he is speaking of *agape*, understanding and creative, redemptive goodwill for all men. Only by following this way and responding with this type of love are we able to be children of our Father who is in heaven.

Let us move on now from the practical *how* to the theoretical *why*: *why should we love our enemies?* The first reason is fairly obvious. Returning hate for hate multiplies hate, adding deeper darkness to a night already devoid of stars. Darkness cannot drive out darkness; only light can do that. Hate cannot drive out hate; only love can do that. Hate multiplies hate, violence multiplies violence, and toughness multiplies toughness in a descending spiral of destruction. So when Jesus says, "Love your enemies," he is setting forth a profound and ultimately inescapable admonition. Have we not come to such an impasse in the modern world that we must love our enemies—or else? The chain reaction of evil—hate begetting hate, wars producing more wars—must be broken, or we shall be plunged into the dark abyss of annihilation.

Another reason why we must love our enemies is that hate scars the soul and distorts the personality. Mindful that hate is an evil and dangerous force, we too often think of what it does to the person hated. This is understandable, for hate brings irreparable damage to its victims. We have seen its ugly consequences in the ignominious deaths brought to six million Jews by a hate-obsessed madman named Hitler, in the unspeakable violence inflicted upon Negroes by bloodthirsty mobs, in the dark horrors of war, and in the terrible indignities and injustices perpetrated against millions of God's children by unconscionable oppressors.

But there is another side which we must never overlook. Hate is just as injurious to the person who hates. Like an unchecked cancer, hate corrodes the personality and eats away its vital unity. Hate destroys a man's sense of values and his objectivity. It causes him to describe the beautiful as ugly and the ugly as beautiful, and to confuse the true with the false and the false with the true.

Dr. E. Franklin Frazier,[3] in an interesting essay entitled "The Pathology of Race Prejudice," included several examples of white persons who were normal, amiable, and congenial in their day-to-day relationships with other white persons, but when they were challenged to think of Negroes as equals or even to discuss the question of racial injustice, they reacted with unbelievable irrationality and an abnormal unbalance. This happens when hate lingers in our minds. Psychiatrists report that many of the strange things that happen in the subconscious, many of our inner conflicts, are rooted in hate. They say, "Love or perish." Modern psychology recognizes what Jesus taught centuries ago: hate divides the personality and love in an amazing and inexorable way unites it.

A third reason why we should love our enemies is that love is the only force capable of transforming an enemy into a friend. We never get rid of an enemy by meeting hate with hate; we get rid of an enemy by getting rid of enmity. By its very nature, hate destroys and tears down; by its very nature, love creates and builds up. Love transforms with redemptive power. . . .

---

[3] Professor Frazier (1894–1962) was a prominent sociologist and author of major works on race relations and African American family life.

The relevance of what I have said to the crisis in race relations should be readily apparent. There will be no permanent solution to the race problem until oppressed men develop the capacity to love their enemies. The darkness of racial injustice will be dispelled only by the light of forgiving love. For more than three centuries American Negroes have been battered by the iron rod of oppression, frustrated by day and bewildered by night by unbearable injustice, and burdened with the ugly weight of discrimination. Forced to live with these shameful conditions, we are tempted to become bitter and to retaliate with a corresponding hate. But if this happens, the new order we seek will be little more than a duplicate of the old order. We must in strength and humility meet hate with love.

Of course, this is not *practical*. Life is a matter of getting even, of hitting back, of dog eat dog. Am I saying that Jesus commands us to love those who hurt and oppress us? Do I sound like most preachers—idealistic and impractical? Maybe in some distant Utopia, you say, that idea will work, but not in the hard, cold world in which we live.

My friends, we have followed the so-called practical way for too long a time now, and it has led inexorably to deeper confusion and chaos. Time is cluttered with the wreckage of communities which surrendered to hatred and violence. For the salvation of our nation and the salvation of mankind, we must follow another way. This does not mean that we abandon our righteous efforts. With every ounce of our energy we must continue to rid this nation of the incubus of segregation. But we shall not in the process relinquish our privilege and our obligation to love. While abhorring segregation, we shall love the segregationist. This is the only way to create the beloved community.

To our most bitter opponents we say: "We shall match your capacity to inflict suffering by our capacity to endure suffering. We shall meet your physical force with soul force. Do to us what you will, and we shall continue to love you.

We cannot in all good conscience obey your unjust laws, because noncooperation with evil is as much a moral obligation as is cooperation with good. Throw us in jail, and we shall still love you. Bomb our homes and threaten our children, and we shall still love you. Send your hooded perpetrators of violence into our community at the midnight hour and beat us and leave us half dead, and we shall still love you. But be ye assured that we will wear you down by our capacity to suffer. One day we shall win freedom, but not only for ourselves. We shall so appeal to your heart and conscience that we shall win *you* in the process, and our victory will be a double victory."[4]

The Six Elements of Nonviolence

In his first book, *Stride toward Freedom*, written after the historic Montgomery bus boycott, King includes a chapter titled "Pilgrimage to Nonviolence" that succinctly summarizes the six key essential elements of nonviolence. These points were reproduced by the Southern Christian Leadership Conference, which King cofounded, and were used for the training of civil rights movement activists.

Since the philosophy of nonviolence played such a positive role in the Montgomery Movement, it may be wise to turn to a brief discussion of some of the aspects of this philosophy.

First, it must be emphasized that nonviolent resistance is not a method for cowards; it does resist. If a person uses this method because he is afraid or merely because he lacks the instruments of violence, he is not truly nonviolent. This is why Gandhi often said that if cowardice is the only alternative to violence, it is better to fight. He made this statement conscious of the fact that there is always another

---

[4] "Loving Your Enemies," sermon delivered at the Dexter Avenue Baptist Church, from A. J. Muste Memorial Institute Essay Series, Montgomery, Alabama, Christmas 1957.

alternative: no individual or group need submit to any wrong, nor need they use violence to right the wrong; there is the way of nonviolent resistance. This is ultimately the way of the strong man. It is not a method of stagnant passivity. The phrase "passive resistance" often gives the false impression that this is a sort of "do-nothing method" in which the resister quietly and passively accepts evil. But nothing is further from the truth. For while the nonviolent resister is passive in the sense that he is not physically aggressive toward the opponent, his mind and emotions are always active, constantly seeking to persuade his opponent that he is wrong. The method is passive physically, but strongly active spiritually. It is not passive nonresistance to evil, it is active nonviolent resistance to evil.

A second basic fact that characterizes nonviolence is that it does not seek to defeat or humiliate the opponent, but to win friendship and understanding. The nonviolent resister must often express his protest through noncooperation or boycotts, but he realizes that these are not ends in themselves; they are merely means to awaken a sense of moral shame in the opponent. The end is redemption and reconciliation. The aftermath of nonviolence is the creation of the beloved community, while the aftermath of violence is tragic bitterness.

A third characteristic of this method is that the attack is directed against forces of evil rather than against persons who happen to be doing the evil. It is evil that the nonviolent resister seeks to defeat, not the persons victimized by evil. If he is opposing racial injustice, the nonviolent resister has the vision to see that the basic tension is not between races. As I like to say to the people of Montgomery: "The tension in the city is not between white people and the Negro people. The tension is, at bottom, between justice and injustice, between the forces of light and the forces of darkness. And if there is a victory, it will be a victory not merely for fifty thousand Negroes, but a victory for justice and the forces of light. We are out to defeat injustice and not white persons who may be unjust."

A fourth point that characterizes nonviolent resistance is a willingness to accept suffering without retaliation, to accept blows from the opponent without striking back. "Rivers of blood may have to flow before we gain our freedom, but it must be our blood," Gandhi said to his countrymen. The nonviolent resister is willing to accept violence if necessary, but never to inflict it. He does not seek to dodge jail. If going to jail is necessary, he enters it "as a bridegroom enters the bride's chamber."

One may well ask: "What is the nonviolent resister's justification for this ordeal to which he invites men, for this mass political application of the ancient doctrine of turning the other cheek?" The answer is found in the realization that unearned suffering is redemptive. Suffering, the nonviolent resister realizes, has tremendous educational and transforming possibilities. "Things of fundamental importance to people are not secured by reason alone, but have to be purchased with their suffering," said Gandhi. He continues: "Suffering is infinitely more powerful than the law of the jungle for converting the opponent and opening ears which are otherwise shut to the voice of reason."

A fifth point concerning nonviolent resistance is that it avoids not only physical violence but also internal violence of the spirit. The nonviolent resister not only refuses to shoot his opponent but he also refuses to hate him. At the center of nonviolence stands the principle of love. The nonviolent resister would contend that in the struggle for human dignity, the oppressed people of the world must not succumb to the temptation of becoming bitter or indulging in hate campaigns. To retaliate in kind would do nothing but intensify the existence of hate in the universe. Along the way of life, someone must have sense enough and morality enough to cut off the chain of hate. This can only be done by projecting the ethic of love to the center of our lives. . . .

A sixth basic fact about nonviolent resistance is that it is based on the conviction that the universe is on the side of justice. Consequently, the believer in nonviolence has deep faith in the future. This faith is another reason why the nonviolent resister can accept suffering without retaliation. For he knows that in his struggle for justice he has cosmic companionship. It is true that there are devout believers in nonviolence who find it difficult to believe in a personal God. But even these persons believe in the existence of some creative force that works for universal wholeness. Whether we call it an unconscious process, an impersonal Brahman, or a Personal Being of matchless power and infinite love, there is a creative force in this universe that works to bring the disconnected aspects of reality into a harmonious whole.[5]

Ends and Means

Like Gandhi, King insisted on the necessity of nonviolent discipline and the compatibility of ends and means. To achieve just ends, he emphasized, we must utilize just means, as he explains in this passage from a 1961 address:

> I would say that the first point or the first principle in the movement is the idea that means must be as pure as the end. This movement is based on the philosophy that ends and means must cohere. Now this has been one of the long struggles in history, the whole idea of means and ends. Great philosophers have grappled with it, and sometimes they have emerged with the idea, from Machiavelli on down, that the end justifies the means. There is a great system of thought in our world today, known as communism. And I think with all the weakness and tragedies of communism, we find its greatest tragedy right here, that it goes under the philosophy that the end justifies the means that are used in the process. So we can read or we can hear the Lenins

---

[5] "Pilgrimage to Nonviolence," in King, *Stride toward Freedom*, 101–7.

say that lying, deceit, or violence, that many of these things justify the ends of the classless society.

This is where the student movement and the nonviolent movement that is taking place in our nation would break with communism and any other system that would argue that the end justifies the means. For in the long run, we must see that the end represents the means in process and the ideal in the making. In other words, we cannot believe, or we cannot go with the idea that the end justifies the means because the end is preexistent in the means. So the idea of nonviolent resistance, the philosophy of nonviolent resistance, is the philosophy which says that the means must be as pure as the end, that in the long run of history, immoral destructive means cannot bring about moral and constructive ends.

There is another thing about this philosophy, this method of nonviolence which is followed by the student movement. It says that those who adhere to or follow this philosophy must follow a consistent principle of noninjury. They must consistently refuse to inflict injury upon another. Sometimes you will read the literature of the student movement and see that, as they are getting ready for the sit-in or stand-in, they will read something like this, "If you are hit do not hit back, if you are cursed do not curse back." This is the whole idea, that the individual who is engaged in a nonviolent struggle must never inflict injury upon another. Now this has an external aspect and it has an internal one. From the external point of view it means that the individuals involved must avoid external physical violence. So they don't have guns, they don't retaliate with physical violence. If they are hit in the process, they avoid external violence at every point. But it also means that they avoid internal violence of spirit. This is why the love ethic stands so high in the student movement. We have a great deal of talk about love and nonviolence in this whole thrust.[6]

---

[6] "Love, Law, and Civil Disobedience," address before the Fellowship of

"Letter from a Birmingham Jail"

No collection of King's writings would be complete without excerpts from his ineffable "Letter from a Birmingham Jail." The letter was written in April 1963 in the midst of the civil rights movement's epic struggle to desegregate the downtown stores of Birmingham, Alabama. King was arrested during the campaign for disobeying local ordinances against protesting. He used his time behind bars to pen a letter to local clergy who opposed the campaign, explaining the reasons why the demonstrations, boycotts, and civil disobedience actions in Birmingham were necessary and just. A great literary work and invaluable guide to effective social action, the letter is one of the most eloquent and inspiring statements ever written on the moral imperative of struggling against racial segregation and the strategy and power of nonviolent resistance.[7]

> My dear Fellow Clergyman,
> While confined here in the Birmingham city jail, I came across your recent statement calling our present activities "unwise and untimely." Seldom, if ever, do I pause to answer criticisms of my work and ideas. . . . But since I feel that you are men of genuine goodwill and your criticisms are sincerely set forth, I would like to answer your statement in what I hope will be patient and reasonable terms.
> I think I should give the reason for my being in Birmingham, since you have been influenced by the argument of "outsiders coming in." . . . Several months ago our local affiliate here in Birmingham invited us to be on call to engage in a nonviolent direct action program if such were deemed necessary. We readily consented and when the hour came

---

the Concerned, November 16, 1961, in *A Testament of Hope: The Essential Writings and Speeches of Martin Luther King Jr.*, ed. James M. Washington (San Francisco: Harper & Row, 1986), 45–46.

[7] For an outstanding analysis of the letter see Jonathan Rieder, *Gospel of Freedom: Martin Luther King Jr.'s Letter from Birmingham Jail and The Struggle That Changed a Nation* (New York: Bloomsbury, 2013).

we lived up to our promises. So I am here, along with several members of my staff, because we were invited here. I am here because I have basic organizational ties here.

Beyond this, I am in Birmingham because injustice is here. Just as the eighth-century prophets left their little villages and carried their "thus saith the Lord" far beyond the boundaries of their hometowns; and just as the Apostle Paul left his little village of Tarsus and carried the gospel of Jesus Christ to practically every hamlet and city of the Greco-Roman world, I too am compelled to carry the gospel of freedom beyond my particular hometown. Like Paul, I must constantly respond to the Macedonian call for aid. . . .

You deplore the demonstrations that are presently taking place in Birmingham. But I am sorry that your statement did not express a similar concern for the conditions that brought the demonstrations into being. I am sure that each of you would want to go beyond the superficial social analyst who looks merely at effects, and does not grapple with underlying causes. I would not hesitate to say that it is unfortunate that so-called demonstrations are taking place in Birmingham at this time, but I would say in more emphatic terms that it is even more unfortunate that the white power structure of the city left the Negro community with no other alternative.

In any nonviolent campaign there are four basic steps: (1) collection of the facts to determine whether injustices are alive, (2) negotiation, (3) self-purification, and (4) direct action. . . .

You may well ask, "Why direct action? Why sit-ins, marches, etc.? Isn't negotiation a better path?" You are exactly right in your call for negotiation. Indeed, this is the purpose of direct action. Nonviolent direct action seeks to create such a crisis and establish such creative tension that a community that has constantly refused to negotiate is forced to confront the issue. It seeks so to dramatize the issue that it can no longer be ignored. I just referred to the creation of tension as a part of the work of the nonviolent resister. This may sound rather shocking. But I must confess that I am not afraid of the word tension. I have earnestly worked and preached against violent tension, but there is a type of constructive nonviolent tension that is necessary for growth. Just as Socrates felt that it was necessary to create a tension in the mind so that individuals could rise from the bondage of myths and half-truths to the unfettered realm of creative analysis and objective appraisal, we must see the need of having nonviolent gadflies to create the kind of tension in society that will help men to rise from the dark depths of prejudice and racism to the majestic heights of understanding and brotherhood. So the purpose of the direct action is to create a situation so crisis-packed that it will inevitably open the door to negotiation. . . .

My friends, I must say to you that we have not made a single gain in civil rights without determined legal and nonviolent pressure. History is the long and tragic story of the fact that privileged groups seldom give up their privileges voluntarily. Individuals may see the moral light and voluntarily give up their unjust posture; but as Reinhold Niebuhr[8] has reminded us, groups are more immoral than individuals.

We know through painful experience that freedom is never voluntarily given by the oppressor; it must be demanded by the oppressed. Frankly, I have never yet engaged in a direct action movement that was "well-timed," according to the timetable of those who have not suffered unduly from the disease of segregation. For years now I have heard the words, "Wait!" It rings in the ear of every Negro with a piercing familiarity. This "Wait" has almost always meant "Never." It has been a tranquilizing thalidomide, relieving the emotional stress for a moment, only to give birth to an ill-formed infant of frustration. We must come to

---

[8] Author of *Moral Man and Immoral Society*, Reinhold Niebuhr was a prominent American theologian who influenced Dr. King's thinking about the reality of sin and the need to confront social evil.

see with the distinguished jurist of yesterday that "justice too long delayed is justice denied." . . . I guess it is easy for those who have never felt the stinging darts of segregation to say, "Wait." But when you have seen vicious mobs lynch your mothers and fathers at will and drown your sisters and brothers at whim; when you have seen hate-filled policemen curse, kick, brutalize, and even kill your black brothers and sisters with impunity; when you see the vast majority of your twenty million Negro brothers smothering in an airtight cage of poverty in the midst of an affluent society; when you suddenly find your tongue twisted and your speech stammering as you seek to explain to your six-year-old daughter why she can't go to the public amusement park that has been advertised on television, and see tears welling up in her little eyes when she is told that Funtown[9] is closed to colored children, and see the depressing clouds of inferiority begin to form in her little mental sky, and see her begin to distort her little personality by unconsciously developing a bitterness toward white people; when you have to concoct an answer for a five-year-old son asking in agonizing pathos: "Daddy, why do white people treat colored people so mean?"; when you take a cross-country drive and find it necessary to sleep night after night in the uncomfortable corners of your automobile because no motel will accept you; when you are humiliated day in and day out by nagging signs reading "white" and "colored"; when your first name becomes "nigger" and your middle name becomes "boy" (however old you are) and your last name becomes "John," and when your wife and mother are never given the respected title "Mrs."; when you are harried by day and haunted by night by the fact that you are a Negro, living constantly at tiptoe stance never quite knowing what to expect next, and plagued with inner fears and outer resentments; when you are forever fighting a degenerating sense of "nobodiness"; then you will understand why we find it difficult to wait. There comes a time when the cup of

---

[9] An amusement park in Atlanta that was segregated at the time.

endurance runs over, and men are no longer willing to be plunged into an abyss of injustice where they experience the blackness of corroding despair. I hope, sirs, you can understand our legitimate and unavoidable impatience.

You express a great deal of anxiety over our willingness to break laws. This is certainly a legitimate concern. Since we so diligently urge people to obey the Supreme Court's decision of 1954[10] outlawing segregation in the public schools, it is rather strange and paradoxical to find us consciously breaking laws. One may well ask, "How can you advocate breaking some laws and obeying others?" The answer is found in the fact that there are two types of laws: there are *just* and there are *unjust* laws. I would agree with St. Augustine that "An unjust law is no law at all."

Now what is the difference between the two? How does one determine when a law is just or unjust? A just law is a man-made code that squares with the moral law for the law of God. An unjust law is a code that is out of harmony with the moral law. To put it in the terms of St. Thomas Aquinas, an unjust law is a human law that is not rooted in eternal and natural law. Any law that uplifts human personality is just. Any law that degrades human personality is unjust. All segregation statutes are unjust because segregation distorts the soul and damages the personality. It gives the segregator a false sense of superiority, and the segregated a false sense of inferiority. To use the words of Martin Buber, the great Jewish philosopher, segregation substitutes an "I-it" relationship for the "I-thou" relationship, and ends up relegating persons to the status of things. So segregation is not only politically, economically, and sociologically unsound, but it is morally wrong and sinful. Paul Tillich has said that sin is separation. Isn't segregation an existential expression of man's tragic separation, an expression of his

---

[10] A reference to the landmark *Brown v. Board of Education* U.S. Supreme Court ruling that struck down the doctrine of "separate but equal," opening the door to legal challenges to segregation.

awful estrangement, his terrible sinfulness? So I can urge people to disobey segregation ordinances because they are morally wrong.

Let us turn to a more concrete example of just and unjust laws. An unjust law is a code that a majority inflicts on a minority that is not binding on itself. This is difference made legal. On the other hand a just law is a code that a majority compels a minority to follow that it is willing to follow itself. This is sameness made legal.

Let me give another explanation. An unjust law is a code inflicted upon a minority which that minority had no part in enacting or creating because they did not have the unhampered right to vote. Who can say that the legislature of Alabama which set up segregation laws was democratically elected? Throughout the state of Alabama all types of conniving methods are used to prevent Negroes from becoming registered voters and there are some counties without a single Negro registered to vote despite the fact that the Negro constitutes a majority of the population. Can any law set up in such a state be considered democratically structured? . . .

I hope you can see the distinction I am trying to point out. In no sense do I advocate evading or defying the law as the rabid segregationist would do. This would lead to anarchy. One who breaks an unjust law must do it *openly, lovingly* (not hatefully as the white mothers did in New Orleans when they were seen on television screaming, "nigger, nigger, nigger"), and with a willingness to accept the penalty. I submit that an individual who breaks a law that conscience tells him is unjust, and willingly accepts the penalty by staying in jail to arouse the conscience of the community over its injustice, is in reality expressing the very highest respect for law. . . .

I had hoped that the white moderate would understand that law and order exist for the purpose of establishing justice, and that when they fail to do this they become dangerously structured dams that block the flow of social progress.

I had hoped that the white moderate would understand that the present tension of the South is merely a necessary phase of the transition from an obnoxious negative peace, where the Negro passively accepted his unjust plight, to a substance-filled positive peace, where all men will respect the dignity and worth of human personality. Actually, we who engage in nonviolent direct action are not the creators of tension. We merely bring to the surface the hidden tension that is already alive. We bring it out in the open where it can be seen and dealt with. Like a boil that can never be cured as long as it is covered up but must be opened with all its pus-flowing ugliness to the natural medicines of air and light, injustice must likewise be exposed, with all of the tension its exposing creates, to the light of human conscience and the air of national opinion before it can be cured. . . .

I had also hoped that the white moderate would reject the myth of time. . . . We must come to see that human progress never rolls in on wheels of inevitability. It comes through the tireless efforts and persistent work of people willing to be coworkers with God, and without this hard work time itself becomes an ally of the forces of social stagnation. We must use time creatively, and forever realize that the time is always ripe to do right. Now is the time to make real the promise of democracy, and transform our pending national elegy into a creative psalm of brotherhood. Now is the time to lift our national policy from the quicksand of racial injustice to the solid rock of human dignity.

You spoke of our activity in Birmingham as extreme. At first I was rather disappointed that fellow clergyman would see my nonviolent efforts as those of the extremist. . . . But as I continued to think about the matter I gradually gained a bit of satisfaction from being considered an extremist. Was not Jesus an extremist in love—"Love your enemies, bless them that curse you, pray for them that despitefully use you." Was not Amos an extremist for justice—"Let justice roll down like waters and righteousness like a mighty stream."

Was not Paul an extremist for the gospel of Jesus Christ—"I bear in my body the marks of the Lord Jesus." Was not Martin Luther an extremist—"Here I stand; I can do none other so help me God." Was not John Bunyan[11] an extremist—"I will stay in jail to the end of my days before I make a butchery of my conscience." Was not Abraham Lincoln an extremist—"This nation cannot survive half slave and half free." Was not Thomas Jefferson an extremist—"We hold these truths to be self-evident, that all men are created equal." So the question is not whether we will be extremist but what kind of extremist will we be. Will we be extremists for hate or will we be extremists for love? Will we be extremists for the preservation of injustice—or will we be extremists for the cause of justice? . . .

I have been so greatly disappointed with the white church and its leadership. . . . In the midst of blatant injustices inflicted upon the Negro, I have watched white churches stand on the sideline and merely mouth pious irrelevancies and sanctimonious trivialities. . . . I have traveled the length and breadth of Alabama, Mississippi, and all the other Southern states. On sweltering summer days and crisp autumn mornings I have looked at her beautiful churches with their lofty spires pointing heavenward. I have beheld the impressive outlay of her massive religious education buildings. Over and over again I have found myself asking: "What kind of people worship here? Who is their God? Where were their voices when the lips of Governor Barnett dripped with the words of interposition and nullification? Where were they when Governor Wallace gave the clarion call for defiance and hatred?[12] Where were their voices of support when tired, bruised, and weary Negro men and women decided to rise from the dark dungeons of complacency to the bright hills of creative protest?"

---

[11] A seventeenth-century Christian reformer and author of *The Pilgrim's Progress* who was jailed for refusing to conform with the Church of England.

[12] Governors Ross Barnett of Mississippi and George Wallace of Alabama were vocal segregationists in the 1960s.

Yes, these questions are still in my mind. In deep disappointment, I have wept over the laxity of the church. But be assured that my tears have been tears of love. There can be no deep disappointment where there is not deep love. Yes, I love the church; I love her sacred walls. How could I do otherwise? I am in the rather unique position of being the son, the grandson, and the great-grandson of preachers. Yes, I see the church as the body of Christ. But, oh! How we have blemished and scarred that body through social neglect and fear of being nonconformists. . . .

I have no fear about the outcome of our struggle in Birmingham, even if our motives are presently misunderstood. We will reach the goal of freedom in Birmingham and all over the nation, because the goal of America is freedom. Abused and scorned though we may be, our destiny is tied up with the destiny of America. Before the Pilgrims landed at Plymouth we were here. Before the pen of Jefferson etched across the pages of history the majestic words of the Declaration of Independence, we were here. For more than two centuries our foreparents labored in this country without wages; they made cotton king; and they built the homes of their masters in the midst of brutal injustice and shameful humiliation—and yet out of a bottomless vitality they continued to thrive and develop. If the inexpressible cruelties of slavery could not stop us, the opposition we now face will surely fail. We will win our freedom because the sacred heritage of our nation and the eternal will of God are embodied in our echoing demands. . . .

One day the South will recognize its real heroes. They will be the James Merediths,[13] courageously and with a majestic sense of purpose facing jeering and hostile mobs and the agonizing loneliness that characterizes the life of the pioneer. They will be old, oppressed, battered Negro women, symbolized in a 72-year-old woman of Montgomery, Alabama, who

---

[13] James Meredith became the first African American student admitted to the University of Mississippi in 1962.

rose up with a sense of dignity and with her people decided not to ride the segregated buses, and responded to one who inquired about her tiredness with ungrammatical profundity: "My feet is tired, but my soul is rested." They will be the young high school and college students, young ministers of the gospel and a host of their elders courageously and nonviolently sitting in at lunch counters and willingly going to jail for conscience's sake. One day the South will know that when these disinherited children of God sat down at lunch counters they were in reality standing up for the best in the American dream and the most sacred values in our Judeo-Christian heritage, and thusly, carrying our whole nation back to those great wells of democracy which were dug deep by the Founding Fathers in the formulation of the Constitution and the Declaration of Independence....

Let us all hope that the dark clouds of racial prejudice will soon pass away and the deep fog of misunderstanding will be lifted from our fear-drenched communities and in some not-too-distant tomorrow the radiant stars of love and brotherhood will shine over our great nation with all their scintillating beauty.[14]

On Power

As a realist influenced by the Christian philosopher Reinhold Niebuhr, King recognized the entrenched power of systems of segregation, economic exploitation, and militarism, which he called the giant "triplet of evil." To overcome these powerful forces of injustice, King urged the creation of alternative systems of people power, as he outlines in this excerpt from his 1967 speech "Where Do We Go From Here?"

Another basic challenge is to discover how to organize our strength in terms of economic and political power. No one

---

[14] "Letter from a Birmingham Jail," April 1963, in Washington, *Testament of Hope*, 290–301.

can deny that the Negro is in dire need of this kind of legitimate power. Indeed, one of the great problems that the Negro confronts is the lack of power. From old plantations of the South to newer ghettos of the North, the Negro has been confined to a life of voicelessness and powerlessness. Stripped of the right to make decisions concerning life and destiny he has been subject to the authoritarian and sometimes whimsical decisions of this white power structure. The plantation and ghetto were created by those who had power, both to confine those who had no power and to perpetuate their powerlessness. The problem of transforming the ghetto, therefore, is a problem of power—a confrontation of the forces of power demanding change and the forces of power dedicated to the preserving of the status quo. Now power properly understood is nothing but the ability to achieve purpose. It is the strength required to bring about social, political, and economic change. Walter Reuther[15] defined power one day. He said, "Power is the ability of a labor union like the UAW to make the most powerful corporation in the world, General Motors, say 'Yes' when it wants to say 'No.' That's power."

Now a lot of us are preachers, and all of us have our moral convictions and concerns, and so often have problems with power. There is nothing wrong with power if power is used correctly. You see, what happened is that some of our philosophers got off base. And one of the great problems of history is that the concepts of love and power have usually been contrasted as opposites—polar opposites—so that love is identified with a resignation of power, and power with a denial of love.

It was this misinterpretation that caused Nietzsche, who was a philosopher of the will to power, to reject the Christian concept of love. It was this same misinterpretation which

---

[15] The President of the United Auto Workers at the time, Walter Reuther was a major supporter of the civil rights movement who marched with Dr. King in the Selma to Birmingham march.

induced Christian theologians to reject the Nietzschean philosophy of the will to power in the name of the Christian idea of love. Now, we've got to get this thing right. What is needed is a realization that power without love is reckless and abusive, and love without power is sentimental and anemic. Power at its best is love implementing the demands of justice, and justice at its best is power correcting everything that stands against love.[16]

"Beyond Vietnam": A Time to Break Silence

As an internationalist and supporter of self-determination for developing nations, King naturally opposed the U.S. war in Vietnam. He made statements against the war as early as 1965, but he refrained from speaking out publicly or joining the growing antiwar movement until 1967. He knew that raising his influential voice against the war meant directly challenging President Lyndon Johnson and jeopardizing the recent gains of the civil rights and antipoverty movements: the 1964 Civil Rights Act outlawing racial discrimination in public facilities, the 1965 Voting Rights Act that guaranteed ballot access, and the administration's War on Poverty program. King recognized that he would pay a price for rebuking the president's war policy, and he did. His previously cordial and cooperative relationship with the White House ended abruptly, and he faced sharp criticism from many of his supporters and even civil rights leaders. The *New York Times*, *Washington Post*, and many other newspapers editorialized against him. King felt compelled to act, though, as the human cost and devastation of the war reached appalling levels, and its disastrous financial and social impacts at home shredded the civil rights and antipoverty agenda. King makes these points and draws the connections between racism, poverty, and militarism in the following excerpt from his historic address at

---

[16] "Where Do We Go from Here?" in Washington, *Testament of Hope*, 246–47.

New York's famous Riverside Church on April 4, 1967, a year to the day before he was assassinated in Memphis.

> I come to this great magnificent house of worship tonight because my conscience leaves me no other choice. I join you in this meeting because I am in deepest agreement with the aims and work of the organization that brought us together, Clergy and Laymen Concerned About Vietnam. The recent statements of your executive committee are the sentiments of my own heart, and I found myself in full accord when I read its opening lines: "A time comes when silence is betrayal." That time has come for us in relation to Vietnam. . . .
>
> Over the past two years, as I have moved to break the betrayal of my own silences and to speak from the burnings of my own heart, as I have called for radical departures from the destruction of Vietnam, many persons have questioned me about the wisdom of my path. At the heart of their concerns, this query has often loomed large and loud: "Why are you speaking about the war, Dr. King? Why are you joining the voices of dissent?" "Peace and civil rights don't mix," they say. "Aren't you hurting the cause of your people?" they ask. And when I hear them, though I often understand the source of their concern, I am nevertheless greatly saddened, for such questions mean that the inquirers have not really known me, my commitment, or my calling. . . .
>
> . . . A few years ago there was a shining moment in [the civil rights] struggle. It seemed as if there was a real promise of hope for the poor, both black and white, through the poverty program. There were experiments, hopes, new beginnings. Then came the buildup in Vietnam, and I watched this program broken and eviscerated as if it were some idle political plaything of a society gone mad on war. And I knew that America would never invest the necessary funds or energies in rehabilitation of its poor so long as adventures like Vietnam continued to draw men and skills and money like some demonic, destructive suction tube. So I was increas-

ingly compelled to see the war as an enemy of the poor and to attack it as such.

Perhaps a more tragic recognition of reality took place when it became clear to me that the war was doing far more than devastating the hopes of the poor at home. It was sending their sons and their brothers and their husbands to fight and to die in extraordinarily high proportions relative to the rest of the population. We were taking the black young men who had been crippled by our society and sending them eight thousand miles away to guarantee liberties in Southeast Asia which they had not found in southwest Georgia and East Harlem. So we have been repeatedly faced with the cruel irony of watching Negro and white boys on TV screens as they kill and die together for a nation that has been unable to seat them together in the same schools. So we watch them in brutal solidarity burning the huts of a poor village, but we realize that they would hardly live on the same block in Chicago. I could not be silent in the face of such cruel manipulation of the poor.

My third reason moves to an even deeper level of awareness, for it grows out of my experience in the ghettos of the North over the last three years, especially the last three summers. As I have walked among the desperate, rejected, and angry young men, I have told them that Molotov cocktails and rifles would not solve their problems. I have tried to offer them my deepest compassion while maintaining my conviction that social change comes most meaningfully through nonviolent action. But they asked, and rightly so, "What about Vietnam?" They asked if our own nation wasn't using massive doses of violence to solve its problems, to bring about the changes it wanted. Their questions hit home, and I knew that I could never again raise my voice against the violence of the oppressed in the ghettos without having first spoken clearly to the greatest purveyor of violence in the world today: my own government. For the sake of those boys, for the sake of this government, for the sake of the hundreds of thousands trembling under our violence, I cannot be silent. . . .

At this point I should make it clear that while I have tried to give a voice to the voiceless in Vietnam and to understand the arguments of those who are called "enemy," I am as deeply concerned about our own troops there as anything else. For it occurs to me that what we are submitting them to in Vietnam is not simply the brutalizing process that goes on in any war where armies face each other and seek to destroy. We are adding cynicism to the process of death, for they must know after a short period there that none of the things we claim to be fighting for are really involved. Before long they must know that their government has sent them into a struggle among Vietnamese, and the more sophisticated surely realize that we are on the side of the wealthy, and the secure, while we create a hell for the poor.

Surely this madness must cease. We must stop now. I speak as a child of God and brother to the suffering poor of Vietnam. I speak for those whose land is being laid waste, whose homes are being destroyed, whose culture is being subverted. I speak for the poor in America who are paying the double price of smashed hopes at home, and dealt death and corruption in Vietnam. I speak as a citizen of the world, for the world as it stands aghast at the path we have taken. I speak as one who loves America, to the leaders of our own nation: The great initiative in this war is ours; the initiative to stop it must be ours. . . .

. . . The words of the late John F. Kennedy come back to haunt us. Five years ago he said, "Those who make peaceful revolution impossible will make violent revolution inevitable." Increasingly, by choice or by accident, this is the role our nation has taken, the role of those who make peaceful revolution impossible by refusing to give up the privileges and the pleasures that come from the immense profits of overseas investments. I am convinced that if we are to get on to the right side of the world revolution, we as a nation must undergo a radical revolution of values. We must rapidly begin the shift from a thing-oriented society to a person-oriented society. When machines and computers, profit motives and property rights, are considered more important than people, the giant triplets of racism, extreme materialism, and militarism are incapable of being conquered.

A true revolution of values will soon cause us to question the fairness and justice of many of our past and present policies. On the one hand we are called to play the Good Samaritan on life's roadside, but that will be only an initial act. One day we must come to see that the whole Jericho Road must be transformed so that men and women will not be constantly beaten and robbed as they make their journey on life's highway. True compassion is more than flinging a coin to a beggar. It comes to see that an edifice which produces beggars needs restructuring.

A true revolution of values will soon look uneasily on the glaring contrast of poverty and wealth. With righteous indignation, it will look across the seas and see individual capitalists of the West investing huge sums of money in Asia, Africa, and South America, only to take the profits out with no concern for the social betterment of the countries, and say, "This is not just." It will look at our alliance with the landed gentry of South America and say, "This is not just." The Western arrogance of feeling that it has everything to teach others and nothing to learn from them is not just.

A true revolution of values will lay hand on the world order and say of war, "This way of settling differences is not just." This business of burning human beings with napalm, of filling our nation's homes with orphans and widows, of injecting poisonous drugs of hate into the veins of peoples normally humane, of sending men home from dark and bloody battlefields physically handicapped and psychologically deranged, cannot be reconciled with wisdom, justice, and love. A nation that continues year after year to spend more money on military defense than on programs of social uplift is approaching spiritual death. . . .

Our only hope today lies in our ability to recapture the revolutionary spirit and go out into a sometimes hostile world declaring eternal hostility to poverty, racism, and militarism. With this powerful commitment we shall boldly challenge the status quo and unjust mores, and thereby speed the day when "every valley shall be exalted, and every mountain and hill shall be made low; the crooked shall be made straight, and the rough places plain."

A genuine revolution of values means in the final analysis that our loyalties must become ecumenical rather than sectional. Every nation must now develop an overriding loyalty to mankind as a whole in order to preserve the best in their individual societies.

This call for a worldwide fellowship that lifts neighborly concern beyond one's tribe, race, class, and nation is in reality a call for an all-embracing and unconditional love for all mankind. This oft misunderstood, this oft misinterpreted concept, so readily dismissed by the Nietzsches of the world as a weak and cowardly force, has now become an absolute necessity for the survival of man. When I speak of love I am not speaking of some sentimental and weak response. I'm not speaking of that force which is just emotional bosh. I am speaking of that force which all of the great religions have seen as the supreme unifying principle of life. Love is somehow the key that unlocks the door which leads to ultimate reality. . . .

We can no longer afford to worship the god of hate or bow before the altar of retaliation. The oceans of history are made turbulent by the ever-rising tides of hate. History is cluttered with the wreckage of nations and individuals that pursued this self-defeating path of hate. As Arnold Toynbee says: "Love is the ultimate force that makes for the saving choice of life and good against the damning choice of death and evil. Therefore the first hope in our inventory must be the hope that love is going to have the last word."

We are now faced with the fact, my friends, that tomorrow is today. We are confronted with the fierce urgency of now. In this unfolding conundrum of life and history, there is such a thing as being too late. Procrastination is still the thief of time. Life often leaves us standing bare, naked, and dejected with a lost opportunity. The tide in the affairs of men does not remain at flood—it ebbs. We may cry out desperately for time to pause in her passage, but time is adamant to every plea and rushes on. Over the bleached bones and jumbled residues of numerous civilizations are written the pathetic words, "Too late." There is an invisible book of life that faithfully records our vigilance or our neglect. Omar Khayyam is right: "The moving finger writes, and having writ moves on."

We still have a choice today: nonviolent coexistence or violent coannihilation. We must move past indecision to action. We must find new ways to speak for peace in Vietnam and justice throughout the developing world, a world that borders on our doors. If we do not act, we shall surely be dragged down the long, dark, and shameful corridors of time reserved for those who possess power without compassion, might without morality, and strength without sight.[17]

---

[17] "Beyond Vietnam," April 4, 1967, Riverside Church, New York, available from Martin Luther King Jr. and the Global Freedom Struggle, King Institute Resources, Stanford University, http://kingencyclopedia.stanford.edu.

3

Pacifism and Nonviolent Action

Pacifism and nonviolence are closely related but are not the same. Gandhi, King, and other pioneers developed the methods of nonviolent action to fight for social, political, and economic justice, not to address the problem of war. Pacifism is a religious and moral belief that opposes all war unconditionally and rejects any participation in military combat. Some of those who engage in nonviolent action are pacifists, but most are not, as Gene Sharp emphasizes in chapter 5. Absolute pacifists who reject all war unconditionally are a minority, even within the peace movement, but they are often among the leaders and most passionate advocates of nonviolent change.

King described himself as a "realistic" pacifist.[1] He rejected violence, but as an African American steeped in the cruelties of segregation he understood all too well the nature of social evil and the human capacity for exploitation and malice toward others. His deep religious commitment to Christian nonviolence was tempered by a sober understanding of the limitations of human nature. King distinguished between violence that is aggressive or retaliatory and violence that is purely defensive, wrote his colleague Andrew Young, citing the example of a black woman in rural Georgia who fired upon Ku Klux Klan terrorists as they

---

[1] Martin Luther King Jr., *Stride toward Freedom: The Montgomery Story* (New York: Harper & Row, 1958), 99.

attempted to break into her home.² The moral presumption and political preference are always against war and violence, but the possibility of a just use of force is left open. Philosopher John Rawls developed a similar position in his concept of contingent pacifism. Violence may be acceptable in theory as a means of upholding justice, but war itself is profoundly unjust and is often waged by the powerful against the weak for purposes of domination. Given the predatory nature of most uses of military force, the pursuit of justice often requires resistance to war.³

Pacifism is often misunderstood as passivity—as weakness or moral abdication. While some religious pacifists follow a tradition of withdrawal from social and political engagement, many pacifists are actively involved in humanitarian service and efforts to prevent and transform armed conflict. Quakers are pacifist but they have always been committed to social action. From the time of their founding in seventeenth-century England to the present, Quakers have sought to transform a sinful world by applying Christian ideals to society and political life. They were leaders of historic social movements for free trade, the end of slavery, and women's suffrage, and they remain active today in many social justice campaigns. In recent decades, Mennonites, some Catholics, and other religious pacifists have joined Quakers in helping to mobilize political resistance to war, opposition to nuclear weapons, and campaigns for racial and social justice.

In the selections that follow, leading pacifists and advocates of nonviolent action reflect upon their commitment to social engagement for economic justice, the rights of workers, and the prevention of war. The authors present perspectives on the philosophy and method of nonviolence as the pathway to a more just and peaceful world. Cesar Chavez and Dolores Huerta offer insights into the farmworkers' movement they helped to

---

² Andrew Young, *An Easy Burden: The Civil Rights Movement and the Transformation of America* (New York: HarperCollins, 1996), 120.

³ John Rawls, *A Theory of Justice*, rev. ed. (Cambridge, MA: Belknap Press of the Harvard University Press, 1999), 335.

lead and the struggle for economic justice and dignity among America's most impoverished and exploited workers. Dorothy Day explains her conversion to Catholicism, her commitment to pacifism and the Catholic Worker movement, and her struggles against the conservatism of the church, which included support for the Vietnam War among leading Catholic clerics in the 1960s. A. J. Muste writes about the linkages between nonviolence and democracy, provides a critical analysis of Gandhi's social and economic program, and discusses the goal of abolishing war. The section ends with excerpts from Albert Camus's *Neither Victims nor Executioners*, cited by Muste but developed more extensively here as a profound philosophical statement on the necessity of nonviolence for human survival and fulfillment.

Cesar Chavez (1927–1993)

It is no accident that the philosophy and methods of Gandhian nonviolence entered American political culture through movements for racial and economic justice among people of color. As King led the African American struggle for civil rights, Cesar Chavez helped to create the United Farm Workers Union (UFW) and led historic campaigns to enhance the dignity and well-being of those who labor in the fields. Like King, Chavez was attracted by the victory of the Gandhian movement in India and the example of brown people challenging the white power structure of the British Raj. He applied the examples of both Gandhi and King in organizing farmworkers and created successful national boycott campaigns. Chavez combined the lessons of nonviolent struggle, the methods of community and labor organizing, and the social justice traditions of Catholic moral teaching to forge a religiously inspired nonviolent campaign for economic and social justice.

Chavez spent much of his early life in poverty, stooped over in the fields picking fruit and vegetables for wealthy food and beverage companies. Farmworkers at the time were paid less than a dollar an hour, had no health insurance or pensions, and often had no toilets or fresh drinking water in the fields where they worked. They were at the mercy of abusive labor contractors and lived in squalid conditions as they moved with the harvest from one field to the next. Farmworker children had little opportunity for education, and many like Chavez never finished secondary school. Despite his limited education Chavez studied intensely and read the works of Gandhi and King. He was a devout Catholic and learned about papal encyclicals and other church teachings that emphasize the dignity of labor and the duty of lifting up the poor and disadvantaged. Like Gandhi and King, Chavez's commitment to social justice was based upon a strong religious foundation.

Impressions of Gandhi

In this passage Chavez tells his biographer Jacques Levy of the strong positive impression Gandhi made upon him and how his own commitment to disciplined nonviolence grew out of the Gandhian model.

> When I read the biography of St. Francis of Assisi . . . there was a reference to Gandhi and others who practiced nonviolence. That was a theme that struck a very responsive chord, probably because of the foundation laid by my mother. So the next thing I read after St. Francis was the Louis Fischer biography of Gandhi.[4]
>
> Since then I've been greatly influenced by Gandhi's philosophy and have read a great deal about what he said and did. But in those days I knew very little about him except what I read in the papers and saw in newsreels. There was one scene I never forgot. Gandhi was going to a meeting with a high British official in India. There were throngs of people as he walked all but naked out of his little hut. Then

---

[4] Louis Fischer, *The Life of Mahatma Gandhi* (New York: Harper & Row, 1950).

he was filmed in his loincloth, sandals, and shawl walking up the steps of the palace.

Not too long ago I was speaking to a group of Indians including three who had worked with Gandhi. When I said I thought Gandhi was the most perfect man, not including Christ, they all laughed. When I asked them why they laughed, they asked, "What do you mean by perfect?"

I said I don't mean he was perfect like a saint in the sense that he didn't move. I said he was perfect in the sense that he wasn't afraid to move and make things happen. And he didn't ask people to do things he couldn't do himself.

I understand Gandhi more and more. To him duty was the first call. He had no compunction whatsoever about sending someone five hundred miles to take care of something, because he himself was willing to do it. I myself can't do all the things that I ask others to do, but then no one can try to imitate him, because it becomes false. You've got to take the whole philosophy and try to adapt it to your needs. I want to experiment with some of the things he did but not imitate him, because I don't think that can be done.

He had tremendous discipline, both personal and around him. He had all kinds of rules and insisted they be obeyed. So a group of thirty, forty, or a hundred men at the most was very effective, because they worked like a symphony. They were totally loyal to him. He wouldn't put up with anybody being half-loyal or 90 percent loyal. It was 100 percent loyal or nothing at all.

Then, of course, there were more personal things, the whole question of the spirit versus the body. He prepared himself for it by his diet, starving his body so that his spirit could overtake it, controlling the palate, then controlling the sex urge, then using all of his energies to do nothing but service. He was very tough with himself.

He believed that truth was vindicated, not by infliction of suffering on the opponent, but on oneself. That belief comes from Christ himself, the Sermon on the Mount, and further back from Jewish and Hindu traditions. There's no question that by setting such an example, you get others to do it. That is the real essence, but that is difficult. That's what separates ordinary men from great men. And we're all pretty ordinary men in those things.

I like the whole idea of sacrifice to do things. If they are done that way, they are more lasting. If they cost more, then we will value them more.

When we apply Gandhi's philosophy of nonviolence, it really forces us to think, really forces us to work hard. But it has power. It attracts the support of the people. I've learned that, if any movement is on the move, violence is the last thing wanted. Violence only seems necessary when people are desperate; frustration often leads to violence.

For example, a supermarket boycott is an effective nonviolent weapon. Fire is not. When a fire destroys a supermarket, the company collects the insurance and rebuilds the store bigger and better, and also marks off the loss on its income tax. But picket lines take away customers and reduce business, and there is no way for the store to compensate for that. It is driven by sheer economics to want to avoid picket lines.

Gandhi described his tactics as moral jujitsu—always hitting the opposition off-balance, but keeping his principles. His tactics of civil disobedience haven't hit this country on a massive scale, but they will. Anybody who comes out with the right way of doing it is going to throw the government into a real uproar. If they have a good issue, and they find a good vehicle for civil disobedience, they're going to be devastating.

Just imagine what would happen to this intricate government we have here. Look what happened with Gandhi's salt march and the civil disobedience that followed after it. He boycotted the salt so the government couldn't collect the tax, but then he showed the people how to make their own salt. He boycotted clothes coming in from England, but he turned around and showed the Indians how to make their own clothes.[5]

Homage to Dr. King

In the following passage marking the tenth anniversary of King's assassination, Chavez dwells upon King's courageous example and reveals some of his own thinking on the power of nonviolence and the necessity of channeling resistance to oppression through peaceful means.

> In honoring Martin Luther King Jr.'s memory we also acknowledge nonviolence as a truly powerful weapon to achieve equality and liberation, in fact, the only weapon that Christians who struggle for social change can claim as their own.
>
> Dr. King's entire life was an example of power that nonviolence brings to bear in the real world. It is an example that inspired much of the philosophy and strategy of the farmworkers' movement. This observance of Dr. King's death gives us the best possible opportunity to recall the principles with which our struggle has grown and matured.
>
> Our conviction is that human life is a very special possession given by God to man and that no one has the right to take it for any reason or for any cause, however just it may be.
>
> We are also convinced that nonviolence is more powerful than violence. Nonviolence supports you if you have a just and moral cause. Nonviolence provides the opportunity to stay on the offensive, and that is of crucial importance to win any contest.
>
> If we resort to violence then one of two things will happen: either the violence will be escalated and there will be

---

[5] Jacques E. Levy, *Cesar Chavez: Autobiography of La Causa* (Minneapolis: University of Minnesota Press, 2007), 91–93.

many injuries and perhaps deaths on both sides, or there will be total demoralization of the workers.

Nonviolence has exactly the opposite effect. If, for every violent act committed against us, we respond with nonviolence, we attract people's support. We can gather the support of millions who have a conscience and would rather see a nonviolent resolution to problems. We are convinced that when people are faced with a direct appeal from the poor struggling nonviolently against great odds, they will react positively. The American people and people everywhere still yearn for justice. It is to that yearning that we appeal.

But if we are committed to nonviolence only as a strategy or tactic, then if it fails our only alternative is to turn to violence. So we must balance the strategy with a clear understanding of what we are doing. However important the struggle is and however much misery, poverty, and exploitation exist, we know that it cannot be more important than one human life. We work on the theory that men and women who are truly concerned about people are nonviolent by nature. These people become violent when the deep concern they have for people is frustrated and when they are faced with seemingly insurmountable odds.

We advocate militant nonviolence as our means of achieving justice for our people, but we are not blind to the feelings of frustration, impatience, and anger which seethe inside every farmworker. The burdens of generations of poverty and powerlessness lie heavy in the fields of America. If we fail, there are those who will see violence as the shortcut to change.

It is precisely to overcome these frustrations that we have involved masses of people in their own struggle throughout the movement. Freedom is best experienced through participation and self-determination, and free men and women instinctively prefer democratic change to any other means.

Thus, demonstrations and marches, strikes and boycotts are not only weapons against the growers, but our way of avoiding the senseless violence that brings no honor to any class or community. The boycott, as Gandhi taught, is the most nearly perfect instrument of nonviolent change, allowing masses of people to participate actively in a cause.

When victory comes through violence, it is a victory with strings attached. If we beat the growers at the expense of violence, victory would come at the expense of injury and perhaps death. Such a thing would have a tremendous impact on us. We would lose regard for human beings. Then the struggle would become a mechanical thing. When you lose your sense of life and justice, you lose your strength.

The greater the oppression, the more leverage nonviolence holds. Violence does not work in the long run and if it is temporarily successful, it replaces one violent form of power with another just as violent. People suffer from violence.

Examine history. Who gets killed in the case of violent revolution? The poor, the workers. The people of the land are the ones who give their bodies and don't really gain that much for it. We believe it is too big a price to pay for not getting anything. Those who espouse violence exploit people. To call men to arms with many promises, to ask them to give up their lives for a cause and then not produce for them afterwards, is the most vicious type of oppression.

We know that most likely we are not going to do anything else the rest of our lives except build our union. For us there is nowhere else to go. Although we would like to see victory come soon, we are willing to wait. In this sense, time is our ally. We learned many years ago that the rich may have money, but the poor have time.

It has been our experience that few men or women ever have the opportunity to know the true satisfaction that comes with giving one's life totally in the nonviolent struggle for justice. Martin Luther King Jr. was one of these unique servants and from him we learned many of the lessons that have guided us. For these lessons and for his sacrifice for the poor and oppressed, Dr. King's memory will be cherished in the hearts of the farmworkers forever.[6]

Dolores Huerta

Known as *La Pasionaria* (the passionate one), Dolores Huerta (b. 1930) was the coleader with Chavez of the United Farm Workers of America (UFW) and for six decades dedicated her life to the farmworkers' struggle for justice. She also supported feminist, social justice, peace, and environmental movements. She met Chavez in California in the 1950s while working for a community service organization on civil rights and social justice issues. A few years later she joined him in organizing the farmworkers' movement and creating the UFW. While Chavez was the public face and spiritual inspiration of the farmworkers' cause (*la causa*), Huerta was the key organizer who focused on the nuts and bolts of building and maintaining a mass movement. She was famous for marching the picket lines and maintaining the spirit of the workers. She spearheaded efforts to organize the national and international boycott of table grapes that pressured growers into signing the first labor contracts with the union.

Huerta helped to bring women into the movement and played a crucial role in maintaining the movement's commitment to nonviolent discipline. She understood the power of nonviolence and emphasized that farmworkers could not succeed in gaining dignity for themselves if they practiced violence toward others. She saw the commitment to principled nonviolence in very practical terms. The movement could not succeed in organizing a successful boycott against the growers without winning the support of many millions of ordinary people, and this would not be possible without a principled commitment to

---

[6] César Chávez, "He Showed Us the Way," *Maryknoll Magazine*, April 1978.

nonviolence. She understood that the dedication to nonviolent methods was necessary to build a broad coalition and attract the support of civil rights, religious, women's, peace, and environmental movements.[7]

The excerpt below captures her commitment to nonviolence and offers insight into the ways she and Chavez sought to overcome the tradition of male machismo in Mexican American culture to build a successful nonviolent movement.

> The whole boycott is a nonviolent tool. It's an economic sanction, so to speak, but it's a way that people can participate. One thing about nonviolence is that it opens the doors for everyone to participate, the children, the women. And women being involved on the picket lines made it easier for men to accept nonviolence. They would always say . . . , "We need some women on our picket line. We need some women here." It makes it a lot easier for them. Then they can justify not being macho tough, or macho revenge, you know. Just having the women there made it possible, I think, for the organization to practice its nonviolence.
>
> I consider nonviolence to be a very strong spiritual force because it's almost like an energy that goes out and it touches people.
>
> In the first strike there was a lot of violence by the growers. So we had to have this big meeting because people said, "It's one thing to be nonviolent against the growers or the labor contractors. But here the Teamsters are coming in and they are beating up our organizers and beating up the farmworkers. So why do we have to use nonviolence against them?" So we had to have this major meeting. We had to have this big discussion with the strikers, and Cesar made everybody take a standing vow for nonviolence. And then some of the organizers and young people were arguing

---

[7] Mario T. Garcia, "Introduction: *La Pasionaria Chicana*," in *A Dolores Huerta Reader*, ed. with an introduction by Mario T. Garcia (Albuquerque: University of New Mexico Press, 2008), xviii–xxiv.

against him. He said, "Well, if one of you wants to take over this union, you can, but I will not be the leader of this union if you're going to use violence." And he said, "If you start using violence against the Teamsters, you're going to use it against each other." So everybody had to take a standing vow for nonviolence and to practice it.

Most of them were either first generation Mexican Americans or recent immigrants. To get them to accept the whole philosophy that you can create a movement with nonviolence was not easy. It was not easy. To get them to understand that—and this you could see happening in people, that they would become transformed. They would actually become stronger through practicing nonviolence. They became much stronger people and had to use strategies and tactics instead of violence to be able to win.

Then Cesar started doing something. He would always do things that would make people feel uncomfortable. . . . He always believed in fasting, again getting that from Gandhi. He would do these seven-day fasts and everybody would do like little fasts when we were going to do something really important. He would ask everybody to please fast and to pray before we embarked on some strike or something. But then he started doing these twenty-five-day fasts for nonviolence. . . .

Every night while Cesar was fasting they would have a big Mass and then farmworkers brought their tents there to the headquarters, the forty acres in Delano.[8] People put up their tents so they could be there with Cesar while he was fasting. It was kind of interesting, too, the reactions of people. They didn't understand it. They couldn't comprehend it. Just like some religious people didn't like—the more traditional—they didn't like the idea that we had the Virgin Mary of Guadalupe on the picket line.[9] They didn't like that.

---

[8] The small farmworkers' community in California's Central Valley where Chavez and his family and closest associates lived and worked.

[9] The image of Our Lady of Guadalupe, Mary the mother of Jesus, is iconic in Mexican religious heritage.

> To Cesar, religion was a very practical thing that you used in your work. It was part of you. It wasn't something that was distant and way up there. It was something that was very, very much a part of you.[10]

Dorothy Day (1897–1980)

Like Chavez, Dorothy Day was strongly influenced by Catholicism. She converted to the church in 1927 at age twenty-nine and embraced the faith with a zeal and passion that marked her as one of the most devout Catholics of her age. She is currently a candidate for canonization as a saint, although she famously said, "Don't call me a saint. I don't want to be dismissed that easily."[11] Day's commitment to social justice and nonviolent activism began during her youth when she wrote for radical newspapers such as *The Masses* and the *New York Call* and participated in antiwar, socialist, and suffragette movements. With colleague Peter Maurin she founded the *Catholic Worker* newspaper in 1933 and opened "houses of hospitality" for the poor and unemployed that spread widely and continue to operate today. She did not organize large-scale action campaigns in the manner of Gandhi, King, or Chavez, focusing more on spiritual transformation than political goals, but she was involved in many social justice campaigns and was strongly opposed to war and nuclear weapons.

For a Vital Religion

In her devotion to serving "Christ in the poor," Dorothy Day was often compared to her contemporary Mother Teresa of Calcutta. But Day wanted to do more to address underlying needs.

---

[10] Garcia, *Dolores Huerta Reader*, 183–85.

[11] Quoted in Jim Forest, *Love Is the Measure: A Biography of Dorothy Day* (New York: Paulist, 1986), 113.

From her youthful experiences of Christianity she had seen the tension between Christian meekness and the duty to resist evil. Here she describes the feelings, as a college student, that had turned her heart from organized Christianity in favor of the radical movements of the day. Curiously, in her question about the need for "saints to change the social order," she would anticipate the later direction of her life.

> Whatever I had read as a child about the saints had thrilled me. I could see the nobility of giving one's life for the sick, the maimed, the leper. Priests and Sisters the world over could be working for the littlest ones of Christ, and my heart stirred at their work.
>
> But there was another question in my mind. Why was so much done in remedying the evil instead of avoiding it in the first place? Disabled men, men without arms and legs, blind, consumptive, exhausted men with all the manhood drained from them by industrialism; farmers gaunt and harried with debt; mothers weighted down with children at their skirts, in their arms, in their wombs, and the children ailing, rickety, toothless—all this long procession of desperate people called to me. Where were the saints to try to change the social order, not just to minister to the slaves but to do away with slavery? . . .
>
> Our Lord said, "Blessed are the meek," but I could not be meek at the thought of injustice. I wanted a Lord who would scourge the moneylenders out of the temple, and I wanted to help all those who raised their hand against oppression.
>
> Religion, as it was practiced by those I encountered, had no vitality. It had nothing to do with everyday life: it was a matter of Sunday praying. Christ no longer walked the streets of this world. He was two thousand years dead, and new prophets had risen up in His place.[12]

---

[12] Ibid., 15.

Conversion to Catholicism

Following her conversion, Day remained deeply disturbed by the church's alliance with reactionary forces in many countries. She agreed with the Catholic Church on matters of religious orthodoxy but strongly opposed the hierarchy when it stood for the interests of the wealthy over those of the poor. She lamented the church's failure to address the underlying economic conditions that produce so many homeless and unemployed for charities like hers to feed and shelter. In this short excerpt, Day reflects upon these issues and vents her dissatisfaction with the "scandal" of the church as an institution.

> That very winter [when I converted] I was writing a series of articles, interviews with the workers, with the unemployed. I was working with the Anti-Imperialist League, a Communist affiliate, that was bringing aid and comfort to the enemy, General Sandino's forces in Nicaragua.[13] I was just as much against capitalism and imperialism as ever, and here I was going over to the opposition, because of course the Church was lined up with property, with the wealthy, with the state, with capitalism, with all the forces of reaction. This I had been taught to think and this I still think to a great extent. . . . But I wanted to be poor, chaste, and obedient. I wanted to die in order to live, to put off the old man and put on Christ. I loved, in other words, and like all women in love, I wanted to be united in my love. . . .
>
> I loved the Church for Christ made visible. Not for itself, because it was so often a scandal to me. Romano Guardini[14] said that the Church is the Cross on which Christ was crucified; one could not separate Christ from His Cross, and one

---

[13] Augusto César Sandino (1895–1934) led the Nicaraguan rebellion against U.S. occupation and was assassinated. He is the namesake for the Sandinista National Liberation Front, which overthrew the Somoza dictatorship in 1979.

[14] Guardini (1885–1968) was a prominent Italian-born priest who had a significant influence on Catholic intellectual development.

must live in a state of permanent dissatisfaction with the Church. . . .

Not long afterward a priest wanted me to write a story of my conversion, telling how the social teaching of the Church had led me to embrace Catholicism. But I knew nothing of the social teaching of the Church at that time. I had never heard of the encyclicals. I felt that the Church was the Church of the poor, that St. Patrick's[15] had been built from the pennies of servant girls, that it cared for the immigrant, it established hospitals, orphanages, day nurseries, houses of the Good Shepherd, homes for the aged, but at the same time, I felt that it did not set its face against a social order which made so much charity in the present sense of the word necessary. I felt that charity was a word to choke over. Who wanted charity? It was not just human pride, but a strong sense of man's dignity and worth and what was due to him in justice, that made me resent, rather than feel proud of, so mighty a sum of total Catholic institutions.[16]

In Solidarity with Workers

In this passage, Day offers impressions of a 1932 protest of unemployed workers. She expresses admiration for the movement but also frustration, as a Catholic, at not being able to join the Communist-led protest. It was immediately after this experience, following her meeting with Peter Maurin, that she decided to launch the Catholic Worker movement.

In the fall of 1932 I had been writing articles for *America* and *The Commonweal*,[17] and the first week in December I went to Washington, DC, to cover the Hunger March of the

---

[15] The famous cathedral on New York's Fifth Avenue that is headquarters of the Catholic Archdiocese of New York.

[16] Dorothy Day, *Selected Writings*, ed. by Robert Ellsberg (Maryknoll, NY: Orbis Books, 1983, 1992), 39.

[17] Two prominent Catholic journals at the time that are still published today.

Unemployed Councils and the Farmers' Convention. Both were Communist-led.[18]

If the journalists and the police of Washington had been coached in their parts, they could not have staged a better drama, from the Communist standpoint, than they did in the events of that week.

Drama was what the Communist leaders of the march wanted, and the drama, even melodrama, was what they got. They weren't presenting their petitions to Congress with any hope of immediately obtaining the cash bonuses and unemployment relief they demanded. (Nevertheless, five years later unemployment insurance became part of Social Security legislation.) They were presenting pictorially the plight of the workers of America, not only to the countless small towns and large cities through which they passed, but through the press to the entire world. And in addition they were demonstrating to the proletariat.

They were saying, "Come, submit yourselves to our discipline—place yourselves in our hands, you union workers, you unemployed, and we will show you how a scant 3,000 of you, unarmed, can terrorize authorities and make them submit to at least some of your demands!"

It does not matter that the victory won was only that of marching to the Capitol. To those unarmed marchers who for two days and two cold nights in December lived and slept on an asphalt highway with no water, no fires, no sanitary facilities, with the scantiest of food, surrounded by hysteria in the shape of machine guns and teargas bombs in the hands of a worn and fretted police force, egged on by a bunch of ghouls in the shape of newspaper men and photographers—to these marchers, the victory was a real one. They had achieved their purpose. . . .

---

[18] The U.S. Communist Party gained influence by organizing broadly based coalitions of workers and the unemployed during the Great Depression and building opposition to the threat of Nazism, but the party never gained much of a following among Americans.

> I watched that ragged horde and thought to myself, "These are Christ's poor. He was one of them. He was a man like other men, and He chose His friends amongst the ordinary workers. These men feel they have been betrayed by Christianity. Men are not Christian today. If they were, this sight would not be possible. Far dearer in the sight of God perhaps are these hungry ragged ones, than all those smug, well-fed Christians who sit in their homes, cowering in fear of the Communist menace."
>
> I felt that they were my people, that I was part of them. I had worked for them and with them in the past, and now I was a Catholic and so could not be a Communist. I could not join this united front of protest, and I wanted to.[19]

Pacifism Against War

From the beginning in the 1930s Day insisted that the Catholic Worker was a pacifist movement—a highly unusual stance for Catholics at the time. She maintained her position throughout World War II, the subsequent Cold War, and all other military actions. Day was a stalwart opponent of nuclear weapons from their very beginning, joining A. J. Muste and other colleagues in publicly disobeying mandatory participation in civil defense air raid drills in New York in the 1950s. She was also a vocal opponent of the Vietnam War, counseling young men faced with the military draft to resist conscription or file for conscientious objection. In these excerpts Day explains the basis for her pacifist stance, beginning with an editorial she published in January 1942, immediately after U.S. entry into World War II.

> Seventy-five thousand copies of the *Catholic Worker* go out every month. What shall we print? We can still print what the Holy Father is saying, when he speaks of total war, of mitigating the horrors of war, when he speaks of cities of refuge; of feeding Europe....

---

[19] Day, *Selected Writings*, 40–41.

We will print the words of Christ, who is with us always, even to the end of the world. "Love your enemies, do good to those who hate you, and pray for those who persecute and calumniate you, so that you may be children of your Father in heaven, who makes His sun to rise on the good and the evil, and sends rain on the just and the unjust."

We are at war, a declared war, with Japan, German, and Italy. But still we can repeat Christ's words, each day, holding them close in our hearts, each month printing them in our paper. In times past Europe has been a battlefield. But let us remember St. Francis, who spoke of peace, and we will remind our readers of him, too, so they will not forget.

In the *Catholic Worker* we will quote our Pope, our saints, our priests. We will go on printing the articles of Father Hugo,[20] who reminds us today that we are all "called to be saints," that we are other Christs, reminding us of the priesthood of the laity.

We are still pacifists. Our manifesto is the Sermon on the Mount, which means we will try to be peacemakers. Speaking for many of our conscientious objectors, we will not participate in armed warfare or in making munitions, or by buying government bonds to prosecute the war, or in urging others to these efforts.

But neither will we be carping in our criticism. We love our country and we love our President. We have been the only country in the world where men and women of all nations have taken refuge from oppression. We recognize that while in the order of intention we have tried to stand for peace, for love of our brothers and sisters, in the order of execution we have failed as Americans in living up to our principles.

We will try daily, hourly, to pray for an end to the war, such an end, to quote Father Orchard (October 28, the *Commonweal*), "as would manifest to all the world, that it was brought about by divine action, rather than by military might

---

[20] Father John Hugo was one of Dorothy Day's spiritual advisers.

or diplomatic negotiation, which men and nations would then only attribute to their powers and sagacity."

Let us add that unless we continue this prayer with almsgiving, in giving to the least of God's children; and fasting in order that we may help feed the hungry; and penance in recognition of our share in the guilt, our prayer may become empty words.

Our Works of Mercy may take us into the midst of war. As editor of the *Catholic Worker*, I would urge our friends and associates to care for the sick and the wounded, to the growing of food for the hungry, to the continuance of all our Works of Mercy in our houses and on our farms. We understand, of course, that there is and that there will be great differences we can have with the government in times like these. There are differences more profound and there will be many continuing to work with us from necessity, or from choice, who do not agree with us as to our position on war, conscientious objection, etc. But we beg that there will be mutual charity and forebearance among us all.[21]

In the selection below Day puts the Vietnam War in context and calls out the church leaders who supported that conflict.

It is not just Vietnam, it is South Africa, it is Nigeria, the Congo, Indonesia, all of Latin America. It is not just the pictures of all the women and children who have been burnt alive in Vietnam, or the men who have been tortured, and died. It is not just the headless victims of the war in Colombia. It is not just the words of Cardinal Spellman and Archbishop Hannan.[22] It is the fact that whether we like it or not, we are Americans. It is indeed our country, right or wrong, as the Cardinal said in another context. We are warm and fed

---

[21] This is taken from an editorial, written immediately after the declaration of war following the attack on Pearl Harbor and published in the *Catholic Worker*, January 1942 (Day, *Selected Writings*, 261–62).

[22] Francis Cardinal Spellman of New York and Bishop Jerome Hannan of Scranton, Pennsylvania, were strongly anticommunist Catholic prelates who supported the Vietnam War.

and secure (aside from occasional muggings and murders amongst us). We are among nations the most powerful, the most armed, and we are supplying arms and money to the rest of the world where we are not ourselves fighting. We are eating while there is famine in the world.

Scripture tells us that the picture of judgment presented to us by Jesus is of Dives sitting and feasting with his friends while Lazarus sat hungry at the gate, the dogs, the scavengers of the East, licking his sores.[23] We are Dives. Woe to the rich! *We* are the rich. The Works of Mercy are the opposite of the works of war, feeding the hungry, sheltering the homeless, nursing the sick, visiting the prisoner. But we are destroying crops, setting fire to entire villages and to the people in them. We are not performing the Works of Mercy but the works of war. . . .

Maybe they are terrified, these Princes of the Church, as we are often terrified at the sight of violence, which is present every now and then in our Houses of Hospitality, and which is always a threat in the streets of the slums. I have often thought it is a brave thing to do, these Christmas visits of Cardinal Spellman to the American troops all over the world, Europe, Korea, Vietnam. But, oh, God, what are all these Americans, so-called Christians, doing all over the world so far from our shores?

But what words are those he spoke—going against even the Pope, calling for victory, total victory? Words are as strong and powerful as bombs, as napalm. How much the government counts on those words, pays for those words to exalt our own way of life, to build up fear of the enemy. Deliver us, Lord, from the fear of the enemy. That is one of the lines in the Psalms, and we are not asking God to deliver us from enemies but from the fear of them. Love casts out fear, but we have to get over the fear in order to get close enough to love them.[24]

---

[23] A reference to Jesus's parable about the Rich Man and Lazarus, Luke 16:19–31.

[24] Day, *Selected Writings*, 337–39.

A. J. Muste (1885–1967)

Abraham Johannes Muste was an ordained minister of the Dutch Reformed Church who became a labor organizer and antiwar activist. He was an opponent of U.S. entry into World War I and joined the Fellowship of Reconciliation soon after its founding in 1916, and he served as executive director of the organization from 1940 to 1953. In the last years of his life he helped to build the National Mobilization Committee to End the Vietnam War and worked tirelessly as a leading figure in the antiwar movement.

Muste was an intellectual as well as an activist. He blended Christian idealism with American pragmatism, linking theory to practice through nonviolent social action. He was critical of conventional liberalism for its often blind faith in capitalism and embrace of cold-war ideology. He advocated an alternative vision of democratic socialism grounded in locally based citizen groups committed to working for racial justice and greater economic and social equality. His books and voluminous articles had a significant influence on the development of nonviolent activism for half a century.[25]

Nonviolence in an Aggressive World

This excerpt from his book *Nonviolence in an Aggressive World* was written on the eve of World War II and offers a glimpse of his deeply rooted critique of the war system, based partly on religious grounds but also on the psychological and social needs of humankind. He examines the racial roots of war and its negative consequences for democracy and social well-being.

---

[25] For a review of Muste's life and intellectual contributions, see Leilah Danielson, *American Gandhi: A. J. Muste and the History of Radicalism in the Twentieth Century* (Philadelphia: University of Pennsylvania Press, 2014).

What we have said implies that the human being is "an end in himself," as the philosophers put it,[26] not a mere tool or domestic animal to serve another's ends. His basic need is to be treated as such an "end in himself," to stand in a relationship of confidence, of affection, of fellowship with others, not in a relation of subjugation or humiliation or of being ignored. To be able to feel that he is a person, he has to "belong" and he has to be "wanted" somewhere, wanted for himself, not for ulterior purposes or for accidental reasons, such as the color of his skin or his economic status—must "belong" and "be wanted" among his fellows as he is in his own family.

When a man grasps and in the degree that he grasps that this is for him the essence of living, he sees others also as ends, not as his means. That is to say, it is in the very nature of human beings, as human, to constitute free fellowships. Only in such a community can they realize themselves. To love and to be loved, to constitute brotherhoods, i.e., democracies, is of the essence of man's nature.

Observe now some of the factors that produce war, that are involved in war-making and the war-system (for whatever purpose it is maintained), and then note how utterly incompatible they are with the very essence of the democratic concept.

One of the concepts upon which war has always openly or covertly been based is that of racism, that the enemy belongs to an "inferior breed." It is the idea on which the wars that accompanied the assumption of "the white man's burden" was based. It is deeply ingrained in the North American attitude toward Latin Americans, which the Latin Americans sense and bitterly resent. It is implicit in our Oriental Exclusion Act and our Jim Crow laws and customs.[27]

---

[26] A reference to philosopher Immanuel Kant's moral principle of treating humanity always as an end in itself, not merely as a means to some other end.

[27] The 1882 Oriental Exclusion Act, also known as the Chinese Exclusion Act, significantly restricted immigration into the United States. Jim

The British regard this attitude of superiority in the Germans as insufferable, and the Germans reciprocate. The forms of "racism" which are promulgated in Germany are but extreme expressions of an assumption which underlies all warmaking, namely, that the enemy is an inferior being with whom normal human relations are impossible—he is savage, he must be kept in subjection "for his own good," he "does not understand any language except that of force." . . .

This whole idea clashes head-on with the democratic concept. Democracy, as we have seen, rests its case on the person, the human being as human, not on this or that breed or class. If, for example, we adopt the idea that Americans are a superior breed who must rule other breeds "for their own benefit," the bottom drops out of the democratic concept. If there are inferior breeds in Asia or Africa, on what ground will you argue that dark-skinned Americans are not inferior to whites, or of course white to black in the estimation of the latter? Furthermore, why is it not then plausible to assume that the present economic and political rulers constitute a superior class? Once you abandon the position that it is man as such who has moral dignity and infinite worth, only brute force and cunning can settle such questions. . . .

I am not for a moment justifying or condoning the violence of strikers, for example, not to mention gangsters. I can see no moral justification for the use of violence, though willingly agreeing that there are cases where resistance to evil and injustice even by violent means is an ethically nobler attitude than cowardly or passive acquiescence in evil. My experience in the labor and radical movements, furthermore, convinced me that violence is self-defeating when workers resort to it, quite as the open and covert violence used by employers or agents of the state is self-defeating. The oppressed will make surer and faster progress if they eschew violence and depend, as they do mainly depend in

---

Crow laws were racial segregation measures adopted by states and local governments primarily in southern states of the United States.

their organizing and strike activities, on their solidarity, courage, capacity for suffering and sacrifice, and on noncooperation where injustice becomes extreme. No saying in all history has, in my opinion, been validated more consistently in all lands and times and in all the relationships of life than Jesus', which may be paraphrased in the words: Put up your sword into its place, for they that take the sword—no matter how great the provocation, how ideal the end, how apparently certain the victory—they that use the sword shall perish by the sword. . . .

Without a fellowship of those who have found the truth, who are in league with the universe, with the very heart of reality, who have surrendered themselves to the good and find all of their joy in its service, who have taken up the Cross and are ready to lose their life so that they may find it; a fellowship which knows no bounds but is universal in character and intention; a fellowship of hope and faith which as all that men have relied on goes to pieces knows that thus the way is open for a better order, that "the Kingdom of God is at hand"—without such a fellowship mankind is lost. It is, to use figures that Jesus employed, like meat with no salt to keep it from putrefying; like a room without a candle; like a dull lump of dough with no yeast to set it fermenting with new life. But such a fellowship of those who believe that they are chosen of God to bring in his Kingdom, that they are the instruments of destiny whom no one and nothing will be able to stop or should be permitted to stop, such a church, such a party is always in danger of becoming a supreme instrument of tyranny, as the history of churches and parties has so often illustrated. There is terrific power in complete surrender of the self to an idea; such a self becomes indeed an agent of elemental forces. But those forces may be demonic as well as divine. The Fellowship, the church, the party of "the elect" will indeed save and redeem men and advance the genuine fulfillment of human history only if the reality, the

God, from whom the dedicated draw their strength is love, and if the only means by which they seek to sway men are reason, love, and sacrificial suffering.

Pacifists, the followers of the nonviolent way in all lands, profess that love is the ultimate reality and that nonviolence, constructive goodwill is the one means for achieving justice, freedom, and brotherhood. So far as words go, they have attained to the truth. But mouthing the words which one does not understand is absurd; to see the truth and then not to embrace it and live by it, that is the sin against the Holy Spirit, the surrender of integrity and respect. So long as pacifists are amiable simpletons who talk what they do not comprehend; or so long as they are imposters who know their Lord and betray him with a kiss, we richly merit the suspicion, the scoffing, the persecution to which we may be subjected. Those who are willing to kill for their convictions at the risk of their own lives are nearer the Kingdom of God than those who will not kill but are in their secret goals even more firmly determined not to die for the faith they profess. It is necessary to emphasize the need of commitment and self-discipline for individual pacifists and of welding the pacifist movement in the Western world into a true church, the party of "the revolution of peace," the universal conquering brotherhood of love.[28]

On the Gandhi Movement

In this essay written in 1941 Muste discusses Gandhi's nonviolent principles in relation to economic and political matters. He is skeptical of some of Gandhi's thinking, especially his rejection of industry and technology, but he sees value in the emphasis on cooperatives, self-help, and manual labor. He also comments on the utility of the Gandhian political method for addressing racial and economic oppression.

---

[28] A. J. Muste, *Nonviolence in an Aggressive World* (New York: Harper & Brothers, 1940), 103–5, 118–19, 186–87.

The Gandhi movement in India is giving the world an example of the use of nonviolence on a mass scale. Not only may we pacifists learn much from Gandhi and his followers in building a mass nonviolence movement in this and other Western countries, but we may hope that people generally in the Western world will be impressed by this oriental example, as the futility and waste of violence becomes more obvious. Furthermore, cooperation between Eastern and Western nonviolence movements may well come to have a decisive influence on world events. . . .

It is an economic and social movement. These elements are symbolized in Gandhi's program by spinning. About some aspects of Gandhi's economic program I am dubious—for instance I am not convinced that it is necessary or desirable to go back to a pre-machine economy—but such elements may, for our present purpose, be put to one side. Three elements implied or suggested by Gandhi's emphasis on spinning are, as I see it, essential to an adequate nonviolence movement.

First, any movement which undertakes to give leadership or help in building a better world must give much attention to the ordering of the economic life. It must clarify its thinking as to the kind of economic order to strive for. It must decide how much socialization is possible without the creation either of a totalitarian state or of a political machine which, besides crushing the liberty of the individual, could fail in the narrow economic sense because of bureaucratic administration and attendant red tape, the deadening of initiative and the accompanying temptation to evade responsibility. It must not only invent, it must experiment with schemes for a more decentralized, human, and cooperative way of living.

The second essential symbolized by Gandhi's spinning plan is the expression of our basic philosophy of life in the economic sphere now rather than someday in the future when a new system is established. To postpone action has been the prevailing tendency among Socialists and Communists: "The day will come when socialism will be established and then we'll be socialists. Meanwhile there is not much that can be done to alleviate the evils of the present order and you personally go on living and doing business much as any capitalist might." One difficulty with this approach is that workers are hungry and cold now and they cannot wait until the revolution to do something about it. But there is a deeper and more subtle difficulty, which may be put this way: If you say that men cannot live as socialists until socialism has been established—or as Christians until a Christian world has been achieved—then you are saying in effect that non-socialists can build socialism and that people who are not Christians except in a theoretical sense can build a Christian order of life. That has an implication which the social democrats never faced squarely, but which the Communists saw clearly and accepted: namely, that if the new system does not represent the general convincement of the people, it has to be set up in the first instance by violence and that human beings must be regimented in the new environment until they are psychologically reconditioned and adapted to the new system. But the Russian experience has reminded us that, in this realm also, violence and coercion are self-defeating and that the product of regimentation is not a finer man, but a degraded human being. We are driven to the conviction that men who are autocrats and lovers of power in their own souls will not build a democratic world; men who are essentially self-seekers will not build a cooperative commonwealth. It equally follows that men who have entered into the spirit of community will inevitably be driven to seek to give expression at once to their inner spirit in economic relationships. As the early Christians, the Franciscans, the early Friends illustrate, there is always creative experimentation in the economic life where there is genuine and fresh religious experience.

Gandhi's spinning program has a third important element for those who seriously desire to build a nonviolence movement. It shows that manual work has important effects on the individual spirit and that corporate manual activity is a powerful agent for unifying pacifist groups within and also for unifying them with their non-pacifist neighbors, especially workers and farmers.

Gandhi's movement, finally, is a political movement. It expresses the determination of the masses of India to free themselves from the yoke of British imperialism without violence and without hatred for the oppressor. For our present purpose it is not necessary to elaborate this point except to observe that, in addition to developing mass resistance to war, a Western nonviolence movement must make effective contacts with oppressed and minority groups such as Negroes, sharecroppers, industrial workers, and help them to develop a nonviolence technique, as Gandhi did in the India National Congress.[29]

Ending War

In this essay written in 1964 near the end of his life, Muste emphasizes the necessity of abolishing war, links this to the global struggle for economic and social justice, and at the end of the excerpt cites Albert Camus's essay, "Neither Victims nor Executioners."[30]

The conviction that war must be abolished, that in every available way we must break with it, must become again central in our thinking and our desire. Then we shall be nonviolent within and various ways will open to us to develop nonviolent activities and brotherhoods.

The labor and socialist movement of a half-century ago, which had such great promise and, alas, did not fulfill it, was a movement which sought economic well-being, social jus-

---

[29] "The World Task of Pacifism," in *The Essays of A. J. Muste*, ed. Nat Hentoff (New York: Clarion Book, Simon and Schuster, 1967), 223–25.

[30] "The Fall of Man," in Hentoff, *Essays of A. J. Muste*, 448–50.

tice, humaneness in all human relationships, equality, and the end of war—all of these together. It believed in man's power to determine his own destiny and to build the beloved community. We need such a movement in our own time and it is not easy to see how it can be gathered in such vastly changed circumstances. But one condition may be emphasized here. That great earlier labor and socialist movement had no doubt that the abolition of war was essential to its program and goal.

Any social and radical movement today which thinks that its goal can be achieved by, and in, an America which does not break sharply with war and devote itself instead to facing its own life problems and helping to advance the emancipation of the disadvantaged masses throughout the world is deluding itself. It tells its followers in effect that they will attain freedom and peace in America as it is today, an America which fails to devote itself to freedom and peace for all men. . . .

In 1947 Albert Camus wrote an essay which sets forth the challenge of breaking with murder and violence, and suggests how that may be done. His is a voice that will be listened to not without a measure of respect on all sides of the lines that divide men into warring camps and sometimes leads to a proliferation of violence on so many levels as to make us wonder whether mankind is dominated by a wish to die.

. . . [Camus's essay] points out that in a world saturated in violence we may not have a choice as to whether or not to be victims but we can still choose not to be executioners. "For my part," he concludes, "I am fairly sure that I have made the choice. . . . I will never again be one of those, whoever they be, who compromise with murder." The basic decision that must be made, he elaborates, is "whether humanity's lot must be made still more miserable in order to achieve far-off and shadowy ends, whether we should accept a world bristling with arms where brother kills brother; or whether, on the contrary, we should avoid bloodshed and misery as much as possible so that we give a chance for survival to later generations better equipped than we are."

Camus, in 1947, assumed that only a few at first would take the course of rejecting murder as a social instrument and of embracing nonviolence, the course of "discovering a style of life." Even so, he felt that precisely such a minority would exhibit a "positively dazzling realism." But may it not be that in the nuclear age multitudes on both sides of barriers indeed may be driven both by necessity—the need for bare survival—and by moral passion, to commit themselves to nonviolence? In this way a movement adapted to our time but reminiscent of that imposing and noble radical movement of an earlier age might spring into life.

Even Camus a decade or so ago could not reject the possibility of such a development and accordingly concluded his essay with this beautiful expression of hope that "the thirst for fraternity which burns in Western man" might be satisfied. He wrote:

> Over the expanse of five continents throughout the coming years an endless struggle is going to be pursued between violence and friendly persuasion, a struggle in which, granted, the former has a thousand times the chances of success than those of the latter. But I have always held that, if he who bases his hopes on human nature is a fool, he who gives up in the face of circumstances is a coward.

Muste could have extended that quote to include the last sentence of Camus's essay: "And henceforth, the only honorable course will be to stake everything on a formidable gamble: that words are more powerful than munitions."[31]

---

[31] Albert Camus, *Neither Victims nor Executioners* (Philadelphia: New Society Publishers, 1986), 55.

Albert Camus (1913–1960)

Born in Algeria, Albert Camus was briefly a member of the Communist Party in the 1930s and thereafter worked with a number of leftist groups and publications. He served in the French resistance during World War II, where he met Jean-Paul Sartre, but the two great writers differed in their philosophies. In his important work *The Myth of Sisyphus*, Camus evokes the story from Greek mythology of the king condemned in Hades to rolling a giant boulder up a hill only to see it roll back down again, eternally repeating the same hopeless task. It is a powerful depiction of the futility of life, from which there is no escape, but Camus argues that we can nonetheless live life to its fullest through rebellion and a passionate commitment to freedom. Knowing that our efforts may not succeed, we are nonetheless committed to the struggle for its own sake, not for any utilitarian purpose it may serve. There is no teleological trajectory that steers history toward utopian ends, he argues. We have only our struggle in the present moment. In this focus on the present rather than ultimate ends, Camus is perhaps close to the Hindu concept of nonattachment. We accept our duty to serve, striving unconditionally and selflessly, regardless of the prospects for success. Our commitment to strive for justice and a better life is not dependent on the likelihood of results. We rebel against the cruelties of injustice and oppression because this expresses who we are, our humanity, our identity as free persons striving to make meaning for ourselves in a world of absurdity.

Camus wrote *Neither Victims nor Executioners* in 1947 after the mass slaughter of two world wars, in the shadow of the atomic bomb, in the midst of widespread despair and uncertainty over the fate of humankind. His famous essay is a passionate outcry against the ideologies and ethics of mass murder and a call for "sociability" and solidarity among individuals and within a community to counter the forces of violence and oppression. In the excerpts that follow, which build upon those quoted above by Muste, Camus offers insight into the dilemmas of his age, with similarities to our own, and also points to the pathways for striving to achieve human dignity and survival.

> The years we have gone through have killed something in us. And that something is simply the old confidence man had in himself, which led him to believe that he could always elicit human reactions from another man if he spoke to him in the language of a common humanity. We have seen men lie, degrade, kill, deport, torture—and each time it was not possible to persuade them not to do these things because they were sure of themselves and because one cannot appeal to an abstraction, i.e., the representative of an ideology. . . .
>
> We live in terror because persuasion is no longer possible; because man has been wholly submerged in History; because he can no longer tap into that part of his nature, as real as the historical part, which he captures in contemplating the beauty of nature and of human faces; because we live in a world of abstractions, of bureaus and machines, of absolute ideas and of crude messianism. We suffocate among people who think they are absolutely right, whether in their machines or in their ideas. And for all who can live only in an atmosphere of human dialogue and sociability, this silence is the end of the world.
>
> . . . For terror is legitimized only if we assent to the principle: "the end justifies the means." And this principle in turn may be accepted only if the effectiveness of an action is posed as an absolute end, as in nihilistic ideologies (anything goes, success is the only thing worth talking about), or in those philosophies which make History an absolute end. . . .
>
> The dizzy rate at which weapons have evolved, a historical fact ignored by Marx, forces us to raise anew the whole question of means and ends. And in this instance, the means can leave us little doubt about the end. Whatever the desired end, however lofty and necessary, whether happiness or justice or liberty—the means employed to attain it

represent so enormous a risk and are so disproportionate to the slender hopes of success, that, in all sober objectivity, we must refuse to run this risk.

This leaves us only the alternative method of achieving a world order: the mutual agreement of all parties. . . .

To save what can be saved so as to open up some kind of future—that is the prime mover, the passion and the sacrifice that is required. . . .

We are asked to love or to hate such and such a country and such and such a people. But some of us feel too strongly our common humanity to make such a choice. Those who really love the Russian people, in gratitude for what they have never ceased to be—the world leaven which Tolstoy and Gorki speak of—do not wish for them success in power-politics, but rather want to spare them, after the ordeals of the past, a new and even more terrible bloodletting. So, too, with the American people, and with the peoples of unhappy Europe. This is the kind of elementary truth we are liable to forget amidst the furious passions of our time.

Yes, it is fear and silence and the spiritual isolation they cause that must be fought today. And it is sociability (*"le dialogue"*) and the universal intercommunication of men that must be defended. Slavery, injustice, and lies destroy this intercourse and forbid this sociability; and so we must reject them. But these evils are today the very stuff of History, so that many consider them necessary evils. It is true that we cannot "escape History," since we are in it up to our necks. But one may propose to fight within History to preserve from History that part of man which is not its proper province. That is all I have tried to say here. The "point" of this article may be summed up as follows:

Modern nations are driven by powerful forces along the roads of power and domination. I will not say that these forces should be furthered or that they should be obstructed. They hardly need our help and, for the moment, they laugh at attempts to enter them. They will, then, continue.

But I will ask only this simple question: What if these forces wind up in a dead-end, what if that logic of History on which so many now rely turns out to be a will-o'-the-wisp? What if, despite two or three world wars, despite the sacrifice of several generations and a whole system of values, our grandchildren—supposing they survive—find themselves no closer to a world society? It may well be that the survivors of such an experience will be too weak to understand their own sufferings. Since these forces are working themselves out and since it is inevitable that they continue to do so, there is no reason why some of us should not take on the job of keeping alive, through the apocalyptic historical vista that stretches before us, a modest thoughtfulness which, without attending to solve everything, will constantly be prepared to give some human meaning to everyday life.[32]

---

[32] Ibid., 27–29, 34, 43–44, 52–55.

4

Women's Voices

The classic authors cited most often in peace studies and nonviolent action courses are usually men, including Gandhi, King, Gene Sharp, Johan Galtung, Adam Curle, and the list goes on. This reflects male bias in publishing and university appointments, and in the leadership of major social organizations. Women have been very active in the study and practice of peacemaking, but their contributions historically have been ignored. This is changing now in many places, as the previously overlooked role of women in social action and scholarship is being acknowledged. Peace studies is enriched today by the integration of gender studies and feminist research and practice, although much more progress is needed to achieve genuine equality.

A greater emphasis on the contributions of women is not just a matter of justice but an essential condition for preventing armed conflict and building peace. Many studies find that the status of women in society strongly predicts the likelihood of peace between and within states.[1] While competing theories explain this phenomenon, the evidence shows that higher levels

---

[1] See, for example, Mary Caprioli and Mark A. Boyer, "Gender, Violence, and International Crisis," *Journal of Conflict Resolution* 45, no. 4 (August 2001): 503–18; Valerie Hudson, Mary Caprioli, Bonnie Ballif-Spanvill, Rose McDermott, and Chad F. Emmett, "The Heart of the Matter: The Security of Women and the Security of States," *International Security* 33, no. 3 (Winter 2008–09): 7–45.

of gender equality as measured by political participation, educational attainment, and socioeconomic status are strongly associated with reduced rates of armed conflict. States characterized by gender equality are less likely to engage in militarized international disputes, have lower rates of military spending, and are less likely to experience internal armed conflict, repression, and human rights abuse. As then-UN secretary-general Kofi Annan stated in 2006, there is no strategy more important for preventing conflict and achieving reconciliation than advancing the economic, social, and political empowerment of women.[2]

Some scholars explain the connection between gender equity and peace on the basis of social dominance theory, which traces hierarchies of status and social norms to the dominance of certain groups over others. According to this theory, political attitudes and values regarding violence are more likely to reflect views on social equality than a person's sex.[3] Preferences for gender equality may be part of a broader normative framework of social equality. Women (and men) hold more peaceful attitudes to the extent that they embrace a more egalitarian worldview. Research indicates that gender equality, democracy, and nonviolence are closely intertwined, with gender equality directly linked to greater democracy and peace.[4] Equalizing the power relations between women and men strengthens democracy, lessens gender-based social dominance, and undermines the legitimacy of violence as a mechanism for settling differences and maintaining social cohesion.

The Women's March movement that emerged in the United States in 2017 significantly advanced the cause of gender equal-

---

[2] Kofi Annan, "No Policy for Progress More Effective Than Empowerment of Women, Secretary-General Says in Remarks to Women's Day Observance," United Nations press conference, March 8, 2006, http://www.un.org.

[3] Felicia Pratto, Lisa M. Stallworth, and Jim Sidanius, "The Gender Gap: Differences in Political Attitudes and Social Dominance Orientation," *British Journal of Social Psychology* 36 (1997): 56.

[4] Monty G. Marshall and Donna Ramsey Marshall, *Gender Empowerment and the Willingness of States to Use Force,* Center for Systematic Peace Occasional Paper Series 2, February 12, 1999, 32.

ity and demonstrated the importance of nonviolent social action. The mobilizations led by women were a transformative experience: the vast numbers of people participating, the positive and loving spirit of the crowds, the collective strength of women taking the lead after a bitter election campaign in which women were so publicly and shamefully demeaned. This was a movement and a moment born of social media, outside the structures of existing social organizations and activist networks. Male leadership hierarchies played no role in its creation.[5] The mobilizations gave birth to campaigns and networks that have since carried on the fight for health care and the protection of immigrants, in defense of science and the environment, and for budget priorities that favor human needs over war. The #MeToo movement against sexual abuse has further energized the struggle for gender equality. Whether the women's movement can maintain this momentum remains to be seen, but already it has introduced into society new forms of resistance to bigotry and inequality that have enormous potential for advancing justice and peace.

The writings below reflect a range of voices addressing issues related to the theory of nonviolence (Deming), feminism and the struggle against violence (hooks), and questions related to maternal thinking and essentialism (Ruddick). They help to deepen our understanding of peace and nonviolence.

Barbara Deming (1917–1984)

The year 1968 was one of tumultuous political tragedy and upheaval in the United States and around the world. Dr. Martin Luther King Jr. fell to an assassin's bullet, Senator Robert Kennedy met the same fate soon afterward, and in Chicago the infa-

---

[5] See Marie Berry and Erica A. Chenoweth, "Who Made the Women's March?", in *The Resistance: The Dawn of the Anti-Trump Opposition Movement*, ed. David S. Meyer and Sidney Tarrow (New York: Oxford University Press, 2018), 75–89.

mous "police riot" against antiwar demonstrators disrupted the Democratic National Convention.[6] In Paris an unprecedented wave of student-led protest and worker strikes shut down much of the country, in Prague government reformers attempting to introduce democratic reform were crushed by Soviet tanks, and in Mexico protesters were massacred in Tlatelolco Plaza. In Vietnam the bloody Tet Offensive exposed the lie of American policy and undermined political support for the war at home and abroad. Revolutionary armed struggles against imperialism were under way in Africa, Asia, and Latin America. Barbara Deming also in that year published her seminal article "On Revolution and Equilibrium," which challenged the advocates of revolutionary violence and raised a passionate and eloquent plea for more powerful and effective forms of nonviolent resistance.

Written partially as a response to Franz Fanon's influential book *The Wretched of the Earth*,[7] Deming's essay stands as one of the most incisive analyses of nonviolent action ever written. She introduced themes of feminism into a discourse that until then was almost entirely dominated by men. She secularized the arguments of Gandhi and King, developing a systematic case for nonviolent resistance based entirely on pragmatic rather than religious foundations. Deming traveled to India in 1959 to study Gandhian nonviolence and in 1960 to Cuba to understand the process of revolution. She sought to combine the achievements of Gandhi and Castro, emphasizing the value of nonviolent action while supporting the need for revolutionary political change. She urged nonviolent activists to adopt more assertive methods of resistance, while asking revolutionists to see the radical potential of substituting nonviolent action for armed

---

[6] The official report on the disruption in Chicago in 1968 labeled it a "police riot" characterized by "unrestrained and indiscriminate police violence" against protesters. See *Rights in Conflict: Convention Week in Chicago, August 25–29, 1968*, a report submitted by Daniel Walker, director of the Chicago Study Team, to the National Commission on the Causes and Prevention of Violence, introduction by Max Frankel (New York: E. P. Dutton, 1968).

[7] Franz Fanon, *The Wretched of the Earth* (New York: Grove Press, 1963, 2004).

struggle. Nonviolent resistance is not simply an appeal to conscience or plea for reform, she argued. It is a more powerful and effective means of exerting social force to overcome oppression.

The effectiveness of the nonviolent method depends not on the goodwill of the adversary, she emphasized, but on the ability of the movement to win the sympathy of third parties and undermine the legitimacy and political foundations of the adversary. Deming described this as the "special genius" of nonviolent action: the ability of nonviolent resistance to attract the support of those who were previously indifferent or opposed to the movement. Unjustified repression against disciplined nonviolent protest tends to generate a sympathetic response in support of the victims and against the oppressors. Chavez referred to this as the "strange chemistry" of nonviolent action. When an adversary unjustly oppresses disciplined nonviolent struggle, the movement gains a tenfold benefit, he said.[8] When authorities are unjustifiably brutal against protesters, their legitimacy and popular support diminish. Even the most dictatorial regimes depend to some extent on the will of the people. When public acceptance and support begin to erode, power shifts. The strategic advantage of nonviolent action, Deming argued, is its ability to attract mass support and erode the legitimacy of the adversary.

"On Revolution and Equilibrium"

In her essay Deming addresses head-on Fanon's arguments about the liberating effect of revolutionary violence. She expresses sympathy for the revolutionary cause in oppressed countries, but she warns against the costs of violence, particularly the psychic and social imbalance it produces.

> The judgments I make are . . . upon the means open to us—upon the promise these means of action hold or withhold.

---

[8] Susan Ferris and Ricardo Sandoval, *The Fight in the Fields: Cesar Chavez and the Farmworkers Movement*, ed. Diana Hembree (New York: Harcourt Brace, 1997), 97.

The living question is: What are the best means for changing our lives—for really changing them?

The very men who speak of the necessity of violence, if change is to be accomplished, are the first, often, to acknowledge the toll it exacts among those who use it—as well as those it is used against. Frantz Fanon has a chapter in *The Wretched of the Earth* entitled "Colonial War and Mental Disorders" and in it he writes, "We are forever pursued by our actions." After describing, among other painful disorders, those suffered by an Algerian terrorist—who made friends among the French after the war and then wondered with anguish whether any of the people he had killed had been people like these—he comments, "It was what might be called an attack of vertigo." Then he asks a poignant question: "But can we escape becoming dizzy? And who can affirm that vertigo does not haunt the whole of existence?"

"Vertigo"—here is a word, I think, much more relevant to the subject of revolutionary action than the word "purity." No, it is not that I want to remain pure; it is that I want to escape becoming dizzy. And here is exactly the argument of my essay: we can escape it. Not absolutely, of course, but we can escape vertigo in the drastic sense. It is my stubborn faith that if, as revolutionaries, we will wage battle without violence, we can remain very much more in control—of our own selves, of the responses to us which our adversaries make, of the battle as it proceeds and of the future we hope will issue from it. . . .

I think of the words with which Fanon opens the final chapter of *The Wretched of the Earth*: "Come then, comrades: it would be as well to decide at once to change our ways." I quote Fanon often—because he is eloquent, but also because he is quoted repeatedly these days by those who plead the need for violence. It is my conviction that he can be quoted as well to plead for nonviolence. It is true that he declares: "From birth it is clear . . . that this narrow world, strewn with prohibitions, can only be called into question by absolute violence." But I ask all those who are readers of Fanon to make an experiment: Every time you find the word "violence" in his pages, substitute for it the phrase "radical and uncompromising action." I contend that with the exception of a very few passages this substitution can be made, and that the action he calls for could just as well be nonviolent action. . . .

Another man with whom I was arguing the other day declared to me, "You can't turn the clock back now to nonviolence!" Turn the clock back? The clock has been turned to violence all down through history. Resort to violence hardly marks a move forward. It is nonviolence which is in the process of invention, if only people would not stop short in that experiment. Fanon again: "If we want humanity to advance a step further, if we want to bring it up to a different level than that which Europe has shown it, then we must invent and we must make discoveries." It is for that spirit of invention that I plead. . . .

At this point suddenly I can hear in my head many voices interrupting me. They all say: "Who among us likes violence? But nonviolence has been tried." It has not been tried. We have hardly begun to try it. The people who dismiss it now as irrelevant do not understand what it could be. And, again, they especially do not understand the very much greater control over events that they could find if they would put this "practice of action," rather than violence, to a real test. . . .

I argue with the contention that nonviolent action can only be prayerful action—must by its nature remain naïve. Too often in the past it has confined itself to petition, but there is no need for it to do so—especially now that so many have learned "change [is] harder to get than they had imagined." There have always been those in the nonviolent movement who called for radical moves. . . . The pressure that nonviolent moves could put upon those who are opposing change, the power that could be exerted this way, has yet to be tested. . . .

To resort to power one need not be violent, and to speak to conscience one need not be meek. The most effective action both resorts to power and engages conscience. Nonviolent action does not have to beg others to "be nice." It can in effect force them to consult their consciences—or to pretend to have them. Nor does it have to petition those in power to do something about a situation. They can face the authorities with a new fact and say: accept this new situation which we have created.

If people doubt that there is power in nonviolence, I am afraid that it is due in part to the fact that those of us who believe in it have yet to find for ourselves an adequate vocabulary. The leaflets we pass out tend to speak too easily about love and truth—and suggest that we hope to move people slowly by being loving and truthful. The words do describe our method in a kind of shorthand. But who can read the shorthand? It is easy enough to recommend "love." How many, even among those who like to use the word, can literally feel love for a harsh opponent—not merely pretending to while concealing from themselves their own deepest feelings? What is possible is to act toward another human being on the assumption that all people's lives are of value—that there is something about every person to be loved, whether one can feel love for that person or not. It happens that, if one does act on this assumption, it gives one much greater poise in the situation. It is easy enough to speak about truth; but we had better spell out how, in battle, we rely upon the truth. It is not simply that we pay our antagonist the human courtesy of not lying. We insist upon telling truths the antagonist doesn't want to hear—telling what seems to us the truth about the injustice being committed. Words are not enough here. Gandhi's term for nonviolent action was "*satyagraha*"—which can be translated as "clinging to the truth." What is needed is this—to cling to the truth as one sees it. One has to cling with one's entire weight. One doesn't simply say, "I have a right to sit here," but acts out that truth—and sits here. One doesn't just say, "I don't believe in this way," but refuses to put on a uniform. One doesn't just say, "The use of napalm is atrocious," but refuses to pay for it by refusing to pay one's taxes. And so on and so on. One brings what economic weight one has to bear, what political, social, psychological, what physical weight. There is a good deal more involved here than a moral appeal. It should be acknowledged both by those who argue against nonviolence and those who argue for it that we, too, rely upon force.

If greater gains have not been won by nonviolent action it is because most of those trying it . . . have stopped short of really exercising their peculiar powers—those powers one discovers when one refuses any longer simply to do another's will. They have stopped far too short not only of widespread nonviolent disruption but of that form of non-cooperation which is assertive, constructive—that confronts those who are "running everything" with independent activity, particularly independent economic activity. There is leverage for change here that has scarcely begun to be applied.

To refuse one's cooperation is to exert force. One can, in fact, exert so very much force in this way that many people will always be quick to call non-cooperators violent. How, then, does one distinguish nonviolent from violent action? It is not that it abstains from force, to rely simply upon moral pressure. It resorts even to what can only be called physical force—when, for example, we sit down and refuse to move, and we force others to cope somehow with all these bodies. The distinction to make is simply that those committed to a nonviolent discipline refuse to injure the antagonist. . . .

But the distinction I have just made is a little too neat. In almost any serious nonviolent struggle, one has to resort to obstructive action. When we block access to buildings, block traffic, block shipments, it can be charged that we go a little further than refusing obedience and impose upon the freedom of action of others. There is some justice to the charge. I nevertheless think it appropriate to speak of nonviolent obstruction, but I would revert to my original description as the definitive one: the person committed to nonviolent action refuses to injure the antagonist. It is quite possible to frustrate another's action without doing that person injury. And some freedoms are basic freedoms, some are not. To impose upon another person's freedom to kill, or freedom to help to kill, to recruit to kill, is not to violate that person in a fundamental way. . . .

This is the heart of my argument: we can put more pressure on the antagonist for whom we show human concern. It is precisely solicitude for the person in combination with a stubborn interference with his or her actions that can give us a very special degree of control (precisely in our acting both with love, if you will—in the sense that we respect the person's human rights—and truthfulness, in the sense that we act out fully our objections to that person violating our rights). We put upon the person two pressures—the pressure of our defiance and the pressure of our respect—and it happens that in combination these two pressures are uniquely effective. . . .

The more the real issues are dramatized, and the struggle raised above the personal, the more control those in nonviolent rebellion begin to gain over their adversary. For they are able at one and the same time to disrupt everything, making it impossible for the adversary to operate within the system as usual, and to temper the response to this, making it impossible for the adversary simply to strike back without thought and with all available strength. They have as it were two hands upon the adversary—the one calming him, making him ask questions, as the other makes him move.

In any violent struggle one can expect the violence to escalate. It does so automatically, neither side being really able to regulate the process at will. . . . In nonviolent struggle, the violence used against one may mount for a while (indeed, if one is bold in one's rebellion, it is bound to do so), but the escalation is no longer automatic; with the refusal of one side to retaliate, the mainspring of the automation has been snapped and one can count on reaching a point where de-escalation begins. One can count, that is, in the long run, on receiving far fewer casualties. . . .

One can, as I say, be certain if one adopts the discipline of nonviolence that in the long run one will receive fewer casualties. And yet very few people are able to see that this is so. It is worth examining the reasons why the obvious remains unacknowledged. Several things, I think, blind people to the plain truth.

First, something seems wrong to most people engaged in struggle when they see more people hurt on their own side than on the other side. They are used to reading this as an indication of defeat, and a complete mental readjustment is required of them. Within the new terms of struggle, victory has nothing to do with their being able to give more punishment than they take (quite the reverse); victory has nothing to do with their being able to punish the other at all: it has to do simply with being able, finally, to make the other move. Again the real issue is depth in focus. Vengeance is not the point; change is. But the trouble is that in most people's minds the thought of victory and the thought of punishing the enemy coincide. If they are suffering casualties and the enemy is not, they fail to recognize that they are suffering fewer casualties than they would be if they turned to violence. . . .

To recognize that men have greater, not less control in the situation when they have committed themselves to nonviolence requires a drastic readjustment of vision. And this means taking both a long-range view of the field and a very much cooler, more objective one. Nonviolence can inhibit the ability of the antagonist to hit back. (If the genius of guerrilla warfare is to make it impossible for the other side really to exploit its superior force, nonviolence can be said to carry this even further.) . . .

In nonviolent struggle the effort is of quite a different nature. One doesn't try to frighten the other. One tries to undo him—tries, in the current idiom, to "blow his mind"—only in the sense that one tries to take him out of former attitudes and force him to reappraise the situation now in a way that takes into consideration your needs as well as his. One is able to do this—able in a real sense to change the other's mind (rather than to drive him out of it)—precisely because one reassures him about his personal safety all the time that one keeps disrupting the order of things that he has known to date. When—under your constant pressure—it becomes to his own interest to adapt himself to change, he is able to do so. Fear for himself does not prevent him. In this sense a liberation movement that is nonviolent sets the oppressor free as well as the oppressed. . . .

One can speak of still another sense in which nonviolence gives one greater control. If the antagonist is unjustifiably harsh in countermeasures, and continues to be, one will slowly win away from him allies and supporters—some of them having consciences more active than his perhaps; but perhaps all of them simply caring about presenting a certain image, caring for one reason or another about public relations. An adversary might seem immovable. One could nevertheless move him finally by taking away the props of his power—those people upon whose support he depends. The special genius of nonviolence is that it can draw to our side not only natural allies—who are enabled gradually to recognize that they are allies because in competition with us their minds are not blurred by fear. . . . Nonviolent tactics can move into action on our behalf those not naturally inclined to act for us; whereas violent tactics draw into actions that do harm us men for whom it is not at all natural to act against us. . . . Violence makes people "dizzy"; it disturbs the vision, makes them see only their own immediate losses and fear of losses. Any widespread resort to violence in this country by those seeking change could produce such vertigo among the population at large that the authorities would be sure to be given more and more liberty to take repressive measures—in the name of "Order." . . .

The words of the Vietnamese Buddhist Thich Nhat Hanh are startling and sound at first naive: "no men are our enemies." By this we do not mean that we think no people will try to destroy us; or that we overlook the fact that people from certain sections of the society are above all likely to try it. We mean, first, of course, that we are committed to try not to destroy them: but we mean furthermore that there is a working chance—if we do refuse to threaten them personally as we struggle with them—that in certain instances at least some of them may be willing to accommodate themselves to the pressure we put on them to change, and so both they and we may be liberated from the state of enmity. . . . And they will only believe that we offer this liberty, only be able to imagine new lives for themselves, if we have refused to threaten them with any personal injury.

If we insist on treating them not as parts of a machine but as people, we gain a much greater control.[9] . . .

May those who say that they believe in nonviolence learn to challenge more boldly those institutions of violence that constrict and cripple our humanity. And may those who have questioned nonviolence come to see that one's rights to life and happiness can only be claimed as inalienable if one grants, in action, that they belong to all men.[10]

"On the Necessity to Liberate Minds"

Deming focuses on the need to win the sympathy and support of third parties and the public officials upon whose support

---

[9] Here and elsewhere in these Deming excerpts, the emphasis is in the original.

[10] "On Revolution and Equilibrium," in Barbara Deming, *Revolution and Equilibrium* (New York: Grossman, 1971), 203–4.

the system of oppression depends. No genuinely democratic transformation can occur without mass support and the involvement of large sectors of the population. If democracy is the goal, popular participation and engagement must be cultivated and encouraged as the means to achieve that goal. The nonviolent method requires that we change minds and attract growing numbers of people to the cause, as she explains below.

> A relatively small number of people can cause a tremendous amount of damage, can throw everything into confusion. But our task is not to wreck. Our task is to transform a society that deals out death into a society that makes life more possible for all. To build such a new society, very many people are needed. So as we strike at the machinery of death, we have to do so in a way that the general population understands, that encourages more and more people to join us.
>
> This is surely the greatest challenge to the movement: How to make the public understand that it's "all right" to attack the death machine—that it is necessary? How to free their minds to see this and to join us?
>
> And here is the preposterous difficulty. We are all living now in a society so deranged that it confronts us not only with the fact that we are committing abominable crimes against others—crimes we shouldn't be able to live with; it confronts us also with threats to our own existence that no people in history have ever had to live with before. And confronts every single member of society with these threats—even the most privileged, even those in control of things, or rather, out of control of them. Confronts us, in the name of "defense," with the threat of nuclear annihilation. Confronts us, in the name of "national profit," with the threat that our environment may be completely destroyed. The society is this insanely deranged. And yet—we have to face the strange fact that most people are very much less terrified of having things continue as they are than of having people like us trying to change things radically.

For most Americans are in deep awe of things-as-they-are. Even with everything this obviously out of control, they still tell themselves that those in authority must know what they are doing, and must be describing our condition to us as it really is; they still take it for granted that somehow what *is*, what is *done*, must make sense, can't really be insane. These assumptions exercise a tyranny over their minds. Those of us committed to trying to bring about change have above all to reckon with this tyranny, have above all to try to find out how to relieve people of it.

I read this past winter of a specially painful example of it, read in the *New York Times* the story of Michael Bernhardt, who was the young soldier who was the first to talk about the massacre at Songmy.[11] He had volunteered for service in Vietnam—full of faith in the words he had heard from his leaders about what this country was trying to do over there. He found himself almost immediately in the action at Songmy. He didn't take part in the killing. As his comrades began to shoot old people, women, babies—the reporter quotes him: "I just looked around and said, 'This is all screwed up.'" But after the action it took him quite a while to come forward and talk about it. Because he very quickly experienced the eerie feeling that neither those in command of the war nor most Americans would agree with him. There is an almost unbearable passage in the story where he is quoted as saying, "Maybe this was the way wars really were . . . I felt like I was left out, like maybe they forgot to tell me something, that this was the way we fought wars, and everybody knew but me." The reporter writes then that the clash between this experience he had at Songmy and his convictions about his country is something he still cannot resolve. "It became almost a question of sanity." But, he writes, "if he were forced to pick, he would choose his convictions over his experiences." He quotes him as insisting, "We hold out hope, you know."

---

[11] A reference to the site of the My Lai massacre in 1928 in which more than five hundred Vietnamese civilians were killed by U.S. troops.

A terrible story, and one worth being very attentive to. Here is a young man who was exceptional. He did not take part. He saw the action for what it was: all screwed up. And yet—*he did not know how to cope afterwards with this vision. It just made him feel left out*. Because he suffered from the bondage I speak of—the awe of what *is*, of what is *done*. He suffered from the anxious sense that if one isn't part of it, *whatever* it is, one is then nowhere. And so in effect he dismisses the insight he had. Or does his best to. He chooses to accept not the truth of his own experience but something he has been told is true: that our country "holds out hope."

The question is: how do we cure people of this bondage? And of course how do we cure our own selves more completely? How do we set all of us free to trust our own experiences of the truth that everything is all screwed up?

The tantalizing thought is that there can hardly be an American living who has not had some glimpse of this truth. This must be so even of those who are most favored by the present system of things. (Even they, for example, must often now try to breathe an air that is unbreathable.) Some among us who want change talk much of the need to "know your enemy." It is of course very necessary to identify those in the society who are going to try the hardest to hold to things as they are. But it is certainly not appropriate to think of oppressed and oppressor as though the distinction between them were absolute. For the first time in history one can say that we are really *all* the oppressed—though some are certainly very much more thoroughly oppressed than others; we are all threatened—as long as things stay as they are.

How can we release the minds of more and more people to be able to see this? See it not just as a nightmare suffered that one tries to put out of mind; see it as meaning that we have to act to change things altogether. How do we give people the courage to trust that if they name things-as-they-are insane, they will not in doing so simply find themselves set adrift?

Much too briefly: I think that those of us who act must always be saying with the actions that we take two things—*and always saying these two things at the same time.*

We have to say very strongly—and not just with words of course: Things are not going to stay as they are. The machinery of things-as-they-are is a machinery of death, and we are going to so disrupt it that it will not be able to continue functioning as it has been. To waken people's minds, *to keep them from postponing and postponing all real thought about our condition*, we have first to give them this necessary shock.

But even as we give that shock, we must be communicating something else, too—again not merely with words, but above all by our actions. We must be saying: don't be afraid of *us*. It is the system we are attacking that you need to fear—that all of us need to fear. For it is reckless with lives. *But we are not*. Don't fear us. What we seek is precisely a new community of people in which we are all careful of each other—and of the natural world around us. And look, we are beginning to build that new world right now—in our relations with each other, in our relations even with you. *Don't be afraid of us. We are trying to release people from fear.*

I think that we have to find more and more ways of making this second point, of acting it out. It is going to be very tempting to take the road of striking at the military machine quite blindly, to think: can't we be more and more effective by being more and more destructive? Especially tempting because, as I have said, in this society a very few people could cause a very great deal of destruction. But again: a very few people could not find a new world among the ruins. This new world can only be built in the company of a great many people.

And so our acts of disruption should be taken in the most careful spirit. The actions through which it is easiest to communicate that spirit of carefulness are actions simply of noncooperation, actions by which we declare to the state: Not with my life!—you'll not commit murder by my hand, or commit it by spending my money, or by applying my wits or my labor. And of course if enough people would declare this by their acts—if enough young people would refuse to fight, and enough of the rest of us support them in that stand, so that more and more would find courage; if enough of us would refuse our taxes; if enough scientists would refuse to loan the state their minds, and enough workers would refuse to work in war industries; if there were enough ready people to launch a general strike—escalating from the recent refusal of students simply to continue their studies as usual—we can end the war by these means alone, and we could also initiate profound changes in the social order.

The trouble is that there are not yet enough people willing to make the changes in their lives that this would involve. And so unless the number of those who are willing grows very rapidly now, there will have to be more of the more aggressive acts taken—such as the blocking and occupation of buildings; and more of the still more aggressive acts such as those taken by the Catonsville Nine, the DC 9, and others.[12] There is such a terrible urgency about halting the machinery of death that is still unimpeded. *For our actions even to be effective as symbolic actions—as actions that speak the truth of our condition—*they must communicate this urgency. They must communicate the utter necessity to stop a machinery so careless of lives.

But when we take actions of this sort, it does become immediately more difficult to communicate at the same time our desire for a new spirit among people, a spirit of respect for one another—more difficult to act out that respect right now. May the men and women who take such actions feel

---

[12] A reference to Catholic antiwar resistance groups during the Vietnam War that destroyed military draft records in Catonsville, Maryland, and broke into the Washington, DC, offices of Dow Chemical, maker of the notorious herbicide and carcinogenic chemical Agent Orange, which was widely sprayed across Vietnam.

the same responsibility to communicate this spirit felt by the Catonsville Nine, the DC 9, the others in that tradition.

May they be careful above all not to harm any person. And careful, too, to make clear that they never would be willing to. May they also be scrupulously careful not to destroy the kind of property that has a valid life meaning for people. Some activists tend to speak of private property as though none of it has ever had such meaning. But some property of course is like the very extension of a person's life—or the extension of many people's lives. When people take patient care to know what they are doing here, make the most sober distinctions—willing to destroy only property that is by its nature deathly or exploitative, and unambiguously so. May they repeat and repeat to themselves the question: can we by these acts release the minds of more and more people—who should be on our side but who have been paralyzed—so that they will feel free to face the truth of our condition, free to join us?

Postscript
. . . Unless you can be sure of finding ways in which to speak a necessary reassurance even as you provide a necessary mental shock, I would say bluntly: Better not to take the action at all. Just as I would say—with even greater emphasis: Do not take the action, interrupt it at any point, unless you can feel sure that it will cause no serious injury to another.[13]

bell hooks

Born Gloria Jean Watkins in 1952 in a small segregated town in rural Kentucky, bell hooks was already writing poetry at age ten and later won fame as a gifted writer of critical essays on

---

[13] "On the Necessity to Liberate Minds," in *We Are All Part of One Another: A Barbara Deming Reader*, ed. Jane Meyerding, with a foreword by Barbara Smith (Philadelphia: New Society, 1984), 199–203.

systems of domination. As her work was published and attracted attention to her as an author, she decided to use the name bell hooks (that of her maternal great-grandmother). She choose not to capitalize her first and last names in an attempt to place the focus on her work, rather than her name.

As a student at Stanford she began writing the work that established her reputation, *Ain't I a Woman*, which was published in 1981. The book contributed significantly to feminist consciousness and became a central focus of discussions on issues of racism and sexism. *Publishers Weekly* later ranked it among the "twenty most influential women's books of the previous twenty years." She went on to become one of the most important female writers of the age. She is the author of more than thirty books and has taught at the University of California at Santa Cruz, Yale, Oberlin College, and the City University of New York.

Writing in a postmodern idiom, bell hooks has addressed the interconnectedness of racism and capitalism and explored linkages among gender, class, sexuality, mass media, and feminism. She is a sharp critic of what she calls "white supremacist capitalist patriarchy." Her writings on feminism have had a profound impact on social and political theory. The following excerpt is from her classic book *Feminist Theory: From Margin to Center*.

> It is essential for continued feminist struggle to end violence against women that this struggle be viewed as a component of an overall movement to end violence. So far feminist movement has primarily focused on male violence, and as a consequence lends credibility to sexist stereotypes that suggest men are violent, women are not; men are abusers, women are victims. This type of thinking allows us to ignore the extent to which women (with men) in this society accept and perpetuate the idea that it is acceptable for a dominant party or group to maintain power over the dominated by using coercive force. It allows us to overlook or ignore the extent to which women exert coercive authority over oth-

ers or act violently. The fact that women may not commit violent acts as often as men does not negate the reality of female violence. We must see both men and women in the society as groups who support the use of violence if we are to eliminate it.

The social hierarchy in white supremacist, capitalist patriarchy is one in which theoretically men are the powerful, women the powerless; adults the powerful, children the powerless; white people the powerful, black people and other non-white peoples the powerless. In a given situation, whichever party is in power is likely to use coercive authority to maintain that power if it is challenged or threatened. Although most women clearly do not use abuse and battery to control and dominate men (even though a small minority of women batter men) they may employ abusive measures to maintain authority in interactions with groups over whom they exercise power. . . .

Male violence against women in personal relationships is one of the most blatant expressions of the use of abusive force to maintain domination and control. It epitomizes the actualization of the concept of hierarchical rule and coercive authority. Unlike violence against children, or white racial violence against other ethnic groups, it is the violence that is most overtly condoned and accepted, even celebrated in this culture. Society's acceptance and perpetuation of that violence helps maintain it and makes it difficult to control or eliminate. That acceptance can be explained only in part by patriarchal rule supporting male domination of women through the use of force. Patriarchal male rule took on an entirely different character in the context of advanced capitalist society. In the precapitalist world, patriarchy allowed all men to completely rule women in their families, to decide their fate, to shape their destiny. Men could freely batter women with no fear of punishment. They could decide whom their daughters were to marry, whether they would read or write, etc. Many of these powers were lost to men with the development of the capitalist nation-state in the United States. This loss of power did not correspond with decreased emphasis on the ideology of male supremacy. However, the idea of the patriarch as worker, providing for and protecting his family, was transformed as his labor primarily benefited the capitalist state. . . .

Until women and men cease equating violence with love, understand that disagreements and conflicts in the context of intimate relationships can be resolved without violence, and reject the idea that men should dominate women, male violence against women will continue, and so will other forms of violent aggression in intimate relationships. To help bring an end to violence against women, feminist activists have taken the lead in criticizing the ideology of male supremacy and showing the ways in which it supports and condones that violence. Yet efforts to end male violence against women will succeed only if they are part of an overall struggle to end violence.

Currently feminist activists supporting nuclear disarmament link militarism and patriarchy, showing connections between the two. Like analysis of violence against women, the tendency in these discussions is to focus on male support of violence—a focus that limits our understanding of the problem. Many women who advocate feminism see militarism as exemplifying patriarchal concepts of masculinity and the right of males to dominate others. To these women, to struggle against militarism is to struggle against patriarchy and male violence against women. . . .

By equating militarism and patriarchy, women who advocate feminism often structure their arguments in such a way as to suggest that to be male is synonymous with strength, aggression, and the will to dominate and do violence to others; to be female is synonymous with weakness, passivity, and the will to nourish and affirm the lives of others. Such dualistic thinking is basic to all forms of social domination in Western society. Even when inverted and employed for a meaningful purpose such as nuclear disarmament, it is nevertheless dangerous because it reinforces the cultural basis of sexism and other forms of group oppression. It promotes a stereotypical notion of inherent differences between men and women, implying that women by virtue of their sex have played no crucial role in supporting and upholding imperialism (and the militarism that serves to maintain imperialist rule) or other systems of domination. Even if one argues that men have been taught to equate masculinity with the ability to do violence and women have been taught to equate femaleness with nurturance, the fact remains that many women and men do not conform to these stereotypes. Rather than clarifying for women the power we exert in the maintenance of systems of domination and setting forth strategies for resistance and change, most current discussion of feminism and militarism further mystifies women's role.

In keeping with the tenets of sexist ideology, women are talked about in these discussions as objects rather than subjects. We are depicted not as workers and activists, who, like men, make political choices, but as passive observers who have taken no responsibility for actively maintaining the value system of the society, which proclaims violence and domination the most effective tools of communication and human interaction, a value system that advocates and makes war. Discussions of feminism and militarism that do not clarify for women the roles we have played and play in all their variety and complexity make it appear that all women are against war and oppose the use of violence, and that men are the problem, the enemy. This is a distortion of women's experience, not a clarification of it or a redefinition. Devaluing the roles women have played necessarily leads to a distorted perspective on women's reality. I use the word "devaluing," for it seems that the suggestion that men have made war and war policies while women have passively watched represents a refusal to see women as active political beings even when we are subordinate to men. The assumption that to be deemed inferior or submissive necessarily defines what one actually is or how one actually behaves is a continuation of sexist patterns that deny the relative powers women have exercised. Even the woman who votes according to her husband's example is making a political choice. We need to see women as political beings. . . .

We must insist that women who do choose (even if they are inspired by motherhood) to denounce violence and domination and their ultimate expression, war, are political thinkers making political decisions and choices. If women who work against militarism continue to imply, however directly or indirectly, that there is an inherent predisposition in women to oppose war, they risk reinforcing the very biological determinism that is the philosophical foundation of notions of male supremacy. . . .[14]

To build a mass-based feminist movement, we need to have a liberation ideology that can be shared with everyone. That revolutionary ideology can be created only if the experiences of people on the margin who suffer sexist oppression and other forms of group oppression are understood, addressed, and incorporated. They must participate in feminist movement as makers of theory and as leaders of action. In past feminist practice, we have been satisfied with relying on self-appointed individuals, some of whom are more concerned about exercising authority and power than with communicating with people from various backgrounds and political perspectives. Such individuals do not choose to learn about collective female experience, but impose their own ideas and values. Leaders are needed, and should be individuals who acknowledge their relationship to the group and who are accountable to it. They should have the ability to show love and compassion, show this love through their actions, and be able to engage

---

[14] bell hooks, *Feminist Theory: From Margin to Center*, 2nd ed. (Cambridge, MA: South End Press, 2000), 118–21, 126–29, 150.

in successful dialogue. Such love, Paolo Freire suggests, acts to transform domination:

> Love is at the same time the foundation of dialogue and dialogue itself. It is thus necessarily the task of responsible subjects and cannot exist in a relation of domination. Domination reveals the pathology of love: sadism in the domination and masochism in the dominated. Because love is an act of courage, not of fear, love is commitment to others. No matter where the oppressed are found, the act of love is commitment to their cause—the cause of liberation. And this commitment, because it is loving, is dialogical.

Women must begin the work of feminist reorganization with the understanding that we have all (irrespective of race, sex, or class) acted in complicity with the existing oppressive system. We all need to make a conscious break with the system. Some of us make this break sooner than others. The compassion we extend to others, the recognition that our change in consciousness and action has been a process, must characterize our approach to those individuals who are politically unconscious. We cannot motivate them to join feminist struggle by asserting a political superiority that makes the movement just another oppressive hierarchy....

To restore the revolutionary life force to feminist movement, women and men must begin to rethink and reshape its direction. While we must recognize, acknowledge, and appreciate the significance of feminist rebellion and the women (and men) who made it happen, we must be willing to criticize, re-examine, and begin feminist work anew, a challenging task because we lack historical precedents. There are many ways to make revolution. Revolutions can be and usually are initiated by violent overthrow of an existing political structure. In the United States, women and men committed to feminist struggle know that we are far outpowered by our opponents, that they not only have access to every type of weaponry known to humankind, but they have both the learned consciousness to do and accept violence as well as the skill to perpetuate it. Therefore, this cannot be the basis for feminist revolution in this society. Our emphasis must be on cultural transformation: destroying dualism, eradicating systems of domination. Our struggle will be gradual and protracted. Any effort to make feminist revolution here can be aided by the example of liberation struggles led by oppressed peoples globally who resist formidable powers.

The formation of an oppositional worldview is necessary for feminist struggle. This means that the world we have most intimately known, the world in which we feel "safe" (even if such feelings are based on illusions), must be radically changed. Perhaps it is the knowledge that everyone must change, not just those we label enemies or oppressors, that has so far served to check our revolutionary impulses. Those revolutionary impulses must freely inform our theory and practice if feminist movement to end existing oppression is to progress, if we are to transform our present reality.[15]

Sara Ruddick (1935–2011)

A philosophy professor who taught at the New School of Social Research in New York for forty years, Sara Ruddick examined the ways in which the practices and mental requirements of mothering can inculcate values of peace and understanding and serve as a basis for opposition to militarism and war. She shifted the focus of feminist thinking away from motherhood as a social institution or biological imperative toward a greater emphasis on the specific activities and values associated with raising and educating children. This work, she argued, can shape the parent as much as the child, giving rise to specific cognitive capacities and values that are oriented toward cooperation and peace and away from aggression and violence. Those who are responsible

---

[15] Ibid., 163–66.

for nurturing children are less likely to countenance violence, she argued, whether in social settings like the playground or the workplace, or as an instrument of state policy. They are, by life experience, trained to resist militarism and war and are inclined toward a politics of nonviolence and peace.[16]

Ruddick distinguished her philosophy from essentialist arguments that women are by nature more peaceful than men. It is not the biological function of having children that generates peaceful values, she argued, but the mental discipline and practices required for child rearing. These behavioral experiences shape our ways of thinking and doing. She did not define mothering as an exclusively female activity. Men can also engage in maternal practices. "Anyone who commits her or himself to responding to children's demands, and makes the work of response a considerable part of her or his life, is a mother."[17] She developed a feminist theory of peace, rooted in the practices and beliefs of women and men who devote themselves to nurturing children and to the demands of preserving, reproducing, and enhancing the prospects for individual and family life.

The following excerpts are drawn from her classic, *Maternal Thinking: Toward a Politics of Peace*:

> Nonviolent peacemaking is governed by four ideals: renunciation, resistance, reconciliation, and peacekeeping. . . . In examining maternal practice through the lens of nonviolence, I look for evidence of an ongoing attempt to renounce and resist violence, to reconcile opponents, and to keep a peace that is as free as possible from assaultive injustice. That is, I ask if there are principles in the practices of mothering that coincide with the four ideals of nonviolence. . . .
>
> I aim to identify principles of maternal nonviolence that I believe could contribute to collective, public understandings

---

[16] William Grimes, "Sara Ruddick Dies at Age 76; Pondered the Role of Mothering," *New York Times*, March 22, 2011, http://www.nytimes.com.

[17] Sara Ruddick, *Maternal Thinking: Toward a Politics of Peace*, with a new preface (Boston: Beacon Press, 1995), xii.

of peacemaking. For my purpose, it is sufficient that there are *some* maternal practices usually governed by the ideals I articulate. Because I am not measuring statistical extent but rather articulating governing ideals, I refer only to those peacemaking maternal practices—atypical as they may be—that I have seen. . . . I always mean only that what *some* mothers do, say, and believe is evidence of a maternal effort and that this effort is characteristic of at least some internal practices of nonviolence. . . .

Mothers aim to nurture and train an adult capable of work and love. They also typically have aims for their children that are related to their religious, political, or intellectual groups. These long-range goals inform some intermediate choices and help a mother to make sense of her work as a whole. Nonetheless, they must be pursued flexibly, with attention to particular challenges and circumstances. Gandhi held on to the distant aim of home rule through years of action, compromises, and settlement. Yet in the course of struggle, the long-range goal was too general to dictate strategy. Rather it was the nonviolence of ongoing struggle that gradually, over time, gave meaning to the goal. Similarly, a mother cannot decide what to do with a bullying or frightened child by appealing to models of adulthood. It is the nonviolence of daily life that is itself the goal to which longer-range aims must be adapted. Gandhi never gave up the goal of home rule. Mothers, by contrast, may be called on to relinquish religious or political aims that are dear to them. All the more important for mothers to learn to interpret long-range goals flexibly as they attend to the specific tasks at hand. As Gandhi would say, "The way is the truth"; or as feminists put it, "The process is the project." . . .

Peace is the more secure, the fewer weapons at hand. In domestic as in public life, there is no substitute for disarmament. Ideally, a mother keeps her house and yard as weapon-free as possible, despite the advertising of toys far more lethal than play pistols and the increasing popularity in the United States of keeping real, dangerous guns at home. She also tries to disarm her neighbors' children. It would be unrealistic to leave weapons about, let alone to pile them up deliberately, and then to expect children not to use them when provoked. But as in public life, disarmament can never be complete. Even if real guns are banned, there are always weapons available to the weak as well as the strong—blocks, rocks, play trucks, and sewing needles, for example. Moreover, bigger children are often as physically capable of seriously injuring a smaller child as is a mother herself. Although weapons should be eliminated wherever possible, there is no substitute for the renunciation of violence. By example and precept a mother has to train children not to stamp on the baby, throw a rock at the head, push a toddler in the river, or squirt insecticide in an enemy's face.

To keep the peace, a peacemaking mother, as best she can, creates ways for children and adults to live together that both appear to be and are fair. She distributes goods and privileges, listens carefully to complaints, and respectfully explains the unavoidable differences in powers and rewards that are inevitable among adults and children of different ages. Faced with rivalry, tyranny, or greed, nonviolent mothers do not sit passively by, letting a stronger or older child annex the possessions or exploit the smaller or more vulnerable one. Arbitrating and restraining, mothers appeal to interests the children share—or invent them. In reinforcing the fragile affections that survive rivalry and inevitable inequality, mothers who are guided by ideals of nonviolence work for the day that their children will come to prefer justice to the temporary pleasures of tyranny and exploitation. . . .

In public battles, where peoples and nations are hatefully and violently abused, to forgive is as intellectually confusing and morally controversial as is renunciation of violence at the outset. For mothers, by contrast, the ideal of responsible reconciliation is a routine aspect of training and education. Mothers name the evils that are done to or by their children. It is wrong (usually) to lie, bully, or humiliate, although children—and mothers—do these things. It is also wrong to suffer such insults in silence or to forgive perpetrators before the deed is named and the agent held responsible. Mothers, like children, are tempted to patch up prematurely, make do, and forget. After all, many "crimes" by and against children are trivial, and some cheerful forgetting is necessary to get through the day. But nonviolence is not simple. There is no rule for distinguishing the trivial "childish" escapade from more serious hurt. While moralism has its clear limits, cheery forgetfulness is no morality at all. Truthful, responsible reconciliation protects children from their own or others' hatred, which "scars the soul," and also from forgetful indifference to pain that they have inflicted or suffered and that, like hate, "corrodes the personality and eats away its vital unity." . . .

The four ideals of nonviolence—renunciation, resistance, reconciliation, and peacekeeping—govern only some maternal practices of some mothers. Yet it is also true that to elucidate these ideals is to describe, from a particular perspective, maternal practice itself. Peacemaking mothers create arrangements that enable their children to live safely, develop happily, and act conscientiously; that is, they preserve, nurture, and train, exemplifying the commitments of internal work. . . .

At its best, maternal nonviolence is a reality in the making, or, to borrow a phrase attributed to the French philosopher Maurice Merleau-Ponty, a *vérité-a-faire*, a truth-to-be-made. The reality is only in the making because failures are many and the ideal marks a struggle that is often lost. Nonetheless there is a reality: there are maternal practices in which ideals of nonviolence actually govern. Mothers can, and often do, renounce the violence to which they are tempted, fight back against the violence done to them and their children, name and insist on responsibility for damages done, yet forswear a scarring hatred in favor of a peace in which they can love and work.

Peacemakers can learn from maternal nonviolence even when mothers themselves do not extend or publicize the nonviolence they imperfectly practice. Conversely, whether or not they take on public militarism, mothers should find it illuminating to look at the ordinary tasks and temptations of their work through the lens of nonviolence. Maternal struggles to achieve nonviolence parallel and illuminate the struggle to achieve a sturdy peace. Whatever their public antimilitarist commitments, nonviolent mothers offer an invigorating image of peace as an active connectedness. All participants resist others' violence and their own temptations to abandon or assault, persisting in relationships that include anger, disappointment, difference, conflict, and nonviolent battle.[18]

---

[18] Ibid., 161–76, 183–84.

5

Strategy and Nonviolent Action

As Gandhi, King, Deming, and others emphasized, nonviolent action is a means of achieving political and social change. Most of those who participate in movements for nonviolent action are not animated by nonviolence as a philosophy. They join a movement because they want to achieve social change and perceive that nonviolent methods are the most effective way of achieving that goal. Within Gandhi's movement, for example, few of his colleagues followed him because of religious and moral beliefs. This was true even among his colleagues in the leadership of the Indian Congress. Future Indian prime minister Jawaharlal Nehru did not share Gandhi's ethic of nonviolence, but he accepted the method of nonviolent resistance "because of a belief in its effectiveness. Gandhiji had placed it before the country not only as the right method but as the most effective one for our purpose."[1]

Gandhi wrote frequently about the principles of nonviolence, but he never attempted to codify the methods of nonviolent action that he successfully developed during his years in South Africa and later in the India freedom struggle. That task was taken up by Gene Sharp, the unassuming American scholar who studied the strategic principles underlying the Gandhian

---

[1] Jawaharlal Nehru, *Toward Freedom: The Autobiography of Jawaharlal Nehru* (New York: John Day, 1941), 80.

method and distilled key lessons for effective social action. No one has done more to codify the strategic principles of nonviolent action than Sharp. Through meticulous analysis of Gandhi's practices and exhaustive study of historic examples, he identified the essential principles of nonviolent strategy and tactical methods that are most strongly associated with achieving political success.

The key variable in many struggles, Sharp argued, is not the dedication or determination of activists but their understanding and application of sound principles of strategy. In nonviolent action as in any form of collective human endeavor, it is necessary to articulate and define objectives, evaluate capacities and obstacles, determine appropriate courses of action, and utilize wise methods. Sound strategic judgment is key to the effectiveness of nonviolent action.

Sharp initially embraced nonviolence philosophically but later emphasized its pragmatic basis. He had been a pacifist as a young man and refused to accept military conscription during the Korean War, serving a two-year sentence in prison. After his release Sharp worked for a time as personal secretary to A. J. Muste at the Fellowship of Reconciliation, and later as a reporter for *Peace News* in London.[2] While studying Gandhi's methods at Oxford, Sharp realized it is not necessary to convert people to pacifism in order to organize effective nonviolent action. This was an important conceptual breakthrough for Sharp, one with enormous implications for the development of nonviolent action as a method of resisting oppression. He devoted himself thereafter to the study of nonviolence as a pragmatic means of achieving change, emphasizing that it could be applied in diverse social, political, and cultural settings without regard for particular belief systems. He developed a systematic analysis of the principles and methods of nonviolent action on an entirely secular basis, drawing from political science and sociology rather than theology and religious studies.

---

[2] John-Paul Flintoff, "Gene Sharp: The Machiavelli of Nonviolence," *New Statesmen*, January 3, 2013, http://www.newstatesmen.com.

The excerpts in this chapter include extensive passages from Sharp on the strategy and method of nonviolent action. Also included are excerpts from the work of Erica Chenoweth and Maria J. Stephan, young scholars whose research over the past decade has revolutionized the study of nonviolent action. Chenoweth and Stephan have applied the quantitative tools of social science to the study of why and how nonviolent action works. Together these readings provide a firm basis for understanding the superiority of nonviolence as a method of social change and identify the key variables of strategy and social action that account for its success.

Gene Sharp (1928–2018)

In the excerpts that follow, drawn from *Waging Nonviolent Struggle*, Sharp emphasizes the critical importance of strategy for the success of nonviolent action. The first section summarizes the key principles of strategy, differentiating grand strategy, campaign strategies, tactics, and methods. This is followed by a discussion of political power and an analysis of the specific political dynamics that account for the ability of nonviolent methods to achieve change. Last is a discussion of repression and how to deal with it, and the necessity to maintain nonviolent discipline for achieving successful political change.

The Strategy of Nonviolent Action

War and other forms of violence have not been universal in the waging of acute conflicts. In a great variety of situations, across centuries and cultural barriers, another technique of struggle has at times been applied. This other technique has been based on the ability to be stubborn, to refuse to cooperate, to disobey, and to resist powerful opponents powerfully.

Throughout human history, and in a multitude of conflicts, one side has instead fought by psychological, social, economic, or political methods, or a combination of them. Many times this alternative technique of struggle has been applied when fundamental issues have been at stake, and when ruthless opponents have been willing and able to apply extreme repression. This repression has included beatings, arrests, imprisonments, executions, and mass slaughters. Despite such repression, when the resisters have persisted in fighting with only their chosen "nonviolent weapons," they have sometimes triumphed.[3] . . .

[The] practice of this type of struggle is not based on belief in "turning the other cheek" or loving one's enemies. Instead, the widespread practice of this technique is more often based on the undeniable capacity of human beings to be stubborn, and to do what they want to do or to refuse to do what they are ordered, whatever their beliefs about the use or nonuse of violence. Massive stubbornness can have powerful political consequences.

The extremely widespread practice of nonviolent struggle is possible because the operation of this technique is compatible with the nature of political power and the vulnerabilities of all hierarchical systems. These systems and all governments depend upon the subordinated populations, groups, and institutions to supply them with their needed sources of power.[4] . . .

[An] important variable in nonviolent struggles is whether they are or are not conducted on the basis of a wisely prepared grand strategy and strategies for individual campaigns. The presence or absence of strategic calculations and planning, and, if present, their wisdom, will have a major impact on the course of the struggle and on determining its final outcome. At this point in the historical practice of nonviolent struggle we can project that a very significant fac-

---

[3] Gene Sharp, *Waging Nonviolent Struggle: 20th-Century Practice and 21st-Century Potential* (Boston: Extending Horizons Books, Porter Sargent Publishers, 2005), 14.

[4] Ibid., 23.

tor in its future practice and effectiveness will be its increasing application on the basis of strategic planning.

Competent strategic planning requires not only an understanding of the conflict situation itself, but also an in-depth understanding of why this technique can wield great power, the major characteristics of nonviolent struggle, the many methods that may be applied, and the dynamics and mechanisms at work in actual struggles of this technique when applied against repressive regimes.[5] . . .

A strategy is the conception of how best to act in order to achieve objectives in a conflict. Strategy is concerned with whether, when, or how to fight, and how to achieve maximum effectiveness in order to gain certain ends. Strategy is the plan for the practical distribution, adaptation, and application of the available means to attain the desired objectives. . . .

There are four levels of strategy: grand strategy, strategy, tactics, and the specific methods. The most fundamental is grand strategy. Then there is strategy itself for more limited campaigns, followed by tactics and methods that are used to implement the campaign strategies. . . .

Grand strategy is the master concept for the conduct of the conflict. A grand strategy is the conception that serves to coordinate and direct all appropriate and available resources (economic, human, moral, etc.) of the population or group to attain its objectives in a conflict. It is an overall plan for conducting the struggle that makes it possible to anticipate how the struggle as a whole should proceed. How can the struggle be won? What is the desired change to be achieved? . . .

The grand strategy needs to sketch in broad strokes how the nonviolent struggle group should conduct the conflict. This would broadly stretch from the present to a future situation in which its objectives have been achieved. . . .

Strategies for campaigns guide how particular conflicts are to be waged within the scope of the broader struggle and the grand strategy. These limited strategies sketch how

---

[5] Ibid., 48.

specific campaigns shall develop, and how their separate components shall be fitted together so as best to achieve their objectives. Strategy also includes the allocation of tasks to particular groups and the distribution of resources to them for use in the conflict. . . .

Campaign strategies will need to be designed to achieve and reinforce the grand strategic objectives. Factors in the formulation of campaign strategies include the development of an advantageous situation, the decision of when to wage a campaign, and the broad schema for utilizing more limited engagements within the strategy to bring success. . . .

The objectives of both the overall struggle and its component campaigns need to be formulated in terms that are clear, understandable, and widely accepted. The objectives should not be expressed as vague platitudes, such as "peace," "freedom," or "justice." Rather, they should be concrete and relatively specific, while always related to the general grievances. . . .

For a limited campaign, it is wise to choose an issue that will be a suitable point of attack. The key is to select an issue that symbolizes the general grievance, or is a specific aspect of the general problem, that is least defensible by the opponents and is almost impossible to justify. The initial objective would then be one for which the nonviolent struggle group could receive maximum support. It should also be an objective that is either within the capacity of the opponents to yield, or within the power of the resisters to take.[6]

Tactics and Methods

A tactic is a limited plan of action, based on a conception of how best in a restricted phase of the conflict to utilize the available means of fighting to achieve a limited objective as part of the wider campaign strategy. To be effective, the tactics and methods must be chosen and applied so that

---

[6] Ibid., 474–75.

they really assist the application of the strategy and contribute to achieving the requirements of its success.

Tactics prescribe how particular methods of action are applied, or how particular groups of resisters shall act in a specific situation. . . .

Tactics are thus the plans for conducting more limited engagements within the selected strategy—limited in scale, participants, time, or specific issues. They specify how a group will act in a specific encounter with the opponents. . . .

In order to achieve the best results and the most effective implementation of the developed strategies, the choice of nonviolent "weapons," or specific methods, will need to be made carefully and wisely. Many past conflicts have started with the choice of the specific methods of action to be used, rather than development of long-term plans for conducting the conflict. This is not recommended.[7] . . .

A multitude of specific methods of nonviolent action, or nonviolent weapons, exist. Nearly 200 have been identified to date, and without doubt, scores more already exist and others will emerge in future conflicts. . . .

Methods of nonviolent action include protest marches, flying forbidden flags, massive rallies, vigils, leaflets, picketing, social boycotts, economic boycotts, labor strikes, rejection of legitimacy, civil disobedience, boycott of government positions, boycott of rigged elections, strikes by civil servants, noncooperation by police, nonobedience without direct supervision, mutiny, sit-in, hunger strikes, sit-downs on the streets, establishment of alternative institutions, occupation of offices, and creation of parallel governments.

These methods may be used to protest symbolically, to put an end to cooperation, or to disrupt the operation of the established system. As such, three broad classes of nonviolent methods exist: *nonviolent protest and persuasion, noncooperation, and the nonviolent intervention*.

Symbolic protests, though in most situations quite

---

[7] Ibid., 454–59.

mild, can make it clear that some of the population is opposed to the present regime and can help to undermine its legitimacy. Social, economic, and political noncooperation, when practiced strongly and long enough, can weaken the opponents' control, wealth, domination, and power, and potentially produce paralysis. The methods of nonviolent intervention, which disrupt the established order by psychological, social, economic, physical, or political methods, can dramatically threaten the opponents' control.[8] . . .

Often it will be wise to target specific sources of the opponents' power in a sequence of priorities. This sequence may be selected on the basis of certain criteria, including at times both their vulnerability and their importance to the opponents.[9]

Power and Obedience

Real and lasting liberation requires significant changes in the power relationships within the society, not merely replacement of personnel. Liberation should mean that the members of the previously dominated and weak population obtain greater control over their lives and greater capacity to influence events.

If we wish to create a society in which people really shape their own lives and futures, and in which oppression is impossible, then we need to explore alternative ways to meet the society's basic need for means of wielding power. We also need to explore the origins of political power at a much more basic level.

The views that power derives primarily from the capacity to wield violence and that the power of rulers is monolithic and relatively permanent are not correct. . . . A major change in the distribution of power happens when the sources of power at the disposal of rulers are weakened or withdrawn,

---

[8] Ibid., 18–19.
[9] Ibid., 480–81.

thereby drastically reducing their effective power. The power relationships also change if formerly weak groups mobilize their unused power potential into effective power. . . .

The social view of power sees rulers or other command systems, despite appearances, to be dependent on the population's goodwill, decisions, and support. As such, power rises continually from many parts of the society. Political power is therefore fragile. Power always depends for its strength and existence upon a replenishment of its sources by the cooperation of numerous institutions and people—cooperation that does not have to continue. . . .

The relationship between command and obedience is always one of mutual influence and some degree of interaction. That is, command and obedience influence each other. Without the expected obedience by the subordinates (whether in the form of passive acquiescence or active consent) the power relationship is not complete, despite the threat or infliction of sanctions. . . .

When the reasons for obedience are weak, the rulers may seek to secure greater obedience by applying harsher sanctions or by offering increased rewards for obedience. However, even then, the results desired by the rulers are not guaranteed. A change in the population's will may lead to its withdrawing its service, cooperation, submission, and obedience from the rulers.

This withdrawal of cooperation and obedience under certain circumstances may also occur among the rulers' administrators and agents of repression. Their attitudes and actions are especially important. Without their support, the oppressive system disintegrates. . . .

Three of the most important factors in determining to what degree rulers' power will be controlled or uncontrolled are

- the relative desire of the populace to control the rulers' power;

- the relative strength of the society's independent organizations and institutions;
- the population's relative ability to withhold their consent and cooperation by concrete actions.

Freedom is not something that rulers "give" the population. The degree of freedom within a society is achieved through the interaction between society and government.

According to this social insight into the nature of political power, people have immense power potential. It is ultimately their attitudes, behavior, cooperation, and obedience that supply sources of power to all rulers and hierarchical systems, even oppressors and tyrants.

The degree of liberty or tyranny in any government is, therefore, in large part, a reflection of the relative determination of the population to be free and their willingness and ability to resist efforts to enslave them. . . .

The power of the rulers is weakened to the degree that the population

- repudiates the moral right of the current rulers to rule;
- disobeys, noncooperates, and refuses to assist the rulers;
- declines to supply the skills and knowledge required by the rulers;
- denies the rulers control over administration, property, natural resources, financial resources, the economic system, communication, and transportation.

Additionally, if the rulers' punishments against a defined population are not available because of disaffection in the military or police forces, or if popular defiance continues and even grows despite harsh penalties, then the power of the rulers will shrink or even dissolve.[10]

---

[10] Ibid., 27–38.

Undermining Pillars of Power

The most efficient way to undermine the opponents' policy or system is to weaken or remove their sources of power. In relatively small campaigns over limited issues, this approach will be only partially required. For example, in a labor strike or a major economic boycott, the withdrawal of labor or halt to purchasing is designed to restrict the opponents' economic resources. In these conflicts, it normally is not necessary for the resisters to undermine other sources of the opponents' power.

However, in larger political struggles—such as attempts to repel a foreign occupation or dissolve a dictatorship—strategists of nonviolent struggle would be wise to attempt to weaken and remove as many of these sources of power as possible. This requires that the weapons of nonviolent struggle be applied against crucial targets, primarily the "pillars of support" of the opponents that are determined to be most vulnerable. . . .

To be most effective, nonviolent action needs to be concentrated against crucial targets. These targets need to be selected after careful consideration of one's own strength, overall objectives, and campaign objectives; the objectives and position of the opponents, including their weaknesses; and the importance of the issues at stake themselves. Napoleon's maxim that it is impossible to be too strong at the decisive point applies here as well.

Campaign strategies need to be designed to utilize the strength of the resisters to expose and attack the opponents' vulnerabilities and weaknesses, while avoiding engagement of the opponents at their strongest and most defensible points. This applies to both the selection of campaign objectives and the choice of tactical targets for attack within those campaigns.[11]

---

[11] Ibid., 482.

... Preserving and strengthening existing independent groups and institutions and creating new ones are important contributions to the capacity to wage effective future resistance. The condition of these bodies must be carefully considered by strategic planners, as they are important in determining the ability of the populace to wage nonviolent struggle successfully.

If such independent social groups and institutions are weak or largely absent, it may be necessary to create new groups or organizations in order to prepare for future strong resistance. Or, it may be possible to turn to certain existing groups or institutions that have not been fully independent into ones with more independence of action, capable of playing major roles in future struggles. The creation and the strengthening of such institutions can significantly increase the future capacity for nonviolent struggle and can expand its effectiveness.[12]

Facing Repression

While noncooperation to undermine compliance and to weaken and sever the sources of the opponents' power are the main forces in nonviolent struggle, one other process sometimes operates. This is "political jujitsu." In this process, brutal repression against disciplined nonviolent resisters does not strengthen the opponents and weaken the resisters, but does the opposite. Widespread revulsion against the opponents for their brutality operates in some cases to shift power to the resisters. More people may join the resistance. Third parties may change their opinions and activities to favor the resisters and act against the opponents. Even members of the opponents' usual supporters, administrators, and troops and police may become unreliable and may even mutiny. The use of the opponents'

---

[12] Ibid., 478.

supposedly coercive violence has then been turned to undermine their own power capacity. Political jujitsu does not operate in all situations, however, and instead heavy reliance must therefore be placed on the impact of large-scale, carefully focused noncooperation.[13] . . .

Faced with repression, nonviolent resisters have only one acceptable response: to overcome, they must persist in their actions and refuse to submit or retreat. *If the resisters show in any way that the repression weakens the movement, they will signal to the opponents that if they make the repression severe enough it will produce submission.*

Fearlessness, or deliberate control of fear, is especially important at this stage of the struggle. Firmness in the face of repression will make it possible for mass noncooperation to produce its coercive effects. Also, persistence may contribute to sympathy for the defiant nonviolent resisters. It is essential that the leadership of the nonviolent struggle be, and be perceived to be, courageous and unbowed in the face of repression and of threatened future punishments.

Sometimes, specific methods of nonviolent struggle will by their nature be much more difficult for the opponents to deal with by repression and less likely to provoke the most extreme brutalities. For example, it may be better not to march down the street in face of potential rifle fire, but instead for everyone to stay at home for 24 hours and therefore paralyze the city.

No change of tactics and methods, however, must be permitted to alter the basic nonviolent counteraction to repression: brave, relentless, and disciplined struggle. . . .

Those planning to initiate nonviolent struggle will need to consider the degree of suffering the volunteers are willing to endure and how firmly they will be able to defy their

---

[13] Ibid., 47.

opponents' repression. A bold action likely to draw a repressive response that the nonviolent resisters are not prepared to endure usually should not be taken. It is generally better to choose methods of action that do not set up resisters as clear targets when more effective and less provocative methods are available. The selected methods of action should be in accord with the degree of repression the resisters are prepared to suffer for such action. Very importantly, it should be understood, only methods should be selected that clearly help to implement the selected strategy for the struggle. . . .

The resisters' persistence will have several effects. Two are:

- The numerical and quantitative effect of many defiant subjects refusing to obey despite repression will significantly limit the opponents' ability to control the situation and to maintain their policies.
- The nonviolent persistence despite repression may produce psychological or qualitative effects on the opponents, their supporters, third parties, and others.[14]

. . . Naturally, opponents whose power, privilege, and control are threatened will be disturbed. When this occurs, powerful opponents are likely to resort to violent repression. Resisters may be beaten, imprisoned, kidnapped, wounded, tortured, or killed.

Such repression is not a sign that the nonviolent struggle has failed. Indeed, this repression is a tribute to the degree to which nonviolent struggle has upset the oppressors. Casualties are not a sign of defeat in nonviolent struggle, any more than they are in military conflict. Casualties are the expected human cost of waging an acute conflict with

---

[14] Ibid., 381–82.

opponents willing and able to kill in order to establish or maintain their control.

The degree to which the opponents' reactions will be crude and brutal, or refined and sophisticated with very little violence, will vary. However, strong responses from the opponents need to be anticipated. The opponents' reactions should be no surprise and the resisters should be prepared for them.[15] . . .

Nonviolent discipline consists of two components: 1) adhering to the strategic plans for the struggle and 2) refraining from violence. Failure of the resisters to adhere to the strategic plan can produce confusion and can deflect strength away from the points at which it needs to be concentrated. The breakdown of nonviolent discipline and the outbreak of violence can have disastrous effects on a nonviolent struggle and can assist the opponents.[16]

Erica Chenoweth and Maria J. Stephan

In 2008 an extraordinary article was published in *International Security*, a top-line academic journal in the field of security studies that usually features work on military strategy, nuclear deterrence, and security policy, often written by male authors. In the summer 2008 issue, the journal published the essay "Why Civil Resistance Works" by two young scholars, Erica Chenoweth and Maria J. Stephan, based on groundbreaking quantitative research into the factors that determine the effectiveness of political action. Their research challenged core realist assumptions about the superiority of military force as an arbiter of political affairs. They presented evidence that, in major struggles for political change in hundreds of cases over

---
[15] Ibid., 486.
[16] Ibid., 488.

the prior century, nonviolent methods of struggle proved to be twice as effective as the use of military force in achieving success. The article created a sensation among political scientists and scholars of nonviolent action and was widely circulated and read. For a number of years afterward it ranked among the top-ten most frequently downloaded articles from the journal. The authors subsequently published their research and a series of case studies in an award-winning book of the same title.[17]

In their study Chenoweth and Stephan examined 323 historical examples of resistance campaigns that occurred over a span of more than one hundred years to compare the relative effectiveness of nonviolent and violent methods. Each case involved an intensive political conflict, sometimes lasting several years, in which sociopolitical movements struggled to change regimes or gain major concessions from government adversaries. They found that nonviolent campaigns were twice as successful as those in which violence was the principal means of struggle. Nonviolent methods were found to be as successful on average in repressive dictatorships as in democratic regimes.

Nonviolent action is not only more effective in achieving change, it is also more likely to generate greater democracy and political freedom. A separate 2005 study of political transitions showed that nonviolent political changes are more likely than violent transitions to yield democratic regimes and an open society. Nonviolent civil resistance campaigns resulted in democratic regimes, while most violent transitions created authoritarian regimes.[18] Chenoweth and Stephan used a different methodology but reached similar conclusions. The use of

---

[17] Erica Chenoweth and Maria J. Stephan, "Why Civil Resistance Works: The Strategic Logic of Nonviolent Conflict," *International Security* 33, no. 1 (2008): 7–44; Erica Chenoweth and Maria J. Stephan, *Why Civil Resistance Works: The Strategic Logic of Nonviolent Conflict* (New York: Columbia University Press, 2011).

[18] The findings are presented in Adrian Karatnycky and Peter Ackerman, "How Freedom Is Won: From Civil Resistance to Durable Democracy," *International Journal of Not-for-Profit Law* 7, no. 3 (2005).

civil resistance methods is much more likely to produce a democratic society than the use of armed struggle.[19]

The excerpts below are drawn from their 2008 article:

Why Civil Resistance Works

Our findings show that major nonviolent campaigns have achieved success 53 percent of the time, compared with 26 percent for violent resistance campaigns. There are two reasons for this success. First, a campaign's commitment to nonviolent methods enhances its domestic and international legitimacy and encourages more broad-based participation in the resistance, which translates into increased pressure being brought to bear on the target. Recognition of the challenger group's grievances can translate into greater internal and external support for that group and alienation of the target regime, undermining the regime's main sources of political, economic, and even military power.

Second, whereas governments easily justify violent counterattacks against armed insurgents, regime violence against nonviolent movements is more likely to backfire against the regime. Potentially sympathetic publics perceive violent militants as having maximalist or extremist goals beyond accommodation, but they perceive nonviolent resistance groups as less extreme, thereby enhancing their appeal and facilitating the extraction of concessions through bargaining.

Our findings challenge the conventional wisdom that violent resistance against conventionally superior adversaries is the most effective way for resistance groups to achieve policy goals. Instead, we assert that nonviolent resistance is a forceful alternative to political violence that can pose effective challenges to democratic and nondemocratic opponents, and at times can do so more effectively than violent resistance. . . .

---

[19] Chenoweth and Stephan, *Why Civil Resistance Works*, 201–19.

Nonviolent resistance can be distinguished from principled nonviolence, which is grounded in religious and ethically based injunctions against violence. Although many people who are committed to principled nonviolence have engaged in nonviolent resistance (e.g., Gandhi and Martin Luther King Jr.), the vast majority of participants in nonviolent struggles have not been devoted to principled nonviolence. The conflation of nonviolent struggle with principled nonviolence, pacifism, passivity, weakness, or isolated street protests has contributed to misconceptions about this phenomenon. Although nonviolent resisters eschew the threat or use of violence, the "peaceful" designation often given to nonviolent movements belies the often highly disruptive nature of organized nonviolent resistance. Nonviolent resistance achieves demands against the will of the opponent by seizing control of the conflict through widespread noncooperation and defiance. . . .

. . . Members of a regime—including civil servants, security forces, and members of the judiciary—are more likely to shift loyalty toward nonviolent opposition groups than toward violent opposition groups. The coercive power of any resistance campaign is enhanced by its tendency to prompt disobedience and defections by members of the opponent's security forces, who are more likely to consider the negative political and personal consequences of using repressive violence against unarmed demonstrators than against armed insurgents. Regime repression can also backfire through increased public mobilization. Actively involving a relatively large number of people in the nonviolent campaign may bring greater and more sustained pressure to bear on the target, whereas the public may eschew violent insurgency because of physical or moral barriers. . . .

. . . Nonviolent resistance campaigns appear to be more open to negotiation and bargaining because they do not threaten the lives or well-being of members of the target regime. Regime supporters are more likely to bargain with resistance groups that are not killing or maiming their comrades.[20]

Proving Dr. King Right

In the passage below from a 2016 academic blog post, Chenoweth and Stephan update their original research findings, revisit their conclusions about key factors of success, and address some of the current debates about social movement strategy. Their latest research shows lower success rates for both violent and nonviolent struggles but a continuing significant effectiveness advantage for nonviolent campaigns.

> Since 2011, the world has been a deeply contentious place. Although armed insurgencies rage across the Middle East, the Sahel, and Southern Asia, violent civil conflicts are no longer the primary way that people seek to redress their grievances. Instead, from Tunis to Tahrir Square, from Zuccotti Park to Ferguson, from Burkina Faso to Hong Kong, movements worldwide have drawn on the lessons of Gandhi, King, and everyday activists at home and abroad to push for change.
>
> Gandhi's and King's emphases on nonviolent resistance—in which unarmed people use a coordinated set of strikes, protests, boycotts, or other actions to confront an opponent—are not without critics. Some critiques are based on a misunderstanding about what civil resistance is, while others doubt the ability of unarmed and suppressed people to organize and challenge a powerful opponent. With each new movement comes the same set of challenges, including questions about the efficacy of nonviolent action in the face of entrenched power and systemic oppression. In 2011, we published a book exploring these questions and found

---

[20] Chenoweth and Stephan, "Why Civil Disobedience Works," *International Security*, 8–12.

unexpectedly that campaigns of nonviolent resistance had succeeded more than twice as often as their violent counterparts when seeking to remove incumbent national leaders or gain territorial independence.

To many people, this conclusion may seem naive, but when we drilled into the data, we found that nonviolent resistance campaigns don't succeed by melting the hearts of their opponents. Instead, they tend to succeed because nonviolent methods have a greater potential for eliciting mass participation—on average, they elicit about 11 times more participants than the average armed uprising—and because this is the source of major power shifts within the opponent regime. Mass participation that draws on diverse segments of society tends to empower and coopt reformers while cutting off hardliners from sources of support. When such participation is nonviolent, it increases the chances of pulling the regime's support from the leadership, allowing security forces, economic elites, and civilian bureaucrats to shift their loyalties with less fear of bloody retribution.

In other words, we found that nonviolent resistance is effective not necessarily because of its conversion potential but rather because of its creative, cooptive, and coercive potential—a theory that Albert Einstein Institution founder Gene Sharp has articulated for decades. Naturally, not all nonviolent campaigns succeed. But in cases where they failed, there was no good systematic evidence to suggest that violent uprisings would have performed any better.

. . . What have we learned about nonviolent resistance in the past five years? Below we sketch some of the key empirical takeaways from political science, some of which have rather surprising implications for skeptics of nonviolent action.

1. Nonviolent campaigns have become increasingly common.

If you feel as though we live in a particularly disruptive time in history, you're right. But it's the kind of disruption that is unique to our time. The Major Episodes of Contention project (a data project run by Professor Erica Chenoweth) suggests that nonviolent resistance campaigns have become the modal category of contentious action worldwide. The NAVCO Data Project, a separate data collection project using different source material and inclusion criteria, shows similar patterns, as do a variety of other protest data sets. Whereas the frequency of violent insurgencies—defined with a 1,000-battle-death threshold—has declined since the 1970s, campaigns relying primarily on nonviolent resistance have skyrocketed. Note that these figures refer specifically to maximalist campaigns, meaning their goals are to remove the incumbent national leadership from power or to create territorial independence through secession or expulsion of a foreign military occupation or colonial power.

In the first five years of the current decade alone, we have seen more onsets of new nonviolent campaigns than during the entire 1990s, and almost as many as were observed during the 2000s. Our current decade is on track to be the most contentious decade on record.

2. Although they are more common, the absolute success rates of nonviolent resistance campaigns have declined.

With this precipitous rise of nonviolent campaigns, we also have seen a steep learning curve. The success rates of nonviolent resistance peaked in the 1990s, but the current decade has seen a sharp decline in the success rates of nonviolent resistance.

There may be a few reasons for this. First, state opponents may be learning and adapting to challenges from below. Although several decades ago, they may have underestimated the potential of people power to pose significant threats to their rule, they may now see mass nonviolent campaigns as truly threatening, devoting more resources to preventing them—perhaps following the implications of Bruce Bueno de Mesquita and Alastair Smith's *Dictator's Handbook*[21]—or deploying "smart repression" to subvert them when they arise....

Second, activists employing methods of nonviolent action may be learning the wrong lessons from their contemporaries around the globe. For instance, one may be tempted to think, based on the news coverage of the mass demonstrations and strikes in Tunisia in 2010 and 2011, that three weeks' worth of demonstrations could unseat a dictator. Yet such understandings completely miss the fact that Tunisia had a unique recent history of robust organized labor activity, which lent its support to the uprising, and that general strikes threatened to cripple the Tunisian economy, such that economic and business elites began to withdraw support from President Zine el Abidine Ben Ali as much as the security forces who defied his order to strafe the demonstrators with automatic weapons.

3. ... Nonviolent campaigns are still succeeding more often than violence.

Violent campaigns have fared much worse, in terms of absolute rates of success, than nonviolent campaigns since 1960. In fact, in the aggregate, from 1900 to 2015, nonviolent campaigns succeeded 51 percent of the time, whereas

---

[21] Bruce Bueno de Mesquita and Alistair Smith, *The Dictator's Handbook: Why Bad Behavior Is Almost Always Good Politics* (New York: PublicAffairs, 2012).

violent campaigns succeeded 27 percent of the time. So far this decade, 30 percent of nonviolent campaigns have succeeded, whereas 12 percent of violent campaigns have succeeded—meaning that, in fact, the proportional success gap between them is now actually wider than average.

4. Violent flanks are typically disadvantageous for nonviolent mass movements.

One of the hot topics since 2011 has been the question of whether employing a little bit of violence alongside a primarily unarmed campaign helps or hurts a nonviolent campaign. This question was often represented in the "diversity of tactics" debate here in the United States. But the question of nonviolent, violent, or mixed methods of contention is common in many movements seeking radical change worldwide. Despite numerous claims, pro and con, by observers, pundits, and activists alike, this question received surprisingly little serious empirical evaluation until fairly recently.

In a recent article in *Mobilization*, Chenoweth and Kurt Schock of Rutgers University use comparative data to study the limited use of violence.[22] They found that violent flanks may achieve some short-term process goals such as media attention, the perception of self-defense, the diffusion of an oppositional culture that builds the commitment of more radical members, or catharsis around the ability to "blow off steam." But violent flanks typically undermine longer-term strategic goals such as maintaining an increasingly large and diverse participation base, expanding support among third parties, and eliciting loyalty shifts among security forces. They find evidence that violent flanks are typically associated with smaller participation rates and more homog-

---

[22] Erica Chenoweth and Kurt Schock, "Do Contemporaneous Armed Challenges Affect the Outcomes of Mass Nonviolent Campaigns"?," *Mobilization: An International Quarterly* 20, no. 4 (2015): 427–51.

enous participation, undermining the main advantage of using nonviolent resistance in the first place. Another study similarly finds that violent flanks tend to increase repression by the state, which tends to be associated with lower participation rates. Thus, on average, violent flanks definitely do not help nonviolent campaigns succeed. . . .

5. Nonviolent conflicts are exceedingly difficult to predict.

The entire field of sociology has long been concerned with the question of when social movements or protest movements occur. . . . [But] people power movements are simply so contextual and contingent that typical forecasting tools and data structures can't quite pin down their causes. Another way to interpret this finding is that people who organize nonviolent uprisings often overcome adverse conditions in creative ways that defy expectations, which brings us to our final point.

6. Repression challenges all dissident campaigns but does not necessarily predetermine the choice of nonviolent resistance or its outcome.

One popular argument about nonviolent resistance is that it can happen and maybe succeed as long as the opponent plays nice. But as soon as the opponent takes off the gloves, nonviolent resistance is impossible or futile. We dealt with this argument a bit in our 2011 book, but some more recent work also speaks to this important question.

In terms of whether brutal repression influences the possibility of nonviolent resistance, Wendy Pearlman argues in her excellent book on the Palestinian national movement that repression alone cannot explain the reasons why the movement has turned from nonviolent action to violence.[23]

---

[23] Wendy Pearlman, *Violence, Nonviolence, and the Palestinian National Movement* (Cambridge University Press, 2014).

She argues that, in fact, repression was just as intense during the nonviolent phase of the First Intifada as it was during several of the movement's violent phases. Instead, she argues, the level of cohesion can best explain the turn to violence. When the movement possessed collective vision, leadership, and a clear set of internal norms and rules, the movement was able to rely on nonviolent resistance despite continued repression by the Israeli government.

Researchers Jonathan Sutton, Charles Butcher, and Isak Svensson likewise point to movement structure and organization as a critical determinant of campaign viability in the face of repression.[24] They use quantitative data to argue that when the state uses one-sided violence or mass killings against unarmed demonstrations, the demonstrators can go on to succeed in the long run only when they are part of a larger, coordinated campaign.

Of course, some research casts doubt on the ability of nonviolent opposition to contend with highly sophisticated repressive regimes—particularly those with genocidal or politicidal ambitions. . . . The Guatemalan security forces' systematic dismantling of the leftist opposition between 1975 and 1985 is a cautionary tale regarding the sophistication and commitment that some regimes pose. As was the brutal, calculated killing of nonviolent protesters by the Bashar al Assad regime in Syria after the protests in Deraa in March 2011—a chilling reminder of why nonviolent mass campaigns fail almost as often as they succeed.

But again, it is difficult to predict when such repressive bureaucracies will be able to compel the full loyalty of their subordinates in the face of a mass uprising. . . . In fact, repressive episodes can often be the cause of a nonviolent campaign rather than its conclusion. The murder of

---

[24] Jonathan Sutton, Charles Butcher, and Isak Svensson, "Explaining Political Jui-Jitsu: Institution-Building and the Outcomes of Regime Violence against Unarmed Protests," *Journal of Conflict Resolution* 51, no. 5 (2014): 559–73.

Emmett Till[25] comes to mind as an example of a horrific episode of violence that ultimately generated an upswell of support, sympathy, and participation for the U.S. civil rights movement.[26]

---

[25] The fourteen-year-old African American boy whose murder in Mississippi in August 1955 galvanized the emerging U.S. civil rights movement.

[26] Erica Chenoweth and Maria J. Stephan, "How the World Is Proving Martin Luther King Jr. Right about Nonviolence," *Washington Post, Monkey Cage*, January 18, 2016, https://www.washingtonpost.com.

6

Africa Rising

In African traditions, peace means much more than the absence of armed conflict. It signifies positive social relationships and the cohesion of communities, a state of social harmony linked to social justice. For many Africans the term for peace is *ubuntu*, which can be translated, "I am because we are." According to philosopher Augustine Shutte, peace and personal fulfillment are achieved through participation and belonging to community.[1] Peace is built upon right relationship with others and the harmonious structuring of society.

Modern African thinking on these issues borrows from these themes in emphasizing the interconnection of peace, development, and human rights. As a continent deeply scarred by the slave trade and the brutal legacies of colonialism, Africa has suffered decades of repression, war, economic exploitation, and corruption, creating grievous social and political wounds. African political and social leaders have argued that peace is not possible without progress in economic development and the free exercise of political and human rights.

Africa led the world in the struggle against colonialism and the movement for political independence and self-determination. Across the continent in the 1950s the repressive structures of

---

[1] Augustine Shutte, *Ubuntu: An Ethic for a New South Africa* (Pietermaritzburg, South Africa: Cluster Publications, 2001), 9.

imperial rule and foreign exploitation began to crumble, beginning with the independence of Ghana. Led by Kwame Nkrumah, the people of that former British colony rose up in nonviolent protest, strikes, and boycotts, emulating the methods of Gandhi. Nkrumah argued that persistent nonviolent resistance, which he called "positive action," offered the best approach for overcoming colonial rule and leading his country to political freedom without the rancor and destructiveness that would result from armed insurgency. After succeeding in this mission and coming to power Nkrumah displayed authoritarian tendencies and was overthrown by a military coup, but his example of nonviolent anticolonial resistance inspired many people in Africa and around the world. Martin Luther King Jr. attended the independence day ceremony in Accra in 1957 and spoke enthusiastically of that experience in his sermon "Birth of a New Nation." The lesson of Ghana, King said, was that "a nation or a people can break free of oppression without violence."[2]

Nelson Mandela (1918–2013)

For some it may seem inappropriate to include Nelson Mandela in a volume on nonviolence and peace. Yes, he was awarded the Nobel Peace Prize and as a political leader spoke out against war and social injustice and helped to mediate international conflicts. During his career in the liberation movement, however, Mandela helped to create and became the first leader of the armed wing of the African National Congress (ANC), also known as Umkhonto we Sizwe (The spear of the nation). Indeed it was precisely because he refused to condemn the use of violence by the ANC that he was imprisoned and held for twenty-seven years on Robbin Island. Even in the late years of his captivity, as white leaders were reaching out to him to negotiate a transition

---

[2] Martin Luther King Jr., "Birth of a New Nation," April 7, 1957, Martin Luther King Papers Project, Stanford University, http://kingencyclopedia.stanford.edu.

to majority rule, Mandela held firm and refused to renounce the use of force. It was a matter of deep principle for him. We will give up our arms, he insisted, only if the government does the same and ceases its brutal repression.

Mandela and the ANC started out fully committed to Gandhian strategies of nonviolence. They adopted the methods of armed struggle reluctantly, only after the 1960 massacre of unarmed civilians in Sharpeville. After decades of nonviolent struggle and the constant rejection of their peaceful demands, and in the face of deepening repression and increasingly violent attacks by the racist regime, Mandela and other ANC leaders felt they had no choice but to fight back with violence. Over the years, the military wing of the ANC committed acts of sabotage and carried out violent attacks, but the armed struggle played only a minor role in the liberation struggle and may have inadvertently given the apartheid regime an excuse to intensify its repression. The victory that came with Mandela's release and South Africa's first free elections did not come at the point of a gun. It was the result of massive civil resistance by the black African population, and the financial and economic isolation of the white regime generated by the worldwide antiapartheid movement.[3]

Mandela was the founder and commander of the ANC's armed wing, but in his autobiography he says very little about his military role. Throughout his distinguished public career he acted nonviolently, using diplomatic rather than violent means, in accord with the principles and spirit of Gandhi and King.

As Mandela states in one of the excerpts below, the freedom movement in South Africa owed much to Gandhi, who lived in the country for more than twenty years and led a significant movement to resist racial oppression and defend the rights of Asian immigrants. Gandhi did not support the emerging African movement for freedom at the time, and some of his early

---

[3] For a concise critical analysis of the role of nonviolence in the final push for liberation, see Stephen Zunes, "South Africa: The Townships Rise Up," in *Civil Resistance and Conflict Transformation: Transitions from Armed to Nonviolent Struggle*, ed. Veronique Dudouet (London: Routledge, 2015), 100–125.

comments on the native population betrayed distinct traces of racial prejudice, although he later tempered his views.[4] Gandhi's successes in using nonviolent resistance and civil disobedience made a huge impression on the founders of the ANC, and his methods were adopted as the primary means of struggle for the new freedom movement. Mandela, Oliver Tambo, and the later generation of ANC leaders adopted similar methods, although purely on a pragmatic basis and only as long as they were deemed effective. The massive wave of noncooperation and civil resistance that arose from the townships in the 1980s made the apartheid system ungovernable and forced the regime to yield.

Mandela was the embodiment of that resistance and the iconic leader of the freedom movement. The demand to free Mandela became the passionate rallying cry to unify all factions and segments of the country's different populations. As president, Mandela guided his country skillfully and gracefully through the early years of political freedom, buffeted by violent currents, working for reconciliation and racial tolerance within South Africa and for peace and transnational cooperation on the continent and globally. His words and courageous action continue to inspire people throughout Africa and the world and will echo through the ages. In *Long March to Freedom* and in his many speeches and public addresses, he argued eloquently for nonviolence and peace with justice. The excerpts below capture some of his key insights on reconciliation, social justice, diplomacy, and the power of nonviolence.

> I always knew that deep down in every human heart, there is mercy and generosity. No one is born hating another person because of the color of his skin, or his background, or his religion. People must learn to hate, and if they can learn to hate, they can be taught to love, for love comes more naturally

---

[4] For a discussion of Gandhi's views toward "Natives," see Joseph Lelyveld, *Great Soul: Mahatma Gandhi and His Struggle with India* (New Delhi: HarperCollins, 2011), 53–77; see also Ashwin Desai and Goolam Vahed, *The South African Gandhi: Stretcher-Bearer of Empire* (Stanford, CA: Stanford University Press, 2016).

to the human heart than its opposite. Even in the grimmest times in prison, when my comrades and I were pushed to our limits, I would see a glimmer of humanity in one of the guards, perhaps just for a second, but it was enough to reassure me and keep me going. Man's goodness is a flame that can be hidden but never extinguished.[5]

I learned that to humiliate another person is to make him suffer an unnecessarily cruel fate. Even as a boy, I defeated my opponents without dishonoring them.[6]

I knew as well as I knew anything that the oppressor must be liberated just as surely as the oppressed. A man who takes away another man's freedom is a prisoner of hatred; he is locked behind the bars of prejudice and narrow-mindedness. I am not truly free if I am taking away someone else's freedom, just as surely as I am not free when my freedom is taken from me. The oppressed and the oppressor alike are robbed of their humanity.[7]

Message to the *Satyagraha* Centenary Conference, New Delhi

We in South Africa owe much to the presence of Gandhi in our midst for 21 years. His influence was felt by freedom struggles throughout the African continent for a good part of the 20th century. And he greatly inspired the struggle in South Africa led by the ANC. His philosophy contributed in no small measure to bringing about a peaceful transformation in South Africa and in healing the destructive human divisions that had been spawned by the abhorrent practice of apartheid.

It is very appropriate, therefore, that India and South Africa are jointly celebrating the centenary of *satyagraha*, which [is] a legacy shared by both the countries. . . .

---

[5] Nelson Mandela, *Long Walk to Freedom* (New York: Back Bay Books, 1995), 622.
[6] Ibid., 10.
[7] Ibid., 624.

In a world riven by violence and strife, Gandhi's message of peace and nonviolence holds the key to human survival in the 21st century. He rightly believed in the efficacy of pitting the soul force of the *satyagrahi* against the brute force of the oppressor and in, effect, converting the oppressor to the right and moral point of view.[8]

Global Peace

Peace and non-violence have not yet become the automatic or predominant modes for living with difference and diversity, in spite of all the progress humankind has seen and achieved in the last century.

Too much of our planet is still embroiled in destructive conflict, strife, and war.

And unfortunately none of us can escape blame for the situation in which humankind finds itself. In almost every part of the world human beings find reasons to resort to force and violence in addressing differences that we surely should attempt to resolve through negotiation, dialogue, and reason.

Development and peace are indivisible. Without peace and international security, nations cannot focus on the upliftment of the most underprivileged of their citizens.

Peace is not just the absence of conflict; peace is the creation of an environment where all can flourish, regardless of race, color, creed, religion, gender, class, caste, or any other social markers of difference. Religion, ethnicity, language, social and cultural practices are elements which enrich human civilization, adding to the wealth of our diversity. Why should they be allowed to become a cause of division, and violence? We demean our common humanity by allowing that to happen. . . .

---

[8] "Video Message by Nelson Mandela to the *Satyagraha* Centenary Conference, New Delhi, January 29–30, 2007," Speeches of Nelson Mandela, Nelson Mandela Foundation, http://www.mandela.gov.za.

South Africa, the country that inspired the Mahatma and that was inspired by the Mahatma, chose a path of peace in the face of all the prophets of doom. We chose his path, the route of negotiation and compromise. And we hope that we honored his memory. And that in remembrance of that great tradition others will follow.[9]

Upon Accepting the Africa Peace Award

[S]ociety's freedom from hunger, ignorance and disease is, more often than not, the dividing line between war and peace. The pursuit of the collective well-being of humanity, to ensure that all persons live life to the full, is an ideal whose time has come.

Humanity is suing for a new world order, premised, above everything else, on this objective. The task is daunting and the obstacles unlimited. But that quest has so captured the imagination of peoples that it can no longer be concealed behind fancy rhetoric.

Africa deserves all these rights. Its children deserve as much of a regular diet of protein as any other. They have the right to computers and instruments of modern communications. . . .

Colonialism and the selfish ordering of world affairs—past and present—have undermined Africa's development. And it is only just that Africa should demand her fair share of world resources; that we should challenge the untenable global division of power and wealth.

But Africa has long traversed past a mind-set that seeks to heap all blame on the past and on others. The era of renaissance we are entering, is, and should be, based on our own efforts as Africans to change Africa's conditions for the better. If Africa's children, like all other children, should

---

[9] "Message by Nelson Mandela to the Global Convention on Peace and Non-Violence, New Delhi," January 31, 2004, Speeches of Nelson Mandela, Nelson Mandela Foundation, http://www.mandela.gov.za.

shelter a light of hope in their hearts about what life can offer, then we, as their parents and leaders, deserve to be judged by the same standards as anyone else.

In this regard, we face the urgent task of deepening the culture of human rights on the continent. We are called upon to ensure that our social structures reflect the will of the people. Our approach to issues of political power should proceed from the premise that it is an expression of popular will, and not a mysterious force wielded by a chosen few. . . .

The continent's challenge is one that equally faces South Africa. For, behind the glitter of city lights, the halo of a relatively advanced technology and the smoothness of paved roads, lies the reality of a rate of illiteracy that is among the highest on the continent; poverty, homelessness, landlessness, and malnutrition that beset millions. . . .

We can only succeed if we work together; in as much as we worked together to succeed against apartheid. And for the enormous sacrifices that Africa endured to complete her emancipation, we in South Africa shall forever be proud and grateful.

Never again shall South Africa be the fountain-head of conflict in the region and further afield. Never again shall our country be the source of armaments used to suppress communities and to wage aggressive wars against neighbors. Never again shall we spend our people's resources to develop weapons of mass destruction.

Democratic South Africa is committed to full equality in our relations with our neighbors and all other nations. . . .

It is with this sentiment that I humbly accept the Africa Peace Award. May peace and prosperity reign on the African continent.[10]

---

[10] "Address by President Nelson Mandela on Upon accepting the Africa Peace Award," March 18, 1995, https://www.sahistory.org.za.

Upon Accepting the Nobel Peace Prize

I am indeed truly humbled to be standing here today to receive this year's Nobel Peace Prize.

I extend my heartfelt thanks to the Norwegian Nobel Committee for elevating us to the status of a Nobel Peace Prize winner.

I would also like to take this opportunity to congratulate my compatriot and fellow laureate, State President F. W. de Klerk, on his receipt of this high honor.

Together, we join two distinguished South Africans, the late Chief Albert Luthuli and His Grace Archbishop Desmond Tutu, to whose seminal contributions to the peaceful struggle against the evil system of apartheid you paid well-deserved tribute by awarding them the Nobel Peace Prize.

It will not be presumptuous of us if we also add, among our predecessors, the name of another outstanding Nobel Peace Prize winner, the late African American statesman and internationalist, the Reverend Martin Luther King Jr.

He, too, grappled with and died in the effort to make a contribution to the just solution of the same great issues of the day which we have had to face as South Africans.

We speak here of the challenge of the dichotomies of war and peace, violence and non-violence, racism and human dignity, oppression and repression and liberty and human rights, poverty and freedom from want.

We stand here today as nothing more than a representative of the millions of our people who dared to rise up against a social system whose very essence is war, violence, racism, oppression, repression, and the impoverishment of an entire people.

I am also here today as a representative of the millions of people across the globe, the anti-apartheid movement, the governments and organizations that joined with us, not to fight against South Africa as a country or any of its peoples, but to oppose an inhuman system and sue for a speedy end to the apartheid crime against humanity.

These countless human beings, both inside and outside our country, had the nobility of spirit to stand in the path of tyranny and injustice, without seeking selfish gain. They recognized that an injury to one is an injury to all and therefore acted together in defense of justice and a common human decency.

Because of their courage and persistence for many years, we can, today, even set the dates when all humanity will join together to celebrate one of the outstanding human victories of our century. . . .

The value of our shared reward will and must be measured by the joyful peace which will triumph, because the common humanity that bonds both black and white into one human race will have said to each one of us that we shall all live like the children of paradise.

Thus shall we live, because we will have created a society which recognizes that all people are born equal, with each entitled in equal measure to life, liberty, prosperity, human rights, and good governance.

Such a society should never allow again that there should be prisoners of conscience nor that any person's human rights should be violated.

Neither should it ever happen that once more the avenues to peaceful change are blocked by usurpers who seek to take power away from the people, in pursuit of their own, ignoble purposes. . . .

Far from the rough and tumble of the politics of our own country, I would like to take this opportunity to join the Norwegian Nobel Committee and pay tribute to my joint laureate, Mr. F. W. de Klerk.

He had the courage to admit that a terrible wrong had been done to our country and people through the imposition of the system of apartheid.

He had the foresight to understand and accept that all the people of South Africa must, through negotiations and as equal participants in the process, together determine what they want to make of their future. . . .

We live with the hope that as she battles to remake herself, South Africa will be like a microcosm of the new world that is striving to be born.

This must be a world of democracy and respect for human rights, a world freed from the horrors of poverty, hunger, deprivation, and ignorance, relieved of the threat and the scourge of civil wars and external aggression and unburdened of the great tragedy of millions forced to become refugees.

The processes in which South Africa and southern Africa as a whole are engaged beckon and urge us all that we take this tide at the flood and make of this region a living example of what all people of conscience would like the world to be.

We do not believe that this Nobel Peace Prize is intended as a commendation for matters that have happened and passed.

We hear the voices which say that it is an appeal from all those, throughout the universe, who sought an end to the system of apartheid.

We understand their call, that we devote what remains of our lives to the use of our country's unique and painful experience to demonstrate, in practice, that the normal condition for human existence is democracy, justice, peace, non-racism, non-sexism, prosperity for everybody, a healthy environment, and equality and solidarity among the peoples.

Moved by that appeal and inspired by the eminence you have thrust upon us, we undertake that we too will do what we can to contribute to the renewal of our world so that none should, in future, be described as the wretched of the earth.

Let it never be said by future generations that indifference, cynicism, or selfishness made us fail to live up to the ideals of humanism which the Nobel Peace Prize encapsulates.

Let the strivings of us all prove Martin Luther King Jr.

to have been correct, when he said that humanity can no longer be tragically bound to the starless midnight of racism and war.

Let the efforts of us all prove that he was not a mere dreamer when he spoke of the beauty of genuine brotherhood and peace being more precious than diamonds or silver or gold.

Let a new age dawn![11]

Desmond Tutu

Ordained an Anglican priest in 1961 Tutu was a bishop of Lesotho who became general-secretary of the South African Council of Churches (SACC) from 1978 until 1984. In 1986 he became the first black archbishop of Capetown, the highest position in the South African Church. Tutu was a prominent leader in the freedom struggle and a vocal opponent of apartheid. He used his position as head of the SACC to organize social and political opposition and was courageous and unrelenting in his criticism of the state's repressive racial laws and its whites-only government. Tutu opposed the policies of "constructive engagement" with apartheid that were advocated by the U.S. government in the 1980s and argued instead for more vigorous international sanctions against the South African government, in keeping with the stance of the ANC and the freedom movement. Better the pain of sanctions, he and his colleagues said, than the agony of apartheid. International sanctions and divestment campaigns against apartheid helped to isolate the South African regime and contributed to its downfall.

Tutu combined his opposition to apartheid with a plea for nonviolence and reconciliation. Like Mandela he did not condemn the decision of the ANC to adopt the methods of armed struggle, emphasizing the severe brutality of the regime that

---

[11] "Address by President Nelson Mandela upon Accepting the Nobel Peace Prize Award," December 10, 1993, https://www.nobelprize.org.

drove people to make that decision, but he consistently advocated and helped to organize peaceful resistance to the regime. The choice of nonviolent methods was not only a moral imperative, he argued, but a practical necessity that would enable the movement to attract greater domestic and international support and more effectively undermine the legitimacy of the regime.

In the excerpts below, drawn from the collection of his sermons and speeches published in *The Rainbow People of God*, Tutu discusses the linkage between peace and social justice, the Christian duty to serve as a peacemaker, and the need for sacrifice and discipline in the struggle for nonviolent social change.

No Peace without Justice

> We see before us a land bereft of much justice, and therefore without peace and security. Unrest is endemic and will remain an unchanging feature of the South African scene until apartheid, the root cause of it all, is finally dismantled. At this time the Army is being quartered on the civilian population. There is a civil war being waged. South Africans are on either side. When the ANC and the PAC were banned in 1960,[12] they declared that they had no option but to carry out the armed struggle. We in the SACC have said that we are opposed to all forms of violence—that of a repressive and unjust system and that of those who seek to overthrow that system. However, we have added that we understand those who say that they have had to adopt what is a last resort for them. Violence is not being introduced into the South African situation de novo from outside.... The South African situation is violent already and the primary violence is that of apartheid, the violence of forced population remov-

---

[12] Founded in 1912 the African National Congress (ANC) was the principal liberation group in the South African freedom struggle and remains the country's largest political party. The Pan Africanist Congress (PAC) was founded in 1959 as a separate faction based on an Africanist ideology.

als, of inferior education, of detention without trial, of the migratory labor system, etc. . . .

There is no peace in Southern Africa. There is no peace because there is no justice. There can be no real peace and security until there be first justice enjoyed by all the inhabitants of that beautiful land. The Bible knows nothing about peace without justice, for that would be crying, "Peace, peace, where there is no peace." God's shalom, peace, involves inevitably righteousness, justice, wholeness, fullness of life, participation in decision-making, goodness, laughter, joy, compassion, sharing, and reconciliation.[13]

Christians as Peacemakers

Now, we are supposed to be witnesses to the love of God. If you say to someone with your mouth, "I love you," and then, when the person is still smiling because you say that you love them, you knock them on the head, your words and your actions don't tally. Then people will say you are a hypocrite, someone who is playacting. And so also with our faith. Many people have said, "Oh, I don't go to church anymore. Have you seen how churchgoers behave? Have you seen how they quarrel? Have you seen how they backbite other people? Have you seen how jealous they are? . . . "

Those people are saying something that is true. We expect Christians to be people of a certain kind, not by what they say through their mouths but by the kind of people they are. We expect them to reflect the character of Jesus Christ. We expect Christians to be gentle, not always quarreling and scratching. We expect Christians to be humble as Jesus was humble, as he said in the Gospel. We expect Christians to be peace-loving and people who work for peace. We expect Christians to be loving. We expect Christians to be those who

---

[13] Desmond Tutu, "Apartheid's 'Final Solution'" (1984), in Tutu, *The Rainbow People of God: The Making of a Peaceful Revolution*, ed. John Allen (New York: Doubleday, 1994), 92.

try to create peace among those who are quarreling. We expect Christians to be people who are caring. We expect Christians to be people filled with love. We expect Christians to be people who forgive as Jesus forgave even those who were nailing him to the Cross. But we expect Christians also to be those who stand up for the truth, we expect Christians to be those who stand up for justice, we expect Christians to be those who stand on the side of the poor and the hungry and the homeless and the naked, and when that happens then Christians will be trustworthy, believable witnesses.[14] . . .

We come as those who are constrained by the Gospel of our Lord Jesus Christ to be peacemakers to those who are at daggers drawn. . . . We ought not to be ashamed that we are going to pray, that we have been praying. We have nothing else to give and we ought to be proud that we can put the world in touch with the greatest resource of all, God. We thank you, too, the people of God, who have responded at short notice. For God will ask us, "What did you do, what did you do when the situation got out of hand?" And you'll say, "Aaah, I didn't know what to do." And yet God told us that we are his coworkers. Doesn't St. Paul say an extraordinary thing about those who are believers—you are fellow workers with God! We are fellow workers with God to change people, to change the darkness, to change oppression, to change chaos into their opposites, their glorious opposites. So we are in touch with an invincible power.[15]

The Costs of Our Calling

You have no option but to be involved in the struggle and I call on you to be involved in the struggle for this new South Africa. I call on you to know that it is God's struggle. You say: But you'll get into trouble. Of course! Who ever saw powerful

---

[14] Tutu, "Perhaps Even to Die" (1987), in Tutu, *Rainbow People of God*, 131–32.

[15] Tutu, "You Give Yourself a Left Hook" (1987), in Tutu, *Rainbow People of God*, 134.

people give up their power without doing anything? The powerful will get angry. So what, what is new? Tell me something else. I invite you to come into this exhilarating enterprise, God's enterprise, to change this country, to transfigure this country, to make this country what it is going to become, a land where all, black, white, green, whatever, will be able to hold hands together because they are then living as those whom God has created in his image, as brothers and sisters, as members of one family.

You must know that there are going to be casualties.... Our children will die, people will be detained in all kinds of strange things, but let the violence come from the system. Let the violence come from the system. Our cause is too noble to be undermined by ignoble methods. I call on you young people especially. I know that you are frustrated many, many, many times. You try to be nonviolent and even a nonviolent procession provokes violence. But that is precisely to show you they [the government] have nothing else. They have no moral authority. They have power but they have no authority. They can beat you up with quirts[16] and people will still go back and then we come, carrying nothing, and we say to our people, "Hold it, get into your buses." And our people go and they get into the buses. We have no power but God gives us a moral authority....

Now, my brothers and sisters, my dear children, let us not allow the enemy to divide us. The enemy is doing everything to divide us. We must not allow the enemy to come between us! Let us not allow the enemy to fill us with hatred! We are hurt, yes, we are hurt. But we have come here to try to pour oil on your hurt. Know that your hurts are our hurts. You are not suffering alone. Your hurts are our hurts. White bishops, black bishops, weep. They weep when they hear of the things that happen to their children. Your pain is our pain. But we have come here to say, "Children of God, let us

---

[16] A short-handled riding whip used against antiapartheid demonstrators by South African security forces.

show that we are the children of God by not being filled with hatred. Let us not be filled with a desire to revenge." You know, they say in the Old Testament that there is a law that says, "An eye for an eye." Okay? ["Yes."] Now, Martin Luther King said something wonderful. He said, "Can you imagine? If we believed in that law of an eye for an eye, very soon all the people will be blind."[17]

Wangari Maathai (1940–2011)

Over the decades our understanding of peace and the meaning of nonviolence has expanded. King, Mandela, Tutu, and many others emphasized the social justice dimensions of peace, the need for greater economic and social equality and opportunity for all. In recent decades, ecological concerns have entered the conversation as scholars increasingly recognize the links between peace and environmental sustainability. Disputes over the control of resources are associated with a greater risk of armed conflict. Climate-induced conditions of severe drought may be among the factors contributing to wars in some ethnically fractionalized states.[18] Peace requires respect for the sanctity of life in all its dimensions and depends upon a nonviolent relationship among peoples and between humankind and the planet. In recognition of these links between peace and environmentalism the Nobel Peace Committee awarded its 2004 Prize to Wangari Maathai.

A scientist trained in biology at the University of Nairobi, Maathai was the first woman to head that university's Depart-

---

[17] Tutu, "The Nadir of Despair" (1990) in Tutu, *Rainbow People of God*, 214.

[18] The evidence linking climate conditions and war is uncertain and contested by some scientists, but a number of studies show at least some connections. See C. F. Schleussner, J. F. Donges, R. V. Donner, and H. J. Schellnhuber, "Armed-Conflict Risks Enhanced by Climate-Related Disasters in Ethnically Fractionalized Countries," *Proceedings of the National Academy of Sciences* (early edition 2016): DOI: 10.1073/pnas.1601611113.

ment of Veterinary Anatomy and was later Kenya's assistant minister for the environment. She served as the head of Kenya's National Council of Women, was a member of Kenya's parliament, and became presiding officer of the Economic, Cultural, and Social Council of the African Union. In 1977 she founded the Green Belt Movement, a broad-based grassroots initiative that has helped women's groups in Kenya and other African countries plant many millions of trees to conserve the environment and improve the quality of life. Maathai was a tireless advocate for democracy, development, human rights, social justice, and environmental sustainability. She received numerous awards in addition to the Nobel Peace Prize, including the Legion d'Honneur of the government of France and the Goldman Environmental Prize.

Below are excerpts from Maathai's acceptance speech for the Nobel Prize, in which she links peace to democracy, the environment, and human rights, followed by an address two years later in Gwangju, South Korea, on development, democracy, and peace.

> Although this [Nobel] prize comes to me, it acknowledges the work of countless individuals and groups across the globe. They work quietly and often without recognition to protect the environment, promote democracy, defend human rights, and ensure equality between women and men. By so doing, they plant seeds of peace. I know they, too, are proud today. To all who feel represented by this prize I say use it to advance your mission and meet the high expectations the world will place on us. . . .
>
> I know that African people everywhere are encouraged by this news. My fellow Africans, as we embrace this recognition, let us use it to intensify our commitment to our people, to reduce conflicts and poverty and thereby improve their quality of life. Let us embrace democratic governance, protect human rights, and protect our environment. I am confident that we shall rise to the occasion. I have always

believed that solutions to most of our problems must come from us.

In this year's prize, the Norwegian Nobel Committee has placed the critical issue of environment and its linkage to democracy and peace before the world. For their visionary action, I am profoundly grateful. Recognizing that sustainable development, democracy, and peace are indivisible is an idea whose time has come. Our work over the past 30 years has always appreciated and engaged these linkages. . . .

Throughout Africa, women are the primary caretakers, holding significant responsibility for tilling the land and feeding their families. As a result, they are often the first to become aware of environmental damage as resources become scarce and incapable of sustaining their families. . . .

Tree planting became a natural choice to address some of the initial basic needs identified by women. Also, tree planting is simple, attainable and guarantees quick, successful results within a reasonable amount of time. This sustains interest and commitment.

So, together, we have planted over 30 million trees that provide fuel, food, shelter, and income to support their children's education and household needs. The activity also creates employment and improves soils and watersheds. Through their involvement, women gain some degree of power over their lives, especially their social and economic position and relevance in the family. This work continues. . . .

In the process, the participants discover that they must be part of the solutions. They realize their hidden potential and are empowered to overcome inertia and take action. They come to recognize that they are the primary custodians and beneficiaries of the environment that sustains them. . . .

Through the Green Belt Movement, thousands of ordinary citizens were mobilized and empowered to take action and effect change. They learned to overcome fear and a sense of helplessness and moved to defend democratic rights. . . .

As we progressively understood the causes of environmental degradation, we saw the need for good governance. Indeed, the state of any county's environment is a reflection of the kind of governance in place, and without good governance there can be no peace. . . .

In the course of history, there comes a time when humanity is called to shift to a new level of consciousness, to reach a higher moral ground. A time when we have to shed our fear and give hope to each other.

That time is now.

The Norwegian Nobel Committee has challenged the world to broaden the understanding of peace: there can be no peace without equitable development; and there can be no development without sustainable management of the environment in a democratic and peaceful space. This shift is an idea whose time has come.[19]

Development, Democracy, and Peace

When the Norwegian Nobel Committee honored me with the Nobel Peace Prize in 2004 it intended to send a new and historic message to the world: to rethink peace and security. It wanted to challenge the world to discover the close linkage between good governance, sustainable management of resources, and peace. In managing our resources, we need to realize that they are limited and need to be managed more sustainably, responsibly, and accountably. . . .

Sustainable management of the resources is only possible if we practice good governance, which calls for respect for the rule of law, respect for human rights, a willingness to give space and a voice to the weak and the more vulnerable in our societies; that we respect the voice of the minority, even while accepting the decision of the majority, and respect diversity. Good governance seeks justice and equity

---

[19] Wangari Maathai, "Nobel Lecture," Oslo, Norway, December 10, 2004, http://www.nobelprize.org.

for all irrespective of race, religion, gender, and any other parameters, which man uses to discriminate and exclude. Good governance is indeed inclusive and seeks participatory democracy.

We call for the strengthening of institutions, such as the United Nations and its many organs to restrain strong nations so that they do not walk all over the weak ones. Security of nations at the global level is as important as security of individuals within the national boundaries. And for individuals, as well for the nations, if they are not secure, no one is secure. This is true whether the threat comes from nuclear power or an AK-47.

When we manage our resources sustainably and practice good governance we deliberately and consciously promote cultures of peace, which include the willingness to dialogue and make genuine efforts for healing and reconciliation, especially where there has been misunderstanding, loss of trust, and even conflict. Whenever we fail to nurture these three themes, conflict becomes inevitable.

I come from a continent that has known many conflicts for a long time. Many of them are glaringly due to bad governance, unwillingness to share resources more equitably, selfishness, and a failure to promote cultures of peace. Leaders fail to care enough for the ordinary citizens and preoccupy themselves with matters that concern them and let their people down. . . .

Indeed all over the world, this is often the root cause of conflicts. Inequities, both national and international, are largely responsible for poverty and all its manifestations. There is hardly any conflict in the world that is an exception. Below the thin layer of racial and ethnic chauvinism, religion, and politics, the real reason for many conflicts is the struggle for the access and control of the limited resources on our planet.

A good number of African leaders have recognized the need for good governance in Africa. This is because, despite all the resources in Africa, development continues to lag behind due to lack of peace and sustainable management of resources. Corruption and mismanagement of resources frustrate development and exacerbate poverty. At the African Union, leaders are encouraging each other to deliberately and consciously promote good governance and peace and give development a chance. Challenges are many and varied, but what is encouraging is the commitment demonstrated by leaders, now willing to shun conflict and violence through peaceful resolutions. More of them are willing to face the fact that no development will take place in a state of conflict and mismanagement of state affairs. . . .

One of the difficult issues we face in sustainable development is consumerism, especially in the rich industrialized countries. In this case technological advancement can assist with the campaign to reduce, reuse, and recycle resources (the 3Rs). . . .

In the area of energy, use of hybrid cars contributes to the reduction of the consumption of fossil fuels. Countries that generate much waste must assume responsibility and take action against threats like climate change. The Green Belt Movement is partnering with some organizations by planting trees in our region to offset some carbon and contribute towards the reduction of the greenhouse gases.

As we planted a tree today at the memorial grounds for the victims of the May 18 Democratic Uprising in 1980,[20] I was very aware of the importance of that symbolism. For trees are symbols of peace and hope. We know that the people of the Korean peninsula have hope. May Peace Prevail.[21]

---

[20] A reference to the massive protests against military rule in the southern Korean city of Gwangju that began in May 1980 and the violent repression of that movement that left more than 150 people dead. Gwangju is now the site of a national memorial and cemetery.

[21] Wangari Maathai, "Sustained Development, Democracy, and Peace in Africa," speech delivered in Gwangju, South Korea, June 16, 2006, http://www.greenbeltmovement.org.

7

The Struggle for Palestine and Israel

The decades-long struggle between Israelis and Palestinians is arguably one of the most bitterly fought and intractable conflicts in the world. On both sides of the political divide, protagonists have employed war and violence to achieve their goals. Israel maintains an oppressive occupation of the West Bank and in recent decades has accelerated the seizure of Palestinian land through illegal settlements. Israeli society is thoroughly militarized, with a large army and advanced weapons technology, while Palestinians are divided politically and have often employed terrorist and military means of struggle.

While the prospects for a political settlement at the governmental level are bleak, movements have emerged within both societies that employ nonviolent strategies for seeking reconciliation and building peace. Many Palestinians and Israelis have spoken out courageously against war, occupation, and terrorism. Groups on both sides of the border are working for human rights and an end to war and violence. The excerpts below capture a few of the Palestinian and Israeli voices advocating nonviolence as a more effective and sustainable strategy for achieving justice and peace between Israel and Palestine.

Jean Zaru

Born in 1940 to a Quaker family in Ramallah, Jean Zaru has been a pioneer for peace and women's equality in Palestine. She was a founding member and vice chair of Sabeel, an ecumenical Palestine liberation theology center in Jerusalem and served on the Central Committee of the World Council of Churches (WCC) and on the WCC Working Group in Interfaith Dialogue. She was also a member of the International Council of the World Conference for Religion and Peace and helped to establish the Friends International Center in Ramallah, which works to nurture a Quaker presence in Palestine and furthers peace and justice issues in the community.

The excerpts below are drawn from her book, *Occupied with Nonviolence*, a collection of her writings on the role of women and the challenges of justice and peace in Palestine.

> I am a Palestinian, a Palestinian woman, a Palestinian Christian woman, and I am also a Quaker and pacifist. Identity is always complex.
>
> As a Palestinian, I am one of about nine million Palestinians both inside and outside Palestine, struggling for justice and freedom for our homeland. . . .
>
> For forty years, I have been walking that edge where the spiritual meets the political. For me, the two have always been integrated. My spirituality is rooted in the human dignity and human rights of all people, and the sacredness of Mother Earth. I feel compelled to work for a world in which human freedom and dignity can flourish. Spirituality can bring life and vibrancy and imagination to my struggle, but of course I recognize that the mixture of religion and politics can also fuel the most extreme and violent acts and lead to systems of self-righteous repression. . . .
>
> Religion involves commitment and relationship, and relationship is action and engagement in the real issues of life. But there is no relationship without love, only waste, strife,

madness, and destruction. Love makes it necessary to find the way of truth, understanding, justice, and peace. My kind of religion is a very active, highly political, often controversial, and sometimes very dangerous form of engagement in active nonviolence for the transformation of our world. . . .

How do I teach a culture of nonviolent action? First, I raise critical and decisive consciousness—consciousness of the value of justice over against injustice, peace over against warfare, humane institutions over against dehumanizing institutions. I try to make it very clear that we are working against evil and not against people. Human well-being is our ultimate goal, and we should be ready to say what we think is the truth and be ready to pay the price.

The biggest obstacle to personal growth and to working for peace is feeling powerless or hopeless. The most important thing I could impart in my classes, then, was a sense of empowerment, a sense of competence to make decisions about how we want to live, and a sense of optimism about the future. While we do not know what the future holds, we do know that we hold the future in our hands. Affirmation is a future-oriented strategy. I affirm what is good and beautiful in our culture, our values, our food, our family relations, our hearts, and our embroidery. I use affirmation instead of negativity, even though there is so much that I reject. This gave my students more self-esteem and made it easier for them to see the good in others, including those with whom we are in conflict.

My students now know that to violate is not only to use force but to treat others who are sacred children of God as nothing. No matter how we are treated, we must not treat anyone else as nothing or less worthy than ourselves. It is not easy for us to learn to think of the sacredness of life and human dignity when our dignity and worth is rarely recognized. But through the hurt, the pain, and the wounds we must try to realize our power and become real agents of change. Real change is not simply transferring power from one group to the other, but changing the relationship between us. It might be a dream but it is my human right to dream and to work toward the reality of this dream.[1] . . .

The endless battering of Palestinians on a daily basis virtually imprisons us in our houses half of the time and the rest of the time within fragmented communities separated from each other by walls, ditches, and checkpoints, making the means of daily life, jobs, education, hospitals, all but inaccessible. This is done as a matter of policy, making life so intolerable that as many of us as possible will leave the country.

But despite the current Israeli government's intention, no degree of violence can succeed in subjugating the will of a people or destroying their spirit when they are struggling for their freedom, dignity, and right to sovereignty on their own land. All Israeli attempts at intensifying the brutality of the occupation against the Palestinians have only led to the escalation of the conflict and increased our determination to gain our liberty. Conflicts can only be resolved politically and legally, on the basis of parity of rights and the global rule of law. I do hope that the Israeli public and the international community will realize the extreme danger of their policies before it is too late and more innocent blood is shed. And I hope the U.S. government will realize that its blind support and military aid to Israel is not necessarily to the long-term advantage of Israel or even in the best interest of the United States.

Our common future as Israelis and Palestinians makes it inevitable for us to try to heal the traumas of the past, right the wrongs of today, and build a better future for all. We should envision a future in which we apply a universal morality, emanating from our common God, measured by a simple standard of behavior, and valid for all people in all lands. These are the universal standards expressed in the

---

[1] Jean Zaru, *Occupied with Nonviolence: A Palestinian Woman Speaks* (Minneapolis: Fortress Press, 2008), 1–10.

Universal Declaration of Human Rights, and we must renew our common commitment to live up to them.[2] . . .

The most basic form of deception in our context is the fabrication of a fake symmetry between occupier and occupied, between oppressor and victim, as if the claims and the power were equal on both sides. The violence of the powerful Israeli occupation army that uses live ammunition, tanks, and helicopter gunships is equated with the violence of Palestinian civilians protesting their victimization and the continued loss of rights, land, and lives. Israel usually presents its military actions and policies of repression to the world as merely a justified reaction to Palestinian violence. In doing so, it frames and controls the discourse on "violence," labeling it as Palestinian. It also ensures that the very word *occupation* disappears from the dominant discourse. But the Israeli occupation is not simply a reaction to "terrorism" or a means of self-defense. It is an expression of a policy of de facto annexation that began immediately after 1967. Occupation equals violence! . . .

Of course, it is also important to recognize that the victims of oppression are not blameless. Too often, they themselves become the oppressors of others. I admit that some Palestinians, in their anger and despair, have resorted to violence. I, personally, do not think that violence can lead us anywhere, neither morally nor strategically. Luckily, this has become the position not only of faith-based organizations, but many Palestinians have adopted it as well. Violence feeds upon itself. While the means of violence are not symmetrical, its results are. Violence creates a symmetry of emotion, pain, fear, mistrust. Violence creates mutual suspicion and mutual accusation. . . .

For me, nonviolence is a religious conviction and a way of life. But I believe it is also highly practical. There is no other effective way to change the dynamics of attack and counterattack, even for someone who does not hold this

---

[2] Ibid., 37–38.

conviction. Look at it: violence has produced counter violence. Violence has become a cycle of despair on both sides. And, practically speaking, violence is not strategically useful, because we and our opponents have asymmetrical access to power. In the West Bank and the Gaza Strip we do not have an army. Israel is a nuclear power and one of the four largest producers of arms in the world. What is the alternative? To submit? To become bitter? To collaborate? To do nothing about the forces that control our lives? Rather than resorting to desperate forms of violence, I am convinced that active nonviolence is still the only path to resist the occupation and the structures of domination. . . .

The alternative is to resist. Resistance challenges the system's values and categories. Resistance speaks its own truth to power, and shifts the ground of struggle to its own terrain. Resistance is often thought of as negative. However, resistance is the refusal to be neglected and disregarded. Today, Palestinians find themselves embedded in structures that neglect and discard their humanity and human rights, and only acts of resistance can transform the structures. And I, along with many others, have opted for the path of active nonviolent resistance. To resist is to be human, and yet nonviolent resistance is not easy. It requires constant, hard work. Indeed, it is not easy to sustain the path of nonviolent resistance for years and years, over many issues. None of us can resist all the time, in every area of life. We must choose our battles, meaning we must choose the priorities of struggle.[3]

Peace is not only the absence of war, but it is the absence of dire poverty and hunger. Peace is freedom from sickness and disease. It is employment and health. Peace is based on a deep sense of human equality and basic justice. Peace is when we have no fear to assemble, to worship, to work, to speak and publish the truth, even to the powerful. Peace is hope for our future and the future of all God's children and

---

[3] Ibid., 59–60, 69–71.

all God's world. Peace is *salaam*, well-being for all, equality and respect for human rights. Peace is when everybody feels at home and is accepted, without barriers based on age, class, sex, race, religion, or nationality. Peace is that fragile harmony that carries with it the experience of struggle, the endurance of suffering, and the strength of love.[4]

Mubarak Awad

Mubarak Awad was born in 1943 and grew up in a pacifist family in Jerusalem. His father was killed in the 1948 Arab-Israeli War. Awad moved to the United States in the 1960s and studied at Bluffton University in Ohio. He spent years as a therapist and counselor of at-risk teenagers before moving to the West Bank in 1983 to establish the Palestinian Centre for the Study of Nonviolence. Awad was greatly influenced by the actions and writings of Gandhi, Martin Luther King Jr., and Gene Sharp, translating their works into Arabic. He worked with young Palestinians who had experienced Israeli violence and trained them in nonviolent resistance. Awad was actively involved in the first Intifada in the 1980s. Named for the Arabic word for "shaking off," the first Intifada was an unarmed, mostly nonviolent struggle in which many thousands of Palestinians engaged in large-scale civil disobedience actions, strikes, pickets, boycotts, and sit-ins to resist Israeli occupation. During that struggle Awad was detained, tortured, and deported by Israel for circulating leaflets encouraging civil disobedience.

In 1984 Awad wrote the important article "Nonviolent Resistance: A Strategy for the Occupied Territories," which served as a blueprint for many of the actions that took place during the Intifada. Excerpts of that article are presented below:

> For the Palestinians who are living in the West Bank and Gaza during this period, the most effective strategy is one

[4] Ibid., 82–83.

of nonviolence.... Such a strategy focuses and increases any beneficial public international attention to our cause by revealing the racist and expansionist features of the Zionist movement and denying it the justifications built on its purported "security." It removes the irrational fear of "Arab violence," which presently cements Israeli society together. By removing this fear, it contributes to the disintegration of hostile Israeli society and helps to isolate Israel politically and morally.

This approach is based on certain assumptions:

First, nonviolent struggle is a total and serious struggle, nothing short of a real war. There is no assurance that the enemy will be nonviolent. On the contrary, there are great sacrifices we should expect in the nonviolent struggle. Martyrs and wounded will fall, and Palestinians will suffer personal losses in terms of their interests, jobs, and possessions. Nonviolent struggle is a real war, not an easy alternative.

Second, nonviolent struggle is not negative or passive. It is an active, affirmative operation, a form of mobile warfare. It will require the enlistment of all resources and capabilities. It requires special training and a high degree of organization and discipline. Secrecy must be maintained in planning, organizing, and coordinating the different operations and campaigns. Most nonviolent activities will be illegal according to the laws and military orders presently imposed on the population.

The Israeli soldier is a human being, not a beast devoid of conscience and feeling. He has an understanding of right and wrong to which it is possible to appeal. Similarly, he can be demoralized. He constantly needs a reasonable justification for his activities. On the other hand, he has the potential for evil and oppression like any other person. He is often an intolerant racist and shares most of his government's evil assumptions.

At another level, the Israeli government is sensitive to public opinion, both local and international. It constantly needs international support and aid, and it has an image it wishes to project. At the same time, this sensitivity is limited: the Israeli government is willing to carry out its plans and maintain its oppression regardless of the views of the international community. Nonetheless, Israel does not possess the internal resources which will enable it to bear international isolation for a long time. . . .

Suffering and pain can be useful in forging unity among the Palestinians to resist oppression. They also achieve for the Palestinians moral superiority over the occupiers and set in motion historical factors which ensure the survival of the Palestinian people and their eventual victory. The Palestinian revolution was built on the blood of the martyrs and the suffering of our people. When a nonviolent person accepts suffering voluntarily in defense of his principles instead of having this suffering imposed upon him involuntarily, he or she increases and accentuates these benefits.

Of course, there is no more assurance that a nonviolent struggle will be victorious than there is an assurance that armed struggle will achieve its end. Victory and success in a nonviolent struggle cannot be measured by easily observable, external, objective criteria. Nonviolent struggle achieves its goals and effect upon the hearts and minds of the Israeli soldiers, for example. It can manifest itself in a higher rate of Israeli emigration, by a loss of fighting spirit for the Israeli soldier, by their complaints and protest against the actions of the Israeli government. Similarly, the increasing moral and political isolation of Israel abroad is difficult to measure, but it can be a real and important phenomenon with definite consequences.[5]

---

[5] Mubarak Awad, "Nonviolent Resistance: A Strategy for the Occupied Territories," *Journal of Palestinian Studies* 13, no. 4 (Summer 1984): 22–36.

In the following interview with Awad from 2015, *In These Times* reporter Waleed Shahid probes the lessons to be learned from the first Intifada.[6] As Shahid notes, the Intifada did not end the Israeli occupation, but it helped to break the decades-long stalemate between Israeli and Palestinian negotiators. It gave legitimacy and urgency to the Palestinian freedom cause and convinced a majority of Israelis for the first time that a diplomatic rather than a military solution to the conflict was necessary. It also gave life to a movement of resistance that emerged within the Israeli military during the 1982 invasion and subsequent occupation of Lebanon. In 1988, more than five hundred Israeli military reservists signed a petition refusing to serve in the Palestinian territories, claiming that the Israeli Defense Force's (IDF) presence in the Palestinian territories was immoral and undermined Israel's own security.

Excerpts from the interview follow.

WS: *In the 1980s, you boldly declared to Palestinians, "We are under occupation because we choose to be under occupation." What does that statement mean?*

MA: . . . I wanted to challenge Palestinians to take responsibility for themselves and their situation. Resisting evil with the gun is one method, but we can also resist evil with nonviolent means. But that means discipline, strategy, training, and knowing your opponent. I wanted Palestinians to push ourselves to create space for elements within our opponent's side to defect to our side. If we cannot convince large amounts of Israelis to agree with us, we will never win.

This is a civil rights struggle. This isn't about expelling the Israeli and the Jewish people. In some way or another, both sides must become friends and see themselves in each other. The goal and objective is simple: end the occupation. We aren't talking about the status of

---

[6] Waleed Shahid, "Lessons in Nonviolent Palestinian Resistance from the First Intifada: An Interview with Mubarak Awad," *In These Times*, October 26, 2015, http://inthesetimes.com.

Jerusalem or refugees or administrative issues. We are just talking about our lives. Nothing else happens until the occupation disappears. And it is up to us to force it to disappear because no one else will. . . .

It's becoming more common for activists to refrain from explicitly condemning violent acts of resistance by Palestinians, but instead contextualize those acts as the product of the structural violence as a result of Israel's occupation. Where do you land on that?

We know what the Israeli government is doing: They wantonly arrest and hurt and even kill Palestinians. But we as Palestinians have to be better than them. Some people don't like when I say that, but it is true and it is not going to change anytime soon. Throwing stones, wielding knives, launching rockets—this is not the right way. It scares our own people and it scares the Israelis even more. It shouldn't be our intention or strategy to make them more afraid and feeling more insecure as individuals. Many Israelis are afraid to leave their homes as well. What kind of strategy would make the Israelis come to us and say, "We need your help to fix this disaster once and for all? As Israelis we are tired of living like this, doing this to you, doing this to ourselves." That means we have to raise the bar for what real reconciliation, acceptance, and coexistence means. We can find that in our three religions if we look for it with honesty.

It sounds like you are saying the main people Palestinians have to convince are the Israeli public?

If you are able to convince many Israelis that it is in their self-interest to have peace with their Palestinian neighbors, then the Israelis would vote for a prime minister who wants real peace. Right now, the Israelis don't think it is in their self-interest, in their values as human beings. That is up to us as Palestinians to decide whether we actually want to use that kind of strategy or not. Nonviolence takes up the question of the occupation and sends it back to the opponent, telling the Israelis that it is now *their* choice to decide. That is exactly what King did in Birmingham and Selma.

Look, I don't have a reason to like Israelis. They killed my father. They destroyed my house. They're destroying my culture. They destroyed my life. They're continuing to destroy the lives of my family back home, coming in the middle of the night and arresting Palestinians from their homes. They block our roads. They take our land. They aren't showing an interest in wanting peace with us.

But we still have to take the strategies of nonviolence and show the way forward. It is very tough and very hard. People on both sides want to take the easy way out and not grapple with fundamental issues. But we have examples of who were able to do the impossible: Gandhi, Martin Luther King, Nelson Mandela, even Northern Ireland. The only conflict that is not resolved is ours. And we must all accept the responsibility for that. It can only truly be resolved when we decide to condemn bloodshed from all sides.

You distinguish between principled nonviolence and strategic nonviolence. Why is that distinction important?

Principled nonviolence is what we learn in religion as Jews, Christians, Muslims, and all people of faith. We all worship a God and that God tells us to make good with each other. We are created by God. And inside every person there exists a piece of God that we should not harm. We don't have the right to harm or kill any person. And if we don't have the right to kill anyone, we have to learn a different kind of discipline.

Strategic nonviolence is about political considerations. You don't have to believe in principled nonviolence to believe in strategic nonviolence. It's not about personal morals and interactions. It's about using nonviolence militantly, like a kind of unarmed warfare. You have to deeply understand power. We have to have thousands of people involved, and active participation—especially from women and older people—severely declines when the resistance is seen as violent.

And for that you really have to understand where the Israelis are coming from. They have the guns and the laws. We don't have those things. We must pick a different method to create the kind of situation that would make them demand an end to the occupation from their own government.

But there is so much anger within both the Palestinian and the Israeli people. How can we understand the Israelis, so that we can trust them and they can trust us as human beings? That is a huge challenge. Some people are not interested in that question. But it is the only way to solve this thing for the long term.

What are the important lessons to draw from the First Intifada?

When thousands of people get together in the street for strategic action, they can achieve something. We were able to get the Israelis and Americans to talk to the PLO for the first time. The PLO didn't make that happen—the people did that. We brought the occupation into television screens all across the globe, and most importantly, we brought our humanity into Israeli living rooms. The second thing we achieved was real negotiations for the first time with the Israelis. We put out the idea that life would be better for both peoples, if our representatives would simply talk to each other.

It didn't turn out the way we thought it might. The Israeli government doesn't want peace. It still doesn't. We were just dreamers, dreaming of peace, trying to get both sides to understand that peace was achievable for everyone. But I don't think the Israeli government wants a two-state solution. They want to keep the status quo going. They think time is on their side. . . .

I still think the Palestinians have to really commit themselves to nonviolence. They can't accept both violence and nonviolence. We really have to come to terms with the idea that we cannot defeat the Israelis with violence. They will always win. I was beaten many times for my people. I am very sad and disappointed. But I still believe that nonviolence is the only way. But it requires real strategy, leadership, training, and discipline.

Youth Against Settlements

Youth Against Settlements (YAS) is a nonviolent direct action group that seeks through nonviolent popular struggle and civil resistance to end the building of illegal Israeli settlements.[7] YAS is based in Hebron, one of the areas hardest hit by the Israeli occupation, where about 800 Israeli fundamentalists guarded by 650 Israeli soldiers have forcibly established a settlement in the heart of a city of some 200,000 Palestinians. In order to protect illegal settlers, the Israeli state has imposed on the Palestinian residents a regime of forced evictions, curfews, market and street closures, military checkpoints, and subjugation to military law. Palestinians face frequent random searches, detentions without charge, and rampant settler violence. Thousands of Palestinian civilians have fled their homes in Hebron's city center, turning the area into a virtual ghost town.

YAS confronts this oppression by empowering and educating Palestinians, especially young people, and urging them to remain in the city, stand firm, and mount nonviolent resistance and resilience campaigns. The coordinator and cofounder of the group is Issa Amro, an activist who has been declared human rights defender of the year in Palestine by the Office of the UN High Commissioner for Human Rights and was recognized as a human rights defender by the European Union. He has been described as "among the most successful community organizers to have come of age" in the crucible of occupied Hebron.[8] Amro has been beaten, shot in the legs three times, and arrested frequently for

---

[7] Youth Against Settlements, Hebron, Palestine, February 2017, http://hyas.ps/about-us/.

[8] Michael Chabon and Ayelet Waldman, "Who's Afraid of Nonviolence?," *New York Times*, January 27, 2017, https://www.nytimes.com.

resisting Israeli occupation, but he refuses to yield. He remains firmly committed to the nonviolent method as "the best strategy for community resistance" and an effective approach that provides "a role for every Palestinian. . . . We can all do something." He argues that nonviolent resistance is necessary for fighting a professional army like the Israeli Defense Force and is "the only realistic way [for] neutralizing their power."[9]

Following is the official statement and philosophy of Youth Against Settlements.

Vision
A 100 percent nonviolent, mass Palestinian uprising of civil disobedience that pressures the Israeli government to dismantle the settlements and end the Occupation.

Strategies
- Establishing direct contact and continuous follow-up with Palestinians in threatened regions.
- Raise awareness through newsletters, advertisements, broadcasting, media, workshops, and conferences, and more.
- Collecting information about settlement activities and organizing, archiving, and distributing it.
- Pursuing legal avenues, such as filing complaints and bringing court cases to Israeli and international courts.
- Building an active network of supportive local, Israeli, and international organizations.
- Nonviolent direct actions and civil disobedience like demonstrations, protests, and defying racist laws of the occupation.
- Recruiting all sectors of the Palestinian community to resist and stand against colonial activities on their lands.
- Spreading the importance of economic and noneconomic boycott of settlements, such as labor in settlements, trade with settlers, and buying settlement products.

---

[9] Issa Amro, "Palestine Field Post: 'I Am Not Your Normal Human Rights Campaigner.'" *The Guardian*, March 10, 2015, https://www.theguardian.com.

Goals
- Study Israel's strategy of colonization, development, and expansion of settlements.
- Raise awareness level in the local and global community about Israeli methods of land confiscation and theft from Palestinian landowners.
- Resist all the stages of Israeli colonization, from settlement planning to construction and expansion.
- Expose Israel's settler colonial plans and strategies.
- Support the presence of the Palestinians on lands vulnerable to confiscation by Israel.
- Build connections between local Palestinians and Palestinian associations and governmental and nongovernmental organizations that work to study and resist Israeli settlement-related activities.

Guiding Principle
- Believing in and committing to our goals and means of struggle.
- Nonviolent direct action, media attention, and advocacy work to resist the occupation.
- Voluntary work to achieve our goals.
- No cooperation with settlers or other parts of the occupation; no participating in any actions or activities that normalize or support settler colonialism.
- Rejection of claiming any of YAS activities for a partisan or individual goal.
- Rejection of any kind of cooperation with fundamentalistic partisan or individuals.
- Respect for the beliefs, traditions, and general values of Palestinian society.
- Recognize and respect women as equal to men in all sectors of society and in all our work with resisting the occupation.
- Respect every person's individual religious beliefs.

Nowhere today is the challenge of advocating and organizing for peace more difficult than in Israel, a militarized country with a long history of war, terrorism, and occupation of Arab lands.[10] The military presence within Israel is pervasive, with troops on duty in public places throughout the country, carrying Uzis in train stations and malls, guarding dozens of checkpoints and border crossings. Looming over all is the grim Separation Wall, which seals off parts of the West Bank and East Jerusalem, separating Palestinians from their families and their land. Within Israel, political discourse has shifted sharply to the right. In this difficult context Israelis who speak out for peace often face criticism and are likely to be considered naïve or even disloyal to the state.

It wasn't always like this. A vibrant peace movement once flourished in Israel, embodied in the organization Peace Now, which mobilized substantial public opposition to war and occupation and encouraged diplomatic dialogue with the Palestinians. Peace Now began in 1978 after 348 officers and enlisted reservists of the Israeli Defense Force (IDF) wrote to then–Israeli prime minister Menachem Begin supporting negotiations with Egypt and more peaceful relations with neighboring Arab countries. Their letter stated,

> We write with a sense of deep alarm. We have doubts about the policy of a government which prefers settlements beyond the Green Line to terminating the historic conflict,[11] and establishing normal relations with the countries in our region.

---

[10] Israel ranks at the top of the Global Militarization Index produced annually by the Bonn International Center for Conversion. The index is based on a comparison of military expenditures with gross domestic product and health spending, the contrast between the total number of military personnel and the overall population and number of physicians, and the ratio of available heavy weapons to total population. See the 2018 ratings at https://www.bicc.de.

[11] The Green Line refers to the pre-1967 demarcation line between Israel and neighboring Arab states, negotiated in the 1949 armistice agreement and officially referenced in UN resolutions.

> The government policy, perpetuating its rule over . . . Arabs, could harm the Jewish-democratic character of the state, and make it difficult for us to identify with its task. Mindful of Israel's security needs and the difficulties on the path to peace, we nevertheless consider that real security can be achieved only when we achieve peace.[12]

Peace Now organized widespread opposition to Israel's invasion of Lebanon in 1982. A Peace Now rally that November attracted four hundred thousand people, approximately 10 percent of Israel's population at the time, the largest political demonstration in the country's history. Peace Now supported the 1993 Oslo Peace Process and the 2005 military disengagement from Gaza. Its Settlement Watch project sought to oppose continued settler encroachments into Palestinian territory.

The hopes for peace of earlier years were shattered, however. The Israeli government reneged on its commitments in the Oslo accord,[13] and Palestinian frustrations at the denial of self-rule led to the violent Second Intifada, beginning in 2000, which left more than four thousand dead, mostly Palestinians, but also more than four hundred civilians within Israel.[14] The result was a hardening of attitudes within Israel and the building of the wall. Political support for peace faded.

Courageous advocates for nonviolent solutions have continued to speak out, however. The selections here include a few examples. Psychologist and peace scholar Julia Chaitin discusses the realities of living in a war zone and the challenges of

---

[12] "The Officer's Letter," March 1978, Peace Now archive, http://archive.peacenow.org.

[13] See the 2013 analysis by Israeli British scholar Avi Shlaim, who originally supported the Oslo agreement: "It's Now Clear: The Oslo Peace Accords Were Wrecked by Netanyahu's Bad Faith," *The Guardian*, September 12, 2013, https://www.theguardian.com.

[14] BBC, "Intifada Toll," based on figures provided by the Israeli Human Rights organization B'tselem, February 8, 2005, http://news.bbc.co.uk.

seeking to address the conflict. This is followed by perspectives from former Israeli ambassador Ilan Baruch, a career diplomat who publicly resigned in 2011 over his disagreement with official policy toward Palestine. Also included are statements by soldiers of the movement Yesh Gvul (There is a limit), which emerged at the time of the Lebanon war and was active during the First and Second Palestinian Intifadas.

Julia Chaitin

The first selection is an essay published in the *Washington Post* at the end of December 2008, in the midst of the first Israel-Gaza war. Chaitin describes the experience of living amid rocket attacks in the Negev region where she lives, adjacent to Gaza, and the necessity of speaking for peace.

> In the winter, the Negev becomes quite beautiful. Though it rains very little here, the rain we get turns everything green, and there is a cleanness in the air that we don't have during the dry summer months. But since Saturday, when a major Israeli offensive began in the Gaza Strip, less than 20 kilometers from my home and less than two kilometers from the college where I teach, all we have had is darkness, despair, and fear.
>
> This war is wrong. It is wrong because it cannot achieve its manifest goals—long-term "normal" life for the residents of the Negev region. The war is morally wrong because most of the victims are Palestinian and Israeli civilians whose only "crime" is that they live in Negev or Gaza. This war is wrong because it is not heading toward a viable solution of the conflict but is instead creating more hatred and greater determination on the part of both peoples to harm one another. It is wrong because it is leading to stronger feelings that we have nothing to lose by striking further, with greater force. This war is wrong because, even before the last smoke rises

from the rubble and the last ambulance carries the dead and wounded to hospitals, our leaders will find themselves signing a new agreement for a cease-fire.

And so this is an unnecessary, cruel, and cynical war—a war that could have been avoided if our leaders had shown courage during the months of the cease-fire to truly work toward creating better lives for people whose only crime is that they live in the south.

Since the Israeli air force began bombing Gaza, it has been almost impossible to speak openly against the war. It is difficult to find public forums that welcome a call for a new cease-fire and for alternative solutions to the conflict—ones that do not rely on military strength or a siege of Gaza. When people are in the midst of war, they are not open to voices of peace; they speak (and scream) out of fear and demand retribution for the harms they have suffered. When people are in the midst of war, they forget that they can harness higher cognitive abilities, their reason and logic. Instead, they are driven by the hot structures of their brains, which lead them to respond with fear and anger in ways that are objective threats to our healthy survival. When people are in the midst of war, voices calling for restraint, dialogue, and negotiations fall on deaf ears, if their expression is allowed at all.

I live in the Negev and teach at the Sapir Academic College—the school located next to Sderot—in the heart of what is called "Qassam-land," after the rockets that fall on us. I know the fast beating of your heart and the awful pit in your stomach that comes when a *tzeve adom*—red alert—is sounded, heralding a rocket attack. I know what it is like to comfort students and colleagues when the rockets strike very, very close—and to wish that someone was there to comfort you as well. I know what it is like to be afraid to get into the car and drive to work because you are not sure you will make it from the parking lot to your classroom alive.

But I know the answer to our conflict will not come with this war. We will know peace only when we accept the fact that the Palestinians in the Gaza Strip have every right to lives of dignity. We will know peace only when we recognize that we must negotiate with Hamas, our enemy, even if we are devastated that the Palestinians did not elect a more moderate party to lead them. We will know peace only when our leaders stop considering our lives cheap and expendable, and help us create a beautiful, green Negev, free of fear and despair.[15]

In the excerpt below, drawn from an academic article in *Peace and Conflict: The Journal of Peace Psychology*, Chaitin explores the cognitive and behavioral impacts of war and the restorative potential of pursuing peace. She also speaks of her local group, Other Voice, which has tried to establish dialogue between the opposing sides.

Conflict is a part of all of our lives; it infuses our deep (inter) personal experiences, often across borders and hemispheres, impacting people around the world. Given that conflict is not only inherent to human life, but often also serves as a trigger for dramatic sociopolitical change, it is essential that we learn how to live with conflict in as healthy a way as possible. This is especially so given that, as individuals, we are usually at a loss for resolving conflicts, certainly the ones that occur on macro and global levels.

Such a perspective . . . leads me to the understanding that it is beneficial, on personal and social levels, to openly and honestly face the conflicts that are hazardous to our psychological and physical health. This is for two main reasons: (a) I see such actions as responsible and moral responses to the sociopolitical world in which we live, the world we helped cocreate with others, even if we were not personally responsible for bringing about or exacerbating the conflict; and (b) I believe that each one of us has the ability to make a dif-

---

[15] Julia Chaitin, "Darkness in Qassam-Land," *Washington Post*, December 31, 2008, http://www.washingtonpost.com.

ference in our world, even when our actions appear to be, at best, miniscule, and at worst, futile attempts to overcome harmful forces that drive people apart. . . .

Israelis who are willing to reflect on the perceptions they hold and on their society's collective narratives concerning the conflict often feel isolated within their communities. They feel that they no longer really fit into their society. It can be difficult for them to openly express new perspectives with close friends or family, because this often leads to conflicts with significant others. Unfortunately, sometimes circumstances become tougher when people who undertake peace work are labeled "traitors" by those members in their communities who see such perspectives and actions as a betrayal of their people and a threat to their very existence. Therefore, it is not difficult to understand why people try to insulate themselves from dealing with the conflict, but by doing so, in effect, help keep the separation, hatred, and violence alive.

Entering into true—that is, honest and open— dialogue with the "other" and making a commitment to jointly working on social actions often challenge everything we "know" to be true about ourselves, about our "side," about the conflict, about the enemy. However, these endeavors, which leave us confused and unsettled, open up doorways to new ways of thinking, feeling, and approaching one's place in this conflictual world, and one's understanding of what one can do to help his or her community move from cycles of conflict to paths of peace and reconciliation with its enemies. If we keep at this work, or at least, do not stray from the path for long periods of time, it can also bring deep meaning and purpose to life. . . .

Other Voice has grown and is now comprised of Israeli citizens from Sderot and *kibbutzim* and *moshavim* [collective agricultural communities] near or on the border with Gaza and Palestinians in the Gaza Strip who believe in peace and coexistence. Other Voice has tried very hard not to become "another leftist group," which tends to alienate many Jewish Israelis who have become cynical concerning prospects of peace, but rather has focused on a platform for bringing together men and women, older and younger, religious and secular, politically right, left, and center, and city and rural Israelis who believe that the Palestinians living in Gaza are ordinary people—not monsters, not terrorists who wish to "throw the Jews into the sea." The uniqueness of the group is that its members are people who live in the very region that is under threat. All of us have been exposed to the rockets; all of us have had very close calls and know people who have been harmed by the rockets. We are all too aware of how frightening this reality is. Yet, in spite of this, or perhaps because of this, the members of Other Voice understand the need to find a nonviolent solution to the conflict, and to work for bettering relations with "ordinary" people in Gaza, even as our leaders refuse to take a different approach. . . .

Although we are still unable to realize many of our wishes—such as joint community actions that can empower ordinary citizens—because our two societies remain at war—our ongoing contact and concern for one another has deepened the bonds between a number of Israelis and Palestinians on opposite sides of the border. In an almost paradoxical manner, the Israelis in the Sderot region and the Palestinians in Gaza understand one another better than Israelis from other parts of the country and Palestinians in the West Bank. Because of the uniqueness of our area, and the ongoing trauma that affects both peoples, we have found that our connections to one another deepen, even though this specific political conflict is far from over. . . .

Over the years of living in Israel and working on these topics, I have come to realize that it is impossible for Jewish Israelis to hide from a confrontation with the significance of the Holocaust, or from the impacts of the Israeli-Palestinian/Jewish-Arab conflicts on their present-day lives. The traumatic past of the Holocaust, and the traumatic past and present of the Middle East conflict, pervades many moments of my own life, the lives of my loved ones, and the lives of people in my community and society. Attempts to insulate ourselves from these traumas and conflicts, or to approach them as problems to be solved by "powerful" political and military leaders, only multiplies the number of people who end up contributing to the hate and conflicts by passively leaving the problems to be handled by others. I have come to see that such inaction is actually action—one with disastrous results. In the case of the Israeli-Palestinian conflict, it makes life more dangerous, because it justifies the status quo of occupation and war, and it makes life more frightening as it colors our present with despair and makes our future appear hopeless.

I believe that, as a Jewish Israeli who lives in a region that is torn apart by cycles of violence, and as a member of a nation that continues to oppress another people, I do not have the privilege to wait for others to solve the conflict. Even as I understand that neither I, nor my fellow citizens, have the power to bring about a formal end to the hostilities, I do believe that by working to identify and understand the psychosocial mechanisms and factors that keep our conflict going, by using these understandings to address our conflict in an honest dialogical manner, and by not giving up on this work, even when many around me continue to tell me that I am naïve or wrong, together with others, I can help cocreate the small safe spaces of peace and dignity that we all deserve.[16]

Ilan Baruch

Ilan Baruch is the former Israeli ambassador to South Africa. He draws on that experience in a July 2013 article in *Haaretz*

---

[16] Julia Chaitin, "Studying and Living Conflict: Working for Peace," *Peace and Conflict: Journal of Peace Psychology* 20, no. 2 (2014): 174–79.

titled "What Netanyahu Should Learn from the Fall of Apartheid," excerpted here.

> The South African example of a negotiated settlement of equals is a possibility that is still just within our grasp, but first, Prime Minister Netanyahu must accept that the occupation has no future.
>
> Prime Minister Benjamin Netanyahu has declared his at least rhetorical willingness to meet with Palestinian Authority President Mahmoud Abbas without preconditions, even if he must do so in a tent on the way from Jerusalem to Ramallah. Netanyahu even committed to confining himself in the tent until peace is concluded. . . .
>
> The most critical juncture in the dismantling of apartheid came when South Africa's white government internalized that apartheid had no future. Pretoria itself initiated secret contacts with the ANC leadership. Their messengers, meeting with the leadership of the struggle against apartheid, did not try to save apartheid. They came with a vision to bring apartheid to an end in a manner that would ensure the safety and wellbeing of the white population in South Africa, the people on whose behalf the regime had existed for 46 years.
>
> This, then, is the first imperative which paves the way to the negotiations tent: The recognition that the occupation, like apartheid, is a political, diplomatic, and national security experience without a future.
>
> The settlement enterprise that is intended to perpetuate the occupation is both immoral and impractical. There is no chance that Israel will perpetuate its control over the Palestinian people in its current format without also risking its own security. Israel does not and will not have the physical, human, and defense resources to rule 2.5 million people in the West Bank and East Jerusalem against their will, and to hold under siege another one and a half million people in the Gaza Strip. There is no future to national self-determi-

nation built upon the negation of another people's national self-determination, upon the regular humiliation of that people and the plundering of their land, water, and resources. Under South Africa's apartheid government, the rights and dignity of blacks were also negated by law, the law of the whites alone, and backed by the force of the whites' security and law enforcement forces acting solely on their behalf.

Thus Prime Minister Benjamin Netanyahu has a historic obligation to lead, in the image of de Klerk. He must send envoys to relay a message wonderful in its simplicity: We seek to bring the occupation to an end on the basis of the 1967 borders, with modifications. Let's conduct negotiations regarding the conditions and timetables that will enable the end of the occupation without harming the safety and well-being of Israeli citizens on both sides of the Green Line.

The second imperative that can be learned from South Africa's example is that both sides must build a model for working together that will shore up their ability to maintain broad public support for a political process that will no doubt be full of painful concessions for both sides. Netanyahu's people must learn in detail the constraints faced by Abbas, not with the tools of the intelligence services, but with diplomatic tools—and this requires listening and trust building. Both sides must sit in the tent as equals, not as superiors and inferiors. As an opening act to build this trust, Netanyahu could think in terms of the freeing of Palestinian security prisoners in Israel, just as Mandela's own release from prison set the tone of future negotiations. At the same time, Abbas' people should be expected to listen in good faith to the constraints faced by Prime Minister Netanyahu.

The third imperative is that both sides must implement steps that will reduce the possibility of violence erupting during the negotiations. This would require restarting the internal Palestinian reconciliation process. Hamas must be able to take part of the responsibility for negotiations. Amid the lack of attentiveness on the part of the Egyptians and the Qataris ..., this would require an Israeli and American revision regarding direct contacts with Hamas. Hamas must tightly enforce ceasefire from the Gaza Strip, while, at the same time, Israel must strictly enforce the law with respect to violent groups among the settler population in the West Bank.

Based upon the South African example, these three imperatives can facilitate both sides' entry into the tent.[17]

Soldiers of Yesh G'vul

When Israel launched its ill-fated invasion of Lebanon in June 1982, more than three thousand Israeli reservists signed a petition to the government that read as follows:

> We have sworn to defend the well-being and security of the state of Israel. We are faithful to that oath. Therefore we appeal to be allowed to render our reserve service within the boundaries of the state of Israel, and not on Lebanese soil.[18]

Thus was born an important movement of nonviolent resistance to Israeli policy. Hundreds of soldiers refused to serve beyond the country's national borders and issued public statements criticizing the government's security policies. The following is a statement sent to the prime minister and minister of defense in 1983:

> We the undersigned, officers and soldiers in reserve military service, turn to you and ask not to be sent to Lebanon, because we can't take it anymore: We have killed, and are being killed too much in the war. We have conquered and bombed and destroyed too much. And for what?

---

[17] Ilan Baruch, "What Netanyahu Should Learn from the Fall of Apartheid," July 10, 2013, *Haaretz*, http://www.haaretz.com..

[18] *Refusnik!: Israel's Soldiers of Conscience*, compiled and ed. Peretz Kidron (London: Zed Books, 2204), 15.

Today it is all clear to us: through this war you are trying to find a military solution for the Palestinian problem. But a people's problem cannot be solved militarily. You are trying to force a "New Arrangement" on the ruins of Lebanon, to shed our blood and the blood of others for the sake of the Phalange.[19] We were not conscripted in the Israel Defense Forces for this purpose.

You have lied to us! . . . Instead of Peace for the Galilee you have brought a war without end.

For this war, for these lies, for this conquest there is no national consensus.

BRING THE SOLDIERS HOME!!!

We took an oath to defend the security and welfare of the State of Israel. We remain faithful to our pledge. We are therefore turning to you to enable us to do our reserve duty within the boundaries of the State of Israel, and not on Lebanese territory.[20]

The excerpt below is from the 1988 letter by reservist Adi Ofir to then–defense minister Yitzhak Rabin.

My decision to refuse is not a rash one. I have thought about it for a long time and shall carry it out with a heavy heart. . . .

Against popular Palestinian resistance, the IDF [Israeli Defense Force] under your leadership employs a series of repressive measures which will continue to afflict the Jewish national memory. The boundaries between preventative and punitive action have been blurred. Thousands of persons have been penalized without trial, in arbitrary fashion, without the control mechanisms normal to a regulated regime.

---

[19] The Phalange was a right-wing Christian militia that carried out the September 1982 massacre of a large number of Palestinian and Lebanese Shiites in the Sabra and Shatilla refugee camp in Beirut.

[20] "Yesh G'vul—There Is a Limit," Information and position paper, April 1983, Israeli-Left-Archive.org, http://israeli-left-archive.org.

> Again and again, collective punishment actions are applied, inflicting suffering upon the innocent. Again and again, excessive force is applied against rioters, children choke to death on tear gas, babies lose their eyes to rubber bullets. Human rights are trampled upon as a daily routine; criminal excesses of various degrees of gravity are continually committed by the authorities and under your aegis, in the twilight zone between law and evil that the occupation regime has created on the far side of the green line, and which has long been spreading to our side too.
>
> The IDF operates in the occupied territories under orders, some of which are flagrantly illegal. Between the militias of the Jewish settlers, maverick soldiers who open fire following illegal rules of engagement, those who detain scores without trial on a daily basis—there has come about a continuum of injustice. . . . Today I am summoned to play an active role in this concert of evil, in which those involved are likely to find themselves implicated in war crimes. I refuse. . . .
>
> Continuation of the occupation is a far greater menace to Israeli democracy than my refusal or that of my colleagues who have already refused, and those who have not yet done so.[21]

The following is a similar letter to Rabin from another soldier resister at the time:

> There were moments when I thought of doing as ordered—even under duress—but I found myself confronted with the pictures of Palestinians being deported from the land of their birth, the great masses of administrative detainees, the demolished homes, and the wanton killings of some 250 Palestinians. During the period that preceded my decision, I took the initiative for a tour of the West Bank and Gaza Street. Having visited military courts, hospitals, and

---

[21] Reprinted in Kidron, *Refusnik!*, 36–38.

the Ansar 3 detention camp, I cannot but affirm that the acts perpetrated by the IDF verge upon war crimes. . . .

What keeps me awake at night is not the personal price I will be called upon to pay, but rather, the future of my own homeland. I can only state that present government policy, beyond being immoral, undermines the legitimacy of the state of Israel. The whole purpose of Zionism is the creation of a focus of positive identification for the members of our people, wherever they may be—not the transformation of the state of Israel into a source of the unease, frustration, and guilt feelings which, more than even before, beset people in Israel and in the Diaspora. . . .

No Israeli will be free as long as there are detention camps in our land; no Israeli will enjoy a secure life as long as the Palestinians are made to feel that they are nothing more than dirt.[22]

---

[22] Published in "About Yesh Gvul: There Is a Limit," August 1988, Israeli-Left-Archive.org, http://israeli-left-archive.org.

8

Religious Sources of Peacemaking

Many of history's great voices for peace and nonviolence have been motivated by religious belief. Religion is a powerful source of inspiration for peacemaking and compassion for those who suffer. Yet religion can also be a catalyst for armed conflict and a justification for violence. Those who kill in the name of God are capable of the most unspeakable cruelties. This ambivalence of the sacred, as Scott Appleby calls it, is one of the searing enigmas of the human condition.[1]

Teachings of love and peace exist within all of the world's great religious traditions, especially the three great Abrahamic faiths: Judaism, Christianity, and Islam. The Bible teaches, "Thou shalt not kill." While passages of Hebrew Scripture justify the resort to war, the dominant messages of the holy book are of love for others, care for the needy, and the commitment to peace and reconciliation. References to repentance, forgiveness, and *shalom* are ubiquitous in classical Jewish sources.[2] *Shalom* is a rich and capacious term, similar to *salaam* in the Islamic tradi-

---

[1] R. Scott Appleby, *The Ambivalence of the Sacred: Religion, Violence, and Reconciliation* (Lanham, MD: Rowman & Littlefield, 2000), 31.

[2] Marc Gopin, *Between Eden and Armageddon: The Future of World Religions, Violence, and Peacemaking* (New York: Oxford University Press, 2000), 77.

tion, embodying the ideals of social harmony and the multiple conditions that are necessary for peace and human flourishing. The concept of holistic peace is especially strong in the books of Isaiah and Micah, where believers are instructed to do justice and love mercy, to beat swords into ploughshares and study war no more.

Christianity is explicit in its commitment to peace, as reflected most prominently in Jesus's command to "love your enemies and pray for those who persecute you." These and other teachings call upon believers to love all unconditionally and renounce war. As Erasmus wrote, the life and sayings of Jesus are "an uninterrupted lesson in peace and mutual love."[3] The early Christians were strict pacifists, but the church accommodated itself to war in the time of Constantine and, through the writings of Augustine and other philosophers and theologians, developed a just war doctrine allowing the use of force for self-defense and the protection of innocents. A tradition of pacifism survived through the ages, however, and gained impetus with the rise of the Anabaptists and Quakers in the sixteenth and seventeenth centuries, the emergence of the social gospel, and the rise of Catholic pacifism and peacemaking more recently.

Islam is often thought of erroneously as a religion of violence, but commitments to peace and nonviolence are prevalent in Islamic Scripture. Benevolence and care for the poor and less fortunate are enduring virtues in the Qur'an.[4] Those who distort Islam in the name of violent jihad defile the religion they claim to espouse. In the teachings of the Prophet, jihad is described primarily as a struggle against the demons within ourselves and not against external enemies. It is the determination and commitment to serve God and avoid evil and immorality. Islam teaches that life is sacred and that believers must uphold truth, justice, and righteousness. Fighting is permissible, but only in

---

[3] José Chapiro and Desiderius Erasmus, *Erasmus and Our Struggle for Peace* (Boston: Beacon Press, 1950), 145.

[4] Reza Aslan, *No God but God: The Origins, Evolution, and Future of Islam* (New York: Random House, 2005), 60.

self-defense and to uphold the right of religion. As writer and activist Rabia Terri Harris observes, the Quranic tradition of war sets limits on the use of force and requires strict protection of noncombatants.[5] By definition this rules out all forms of terrorism and the indiscriminate use of force.

The selections below offer excerpts from important voices for peace within Jewish, Christian and Islamic traditions.

Abraham Joshua Heschel (1907–1972)

Abraham Joshua Heschel was a Polish-born rabbi and one of the most prominent Jewish theologians of the twentieth century. He earned his doctorate at the University of Berlin in 1933 and taught in Frankfurt for several years before being arrested and deported back to Poland in 1938. He escaped to London in 1939 a few weeks before the start of World War II. His mother and sister were killed in the war, and two other sisters were sent to their deaths in concentration camps. He arrived in New York in 1940 and became a professor of Jewish ethics and mysticism at the Jewish Theological Seminary of America.

Heschel constructed a modern philosophy of religion rooted in the ancient Jewish tradition of piety. He sought to convey the inner depth of devotion in traditional Jewish teachings to the modern human experience. He believed in a God of pathos, a creator in intimate relationship with the world. This divine pathos, he wrote, calls forth a human response of sympathy for God. The individual learns about God not by reason and intellect, but through experience, revelation, and sacred deeds, through a "leap of action," not merely a leap of faith.

Heschel considered the teachings of the Hebrew prophets a call for social engagement on behalf of the poor and oppressed.

---

[5] Rabia Terri Harris, "Interpreting a Qur'an of Nonviolence," in *Peace Primer II: Quotes from Jewish Christian Islamic Scripture and Tradition*, ed. Lynn Gottlieb, Rabia Terri Harris, and Ken Sehested (Charlotte, NC: Baptist Peace Fellowship of North America, 2012), 61–63.

His concern for the marginalized led him to sympathize with and support the civil rights movement. He joined hands with Dr. King to lead the famous march in Alabama from Selma to Montgomery in 1965. He was an early opponent of the escalating war in Vietnam and joined with Reverend William Sloane Coffin Jr. and other prominent religious leaders in founding Clergy and Laymen Concerned About Vietnam (later Clergy and Laity Concerned). He introduced Martin Luther King Jr. at New York's Riverside Church when King delivered his historic "Beyond Vietnam" address.

The excerpt below is from his 1955 book, *God in Search of Man*:

> In what dimension of existence does man become aware of the grandeur and earnestness of living? What are the occasions in which he discovers the nature of his own self? . . .
>
> It is in *deeds* that man becomes aware of what his life really is, of his power to harm and to hurt, to wreck and to ruin; of his ability to derive joy and to bestow it upon others; to relieve and to increase his own and other people's tensions. It is in the employment of his will, not in reflection, that he meets his own self as it is; not as he should like it to be. In his deeds man exposes his immanent as well as his suppressed desires, spelling even that which he cannot apprehend. What he may not dare to think, he often utters in deeds. The heart is revealed in the deeds.
>
> The deed is the test, the trial, and the risk. What we perform may seem slight, but the aftermath is immense. An individual's misdeed can be the beginning of a nation's disaster. The sun goes down, but the deeds go on. Darkness is over all we have done. If man were able to survey at a glance all he has done in the course of his life, what would he feel? . . .
>
> . . . The ethical question refers to particular deeds; the meta-ethical question refers to all deeds. It deals with doing as such: not only what we ought to do, but what is our right to act at all? We are endowed with the ability to conquer

and to control the forces of nature. In exercising power, we submit to our will a world that we did not create, invading realms that do not belong to us. Are we the kings of the universe or mere pirates? By whose grace, by what right, do we exploit, consume, and enjoy the fruits of the trees, the blessings of the earth? Who is responsible for the power to exploit, for the privilege to consume?

It is not an academic problem but an issue we face at every moment. By the will alone man becomes the most destructive of all beings. This is our predicament: our power may become our undoing. We stand on a razor's edge. It is so easy to hurt, to destroy, to insult, to kill. Giving birth to one child is a mystery; bringing death to millions is but a skill. It is not quite within the power of the human will to generate life; it is quite within the power of the will to destroy life.

In the midst of such anxiety we are confronted with the claim of the Bible. The world is not all danger, and man is not alone. God endowed man with freedom, and He will share in our use of freedom. The earth is the Lord's, and God is in search of man. He endowed man with power to conquer the earth, and His honor is upon our faith.[6] . . .

As surely as we are driven to live, we are driven to serve spiritual ends that surpass our own interests. "The good life" is not invented by society but is something which makes society possible; not an accidental function but of the very essence of man. We may lack a clear perception of it, but we are moved by the horror of its violation. We are not only in need of God, but also in need of serving His ends, and these ends are in need of us.[7]

The following brief passage from an address in 1967 captures his profound respect for King and his moral revulsion at the slaughter then under way in Vietnam:

---

[6] Abraham Joshua Heschel, *God in Search of Man: A Philosophy of Judaism* (New York: Octagon Books, 1972), 283–86.
[7] Ibid., 291.

Martin Luther King is a sign that God has not forsaken the United States of America. God has sent him to us. His presence is the hope of America. His mission is sacred, his leadership of supreme importance to every one of us. . . .

To speak of God and remain silent on Vietnam is blasphemous. . . . In the sight of so many thousands of civilians and soldiers slain, injured, crippled, of bodies emaciated, of forests destroyed by fire, God confronts us with this question: Where are you? Is there no compassion in the world? No sense of discernment to realize that this war is a war that refutes any conceivable justification of war? . . . Men slaughtering each other, cities battered into ruin: such insanity has plunged many nations into the abyss of disgrace. . . .

The most basic way in which all men may be divided is between those who believe that war is unnecessary and those who believe that war is inevitable; between those to whom the sword is the symbol of honor and those to whom seeking to convert swords into plowshares is the only way to keep our civilization from disaster. . . .

O Lord, we confess our sins, we are ashamed of the inadequacy of our anguish, of how faint and slight is our mercy. . . . We must continue to remind ourselves that in a free society all are involved in what some are doing. *Some are guilty; all are responsible.* [Emphasis in original][8]

Lynn Gottlieb

Lynn Gottlieb is a feminist rabbi, community activist, and storyteller. She served as rabbi from 1973 to 1980 of Temple Beth Or of the Deaf and Mishkan, an experimental synagogue in New York. From 1981 to 2005 she was rabbi of Congregation Nahalat Shalom in Albuquerque, New Mexico, which she cofounded. She has spent her life engaged in organizing around

---

[8] *Abraham Joshua Heschel, Essential Writings*, selected with an introduction by Susannah Heschel (Maryknoll, NY: Orbis Books, 2011), 84–85.

issues of economic and racial justice, gender equality, and demilitarization. She worked extensively with the Fellowship of Reconciliation and has supported efforts for reconciliation and nonviolence in Israel-Palestine.

In 2012 Gottlieb joined with Ken Sehested, founding director of the Baptist Peace Fellowship of North America, and Rabia Terri Harris of the Muslim Peace Fellowship to produce an updated version of the *Peace Primer*, an online educational resource to help local religious communities understand the scriptural foundations of peace and address challenges related to interreligious dialogue and cooperation. The *Peace Primer* contains scriptural citations on the teachings of peace and nonviolence contained in the three Abrahamic faith traditions. The original 2002 version of the *Primer* included Christian and Muslim teachings and was intended to help members of local churches and mosques deal with the heated debates about religion and violence that followed in the wake of the 9/11 attacks. The second edition in 2012 incorporated teachings from the Torah and other Jewish scriptural sources.

In the excerpts below, Gottlieb interprets Jewish rabbinical teachings in the context of the divine commandment to serve the stranger and the oppressed and to work for the healing peace of shalom. The selection also includes citations from biblical passages.

The Practice of Shalom

> Jewish tradition is crafted around a system of ethical and ritual behaviors called *mitzvot*. *Mitzvot* are meant to promote restorative justice and peace while discouraging violence. *Shmirat shalom*, or nonviolent peace stewardship, is the practice of this system based on the principles of nonviolence found within the tradition as well as contemporary anti-oppression work. Judaism is a deed-oriented system rather than a belief-oriented system. For this reason, Judaism has developed a system of practice known as *halakha*

or walking on the Way. The following *middot*, or guiding principles, represent the foundational principles of *shmirat shalom*. They are drawn from both the written and oral traditions of Torah.

(*Deuteronomy* 6:7) Life is sacred and interrelated. (Jewish people do not pronounce the ineffable Name.) When we recite the biblical prayer *Shema Yisrael*, "Listen Israel . . . YHVH is one!" the intention is to honor the oneness of all life. If we are all interconnected, then every action we take either heals or harms the great web of being. Judaism teaches us to be awake to the sacredness of all living beings as the first step on a spiritual pathway.

(*Leviticus* 19:18) Do not do to others that which is hateful to you (BT *Shabbat* 31a). The commandment to love your neighbor is amplified by the instruction to cause no harm. Both are considered foundational to all of Torah. . . . Loving others is a way to love the Creator. Love is revealed in deeds of compassion and, on occasion, acts of restraint.

(BT *Berakhot* 19b) Our tradition teaches that human dignity—*kavod ha-adam*—trumps all other obligations. Pious observance cannot offset actions that compromise human dignity. The sages taught, "A person should be concerned more that he or she not injure others than that he or she not be injured." Each face mirrors a divine reflection to be cherished. Righteousness occurs when dignity is preserved in our interactions with fellow humans and creatures that share planet earth.

It is written, "By three things the world is preserved, by [restorative] justice, by truth, and by peace, and these three are one: if [restorative] justice has been accomplished, so has truth, and so has peace" (JT *Ta'anit* 4:2). The voice of the prophets insist on the relationship between justice, truth, and peace. Speaking truth to power is urgent. Addressing oppression involves understanding the way we profit from it. Repairing the wounds of injustice requires transforming underlying social conditions.

Practice *teshuvah* [reconciliation]. The goal of conflict transformation is not to defeat the enemy, but to transform the conditions that produce injustice. *Teshuvah* is a response to injustice that involves taking responsibility for one's deeds (confession) along with an acknowledgment of the collective accountability for injustice. Only then can we successfully engage healing, forgiveness, and restoration. . . .

"Not by military might, and not by force of arms. By spirit [nonviolence] alone, says Adonai" (*Zechariah* 4:6). Therefore, refuse to cooperate with oppression and nonviolently resist structural violence. This principle requires Jews who follow the path of *shmirat shalom* to refrain from participating in war or occupation. It is an act of both noncooperation and constructive peace building.

Interpreting a Torah of Nonviolence

Although there are many acts of violence in the written Torah, the rabbinic sages that developed the oral Torah created a series of strategies that altogether eliminated or severely circumscribed the application of these passages to the real world. The process of curtailing the application of biblical laws that promote violence led to the evolution of rabbinic Judaism's preference for nonviolence as a way of life. Rabbinic Judaism rarely honors warriors. Rather, classical Judaism shows a preference for the wisdom of sages committed to study, community service, and prayer, and views violence as *muktzeh*, something which should be avoided altogether. . . .

There are hundreds of . . . examples that amount to a trend in rabbinic literature favoring nonviolence and expressing disdain for violence. They call anyone who lifts a hand against another person a *rasha* or evil person. Hillel's famous phrase, "Do not do unto others that which is hateful to you. That is the entire Torah. Now go study," is a foundational principle of Jewish nonviolence. A *shom-*

eret shalom believes that the Torah must never be used to cause harm. Rather, everything in Torah must prevent harm and cultivate peace.

Nonetheless, some people use Jewish scriptures, both oral and written, to promote violence. If one is an angry person, one will find an angry Torah. If one is a compassionate person, one will find a compassionate Torah. Therefore, as the Torah teaches us, we must choose life and not death, a blessing and not a curse.[9]

Quotes from Scripture

Seek shalom and pursue it (*Psalm* 34:15).

A stranger you shall not harm, neither shall you violently oppress, for you are no strangers to oppression. The stranger who resides with you shall be to you as one of your citizens; you shall love him as yourself, for you were strangers in the land of *Mitzrayim*. (*Leviticus* 19:33–34; *Exodus* 22:20)

You shall have one law for stranger and citizen alike. (*Leviticus* 24:22)

Do not pervert justice for the stranger or the orphan, do not take a widow's garment as security for a loan. You must remember that you were enslaved in Egypt. (*Deuteronomy* 24:17–18)

Leonardo Boff

A former Franciscan priest and professor of theology at Rio De Janeiro State University, Leonardo Boff was one of the founders of liberation theology and a leading voice in advo-

---

[9] *Peace Primer II: Quotes from Jewish, Christian, Islamic Scripture & Tradition*, ed. Lynn Gottlieb, Rabia Terri Harris, and Ken Sehested (Charlotte, NC: Baptist Peace Fellowship of North America, 2012), http://www.bpfna.org.

cating for human rights and empowerment of the poor. He believed that the church should focus on human needs rather than a narrow focus on doctrine and urged greater institutional efforts on behalf of the poor and oppressed. Because of his theological writings he came into conflict with certain church officials and in the 1980s he was silenced by the Vatican and subjected to censorship. In 1992 he chose to resign from the priesthood. Nevertheless, his prolific writing continued, including the influential work *Cry of the Earth, Cry of the Poor*.[10] He developed an integrative ecotheology combining care for God's creation with the need to overcome the marginalization and oppression of the poor. Pope Francis reached out to Boff early in his papacy and reportedly drew from his work in writing his groundbreaking encyclical on the environment, *Laudato Si* (Praise to thee).[11]

Below are excerpts from the essay Boff wrote in 1989 as a foreword to the volume *Relentless Persistence: Nonviolent Action in Latin America*. In this selection he describes the various forms of violence and elaborates the spiritual meaning and power of nonviolence as a means of moral resistance to oppression.

> Besides everyday violence, three great forms of violence confront us today: originating violence, consequential violence, and revolutionary violence. Originating violence has its roots in the elite institutions of power, in a social structure that protects the interests of the dominant groups, and in the extreme right, which will not tolerate any social change out of fear of losing its privileged status. As a result, many countries of the Third World are in the grips of state terrorism. Those who oppose the interests of capital or of the totalitarian state find themselves monitored, imprisoned, tortured, "disappeared," or assassinated.

---

[10] Leonardo Boff, *Cry of the Earth, Cry of the Poor* (Maryknoll, NY: Orbis Books, 1995).

[11] Wen Stephenson, "How Pope Francis Came to Embrace Not Just Climate Justice but Liberation Theology," *The Nation*, September 9, 2015, https://www.thenation.com.

Out of this first violence comes a second: consequential violence. To counter the first violence, or to show that they can and will fight back, resistance groups or terrorists use violent means. Undeniably, consequential violence has a component of legitimate indignation at injustice. At the same time it reflects a less admirable sentiment: revenge. Revenge is an attempt to pay back in kind. But returning violence to the violent does not change the social structure that produces the violence. To the contrary, as the Brazilian religious leader Dom Hélder Câmara says, it creates an endless spiral of violence.

Finally, there is revolutionary violence. Behind revolutionary movements there is an immense thirst for justice in the face of a fundamentally unjust social system. A revolutionary desires an alternative society that offers a greater possibility of life, the full participation of all citizens, and greater equity among them. Revolution is complex, perhaps the most complex process of history. After all, it involves nothing less than remaking an entire social edifice and cultivating new values and new ways of relating. A revolution has many fronts: the popular, the legal, the diplomatic, the political, the pedagogical, the religious, the class, and historically, also the military front. It is with the military front that the question of violence as a means to overthrow the old, oppressive regime surfaces most obviously. For revolutionary violence may have a different purpose than originating violence, but it also produces victims.

History is full of examples of these three responses to a situation of social inequity. Can we break this vicious cycle of violence? Is it at least possible to limit violence in such a way that we neither become accomplices of injustice nor lose our human dignity?

Throughout the world an alternative movement called *active nonviolence* answers with an emphatic "Yes!" This answer is inspired in part by the extraordinary example of persons who have successfully demonstrated another way of confronting highly conflicted situations. Some of the best known are Mahatma Gandhi, Martin Luther King Jr., Dom Hélder Câmara, and Adolfo Pérez Esquivel.[12] . . . They demonstrate that the path of active nonviolence is viable and, in a world threatened by nuclear holocaust and the destruction of its ecosystems, is perhaps the only way to safeguard creation and life in all its forms.

These stories reveal that behind every concerted nonviolent struggle there is a powerful *mística*: the conviction that truth, justice, and love are ontological. That is to say, these are objective forces tied to the very structure of reality, of human society, of being human. No matter how much they are violated, they always persist, and they find an echo in both the consciousness of people and in historical processes. These are the banners that never fall. Under them people accept death with honor.

The *mística* of active nonviolence implies changing ourselves as well as working to change the world. We must live the truth. We must be just, our integrity transparent. We must be peacemakers. It is not enough simply to confront external violence. We must also dig out the roots of violence in our own hearts, in our personal agendas, and in our life projects. In both a personal and a political sense we must seek to live today in miniature what we are seeking for tomorrow. Otherwise the glorious tomorrow of the revolution will never come.

Nothing is more subversive and transforming than love. . . . Not being violent—in and of itself—is not the key to the praxis of Christ. The key is the capacity to love, which

---

[12] Dom Hélder Câmara was the archbishop of Olinda and Recife in Brazil and a defender of the poor and champion of liberation theology. He said famously, "When I give food for the poor, they call me a saint. When I ask why they are poor, they call me a communist." Adolfo Pérez Esquivel was cofounder of the pacifist human rights group SERPAZ (Service, Peace, and Justice Foundation). During Argentina's "dirty war" he was arrested, imprisoned, and tortured because of his advocacy for human rights. He was awarded the Nobel Peace Prize in 1980.

in turn means to be in solidarity with the socially and religiously marginalized. Such solidarity is faithful to the promise of the coming of the Kingdom, even at risk of death. These are the ideas which committed Christ to nonviolence and made him a preacher and peacemaker.

Human history is not ruled by our desires, nor by the high-mindedness of our ethical and political ideals. It is dramatic and at times tragic. For Christians, the brokenness of our world reflects the presence of sin and evil. And that brokenness results in violence, whether through weakness, malice, or the selfish interests of individuals or groups. In this world the struggle is for life, for justice, and for solidarity in social relations. It is not against the bosses or the powerful. Struggle *with* compassion but never *for* passion. And always struggle with compassion. With good reason Gandhi used to say, "Nonviolence has as an essential condition the ability to both move others and to be moved to compassion by others."

The theology of liberation is not an alternative to active nonviolence, nor vice versa. On the contrary, they are born of the same inspiration, which is the commitment to transform a violent social reality to one based on justice and fraternity through peaceful means. Theologians of liberation always speak with confidence of the historic power of the poor. The process of liberation comes from the oppressed themselves.

It begins with a pedagogy of liberation. Paulo Freire, the great pedagogue of the poor of the Third World, has outlined this. The first task of the process consists of ejecting the oppressor who lives within the oppressed. The goal is not to become another oppressor, but to be free and to establish ties of solidarity, which are the building blocks of collective freedom. When popular movements turn to action, their vision may be initially more tactical than strategic. They may struggle to fill a very particular need or to claim a specific right. But their small victories serve both to redeem hope and gradually to destabilize the oppressive system.

In the struggle, theologians of liberation give clear preference to peaceful means because they are the means that generate life. We find in the gospel the renunciation of all vengeance, of all domination of one over another. We learn solidarity and love of enemy. But traditionally this gospel has only been preached at the personal level. We must reclaim it for our politics as well.

Like liberation theology, active nonviolence—also called *firmeza permanente* or relentless persistence—is centered on the conviction that liberation is only possible when the oppressed are the subjects of their own history. Active nonviolence has contributed to the theology of liberation through its pedagogy, through its gospel-based *mística* of peace based on justice, and through its creative means of confronting conflict by applying gospel teachings in political action.

Thus active nonviolence and liberation theology are two facets of a single reality. The two facets are not opposed. On the contrary, they inform and complete each other. As the Chilean Bishop Jorge Hourton[13] observed at an international meeting on active nonviolence in 1977, nonviolence is "a vibrant, rich, and valid vein of liberation theology."

To a great degree the future of active nonviolence depends on nurturing a culture of solidarity, dialogue, and participation. It is in the absence of these practices that a society turns violent. When such values are real social practices, they constitute the necessary preconditions for a network of cooperative relationships and for controlling the violence that continues to plague humanity.

Finally, we must not limit the renunciation of violence to human relations. It must also include relations with nature. The stones, the plants, the animals, the air, and the water are our sisters and brothers. We need to cultivate tenderness for all beings. Democracy should be not only political,

---

[13] An auxiliary bishop who supported human rights defenders during the Pinochet dictatorship and was an advocate of reform within the church.

but cosmic. When there are open relationships based on solidarity with all of creation and especially between people, then we can hope that the era of violence will belong to the dark past of humanity and that a new era of universal love will be inaugurated.[14]

Jim Wallis

Founder of the Sojourners community in the United States and author of numerous books on faith and politics, including the best-selling *God's Politics: Why the Right Gets It Wrong and the Left Doesn't Get It* (HarperCollins, 2005), Jim Wallis is a leading progressive evangelical voice for peace and social justice. In this excerpt, often used in his speeches and sermons, Wallis calls attention to the abiding biblical commitment to serve the poor and care for "the least of these."

Many years ago, I was part of a group of seminary students in Chicago. We decided to do a study to find every biblical reference to one particular subject—the poor and oppressed. We researched the scriptures for each mention of the subject and found, to our astonishment, that there are thousands of verses about the poor in the Bible. Those who are marginalized and forgotten by everyone else, those who are mistreated and abandoned on the bottom of society keep appearing in the Bible as a central concern. The Bible, we discovered, was full of poor people. And even more startling to discover, God is portrayed throughout the Bible as the deliverer of the oppressed.

In the Old Testament, the subject of the poor is the second most prominent theme. Idolatry is the first, and the two

---

[14] Leonardo Boff, "Active Nonviolence: The Political and Moral Power of the Poor," in *Relentless Persistence: Nonviolent Action in Latin* America, ed. Philip McManus and Gerald Schlabach (Philadelphia: New Society Publishers, 1991), vii–x.

are often connected. In the New Testament, one out of every 16 verses is about the poor! In the Gospels, the number is one out of every 10 verses; in Luke's Gospel one of every seven, and in the book of James one of every five.

One zealous seminarian in our group decided to try an experiment. He found an old Bible, took a pair of scissors, and then proceeded to cut out every single reference to the poor. It took him a very long time.

He came to the prophet Amos and read, "Take away from me the noise of your songs; I will not listen to the melody of your harps. But let justice roll down like waters, and righteousness like an ever flowing stream." Then he cut it out. He got to Isaiah and found the prophet thundering, "Is not this the fast that I chose: to loose the bonds of wickedness, to undo the throngs of the yoke, to let the oppressed go free, and to break every yoke? Is it not to share your bread with the hungry, and bring the homeless into your house; when you see the naked, to cover them, and not hide yourself from your own kin?" He cut that out, too.

The books of the prophets were all decimated. So were the Psalms, where God is revealed as the comforter of the afflicted. The Exodus story of God's deliverance of an enslaved people out of the hands of their oppressors, likewise, disappeared. So did the record of the Jubilee, a Hebrew tradition for the periodic forgiving of debts, redistribution of land, and sharing of wealth.

In the New Testament, the young seminarian put his scissors to work again when he came to the Song of Mary, the *Magnificat* that prophesied the mission of the child she carried in her womb: "He has scattered the proud in the thoughts of their hearts. He has brought down the powerful from their thrones, and lifted up the lowly; he has filled the hungry with good things, and sent the rich away empty." After a few snips it was gone. You can imagine what happened to Jesus' teaching in Matthew 25 about caring for "the least of these."

He also cut out Jesus' first sermon at Nazareth where he announced the manifesto of his ministry, "The Spirit of the Lord is upon me, because he has anointed me to bring good news to the poor. He has sent me to proclaim release to the captives and recovery of sight to the blind, to let the oppressed go free, to proclaim the year of the Lord's favor." A few quick cuts, and the prophetic vision of Jesus' ministry had disappeared.

The beatitudes from the Sermon on the Mount, "Blessed are you who are poor," and "Blessed are the poor in spirit," had to go, too. All those teachings had to be removed, since they announce a whole new way of living that turns all our cultural assumptions and established status quos on their heads. The clear injunctions in the epistle of James not to treat the rich differently than the poor didn't survive the scissors, nor did the exhortation in John's letters that if we do not love our neighbor in need, we simply do not love God. Of course, the testimony of the early church where goods and property were shared freely and "There was not a needy person among them" quickly disappeared.

All of that and more was snipped right out of the Bible. When the seminarian was finished, that old Bible hung in threads. It wouldn't hold together; it fell apart in our hands. It was a Bible full of holes. . . .

In America and throughout the Western world, we have responded to all that the Scriptures say about the poor by pretending it just isn't there. We have cut the poor out of the Bible.

The God of the Bible is the deliverer of the poor. This God has a special love for the disenfranchised and marginalized—those who are on the bottom of everybody else's priority list. If that isn't clear from the Bible, then nothing is. It is evident from start to finish.

Therefore, from a biblical point of view, questions concerning the poor and oppressed cannot simply be regarded as matters of politics, or safely delegated to the social concerns committee of a religious congregation. Instead, what is at stake is nothing less than restoring our biblical integrity. It is a matter of conversion.

To place the reality of the poor at the center of our attention will require a fundamental change in priorities and direction. Our task is much deeper than social charity; it is to put our decimated Bibles back together again, to recover the meaning of the sacred text in our personal lives, our congregations and communities, and in the world.[15]

William J. Barber II

A Disciples of Christ (Christian Church) pastor, Reverend Barber has been the leader of the Moral Mondays movement, which began in 2013 as a series of demonstrations to challenge unjust policies in North Carolina that cut unemployment benefits, health-care funding, and environmental regulations. He also campaigned tenaciously against voter suppression laws in North Carolina.

In 2017 Barber became cochair of the new Poor People's Campaign, a diverse coalition of faith-based, labor, and community groups that seeks to keep alive the spirit and intent of Dr. King's original campaign of fifty years earlier. In 2018 Barber received the MacArthur Foundation "genius award" for his effectiveness at building "unusually inclusive fusion coalitions" that are multiracial and interfaith; reach across gender, age, and class lines; and are dedicated to addressing poverty, inequality, and systemic racism.

In these excerpts, drawn from his 2016 book, *The Third Reconstruction*, Barber explains how repression can be the sign of a movement's strength and should not deter organizers from keeping up the pressure for change, nor from seeking reconciliation with adversaries. He notes the value of broadly based coali-

---

[15] Jim Wallis, *The Soul of Politics: A Practical and Prophetic Vision for Change* (New York: New Press and Orbis Books, 1994), 149–52.

tions and cites the vision of Dr. King in calling for an alliance between labor and the struggle for social justice.

> Faith-rooted moral battles . . . do not always advance on schedules that make sense to us. But of this we can always be sure: when we stand for what is good and right, evil will employ every power at its disposal to take us out. A heavy backlash against our movement for justice may hurt. It may well make us weep and moan. But it must not deter us. In fact, it should encourage us. Because resistance is our confirmation that we are on the right track.
> Frederick Douglass taught us back in the 19th century that power concedes nothing without a demand. Because power blinds broken human beings to injustice, the most powerful among us will always ignore and laugh at the cries of those who suffer. But when the balance of power tips far enough to threaten those who think they are in control—when the people come together in a demonstration of our political force—*then* those in power fight back. Their resistance is our confirmation that we are gaining ground. When they stop laughing and start fighting, you can be sure they are worried that you are winning.
> . . . Years of struggle solidified in our coalition the need for a faith-rooted moral movement that welcomes people of all faiths, as well as those who struggle with faith. A diverse coalition of liberals and conservatives, Christians, Jews, and Muslims, the documented and the undocumented, black, white, and brown sisters and brothers were learning that we could trust one another. What's more, we could trust a Higher Power to have our back when things got rough. This faith even gave us hope to pray that our enemies might become our friends. . . .
> As St. Paul says in the book of Romans, we are *more than conquerors* when we engage in a moral struggle. It's not enough to conquer the opposition. In a nonviolent struggle, we are committed to fight on until we win our adversaries as

friends. As King explained to his Montgomery congregation, "The significant thing is that when you follow this way, when the battle is almost over, a new friendship and reconciliation exists between the people who have been the oppressors and the oppressed."

This is the end goal of nonviolent struggle: a new nation—a new world—where former enemies become co-laborers for the common good. We can never be friends with our enemies, of course, until they stop trying to destroy us. But even in the midst of a struggle, Jesus said, we can love our enemies. As love seeks understanding, we can learn from them. Sometimes, in fact, they become our most important teachers as we develop tactics for the next stage of battle.

Because our coalition has inherited this philosophy of nonviolent struggle from the Southern freedom movement, we did not stop at seeing the resistance of extremist forces as a confirmation of our moral cause. We also considered their massive attack against us as an opportunity to learn. . . .

In a 1965 speech to the Illinois State AFL-CIO, Dr. King had outlined the need for civil rights and labor activists to join forces. "The two most dynamic Movements that reshaped the Nation the past three decades are the labor and civil rights Movements," he said. "If our two Movements unite their social pioneering initiative, 30 years from now people will look back on this day and honor those who had the vision to see the full possibilities of modern society and the courage to fight for their realization." It had taken us over 40 years, but we were beginning to catch up to Dr. King's vision. We learned from experience that he was right: at the heart of a moral movement for a just economy we had to bring workers together with freedom fighters who had a deeply antiracist analysis of our nation's economic problems. Conversations about "fair wages" or "civil rights" could not be reduced to the self-interest of separate groups. No, we were engaged together in a conversation about what kind of economy builds up the common good. . . .

We began to identify pro-labor, anti-poverty policies that ensure economic sustainability as a centerpiece of our agenda. A fusion coalition committed to the common good could bring black, white, and brown together, insisting on an economy that works for everyone. But to stand together, we would have to listen to one another and understand the other pressures that weighed heavily on some of our partners as they struggled to survive in this economy.[16]

Pope Francis

When Cardinal Jorge Mario Bergoglio of Buenos Aires was named pope in 2013, he became the first Jesuit and only prelate from the Americas to lead the worldwide Roman Catholic Church. He immediately distinguished himself by his courageous stands on behalf of the exploited and oppressed. He also displayed extraordinary humility, choosing to live in a modest guesthouse rather than the Apostolic Palace and washing the feet of impoverished immigrants after terror attacks in Brussels. He earned worldwide respect as a progressive innovator dedicated to interfaith dialogue, support for the poor, and promotion of justice and peace. In his first encyclical, *Evangelii Gaudium* (Joy of the Gospel) Pope Francis emphasized the connection between social equality and peace:

> Until exclusion and inequality in society and between peoples are reversed, it will be impossible to eliminate violence. . . . When a society . . . is willing to leave a part of itself on the fringes, no political programs or resources spent on law enforcement or surveillance systems can indefinitely guarantee tranquility. This is not the case simply

---

[16] William J. Barber II, with Jonathan Wilson-Hartgrove, *The Third Reconstruction: How a Moral Movement Is Overcoming the Politics of Division and Fear* (Boston: Beacon Press, 2016), 65–68, 71.

because inequality provokes a violent reaction from those excluded from the system, but because the socioeconomic system is unjust at its root.[17]

Francis expanded upon these same themes in *Laudato Si*, which directly links environmental sustainability with ending poverty and exploitation of the poor. He writes in words no doubt inspired by Leonardo Boff: "Today . . . we have to realize that a true ecological approach always becomes a social approach; it must integrate questions of justice in debates on the environment, so as to hear *both the cry of the earth and the cry of the poor* [emphasis in the original]." Francis's use of the title of Boff's book could not have been coincidental.[18]

In April 2016 some eighty-five laypeople, theologians, members of religious congregations, priests, and bishops traveled from all over the world to Rome for a landmark gathering, "Nonviolence and Just Peace Conference: Contributing to the Catholic Understanding of and Commitment to Nonviolence." Cosponsors included the Vatican's Pontifical Council for Justice and Peace and the Catholic peace movement Pax Christi International. The conference sought to elevate the importance of nonviolence in Catholic doctrine and urged the church to make a greater commitment to nonviolent strategies and tactics.[19] The report of the conference was delivered to Pope Francis along with a request for a papal encyclical committing the church more firmly to nonviolence. The pope's response came a few months later in the Vatican's annual World Day of Peace

---

[17] *Apostolic Exhortation Evangelii Gaudium of the Holy Father Francis* (2013), par. 59, w2.vatican.va.

[18] I am indebted to Wen Stephenson for noting this connection. See Wes Stephenson, "How Pope Francis Came to Embrace Not Just Climate Justice but Liberation Theology," *The Nation*, September 9, 2015, https://www.thenation.com.

[19] For a report on the conference, see Ken Butigan, "Historic Vatican Conference Calls for Nonviolence and 'Just Peace,'" *Waging Nonviolence*, April 21, 2016, http://wagingnonviolence.org. For a comprehensive report, see Marie Dennis, ed., *Choosing Peace: The Catholic Church Returns to Gospel Nonviolence* (Maryknoll, NY: Orbis Books, 2018).

message for 2017, which broke new ground in the depth of its commitment to nonviolence and peace.[20]

Most of the text of the message is presented below.

Nonviolence: A Style of Politics for Peace

1. At the beginning of this New Year, I offer heartfelt wishes of peace to the world's peoples and nations, to heads of state and government, and to religious, civic, and community leaders. I wish peace to every man, woman, and child, and I pray that the image and likeness of God in each person will enable us to acknowledge one another as sacred gifts endowed with immense dignity. Especially in situations of conflict, let us respect this, our "deepest dignity," and make active nonviolence our way of life.

This is the fiftieth Message for the World Day of Peace. In the first, Blessed Pope Paul VI addressed all peoples, not simply Catholics, with utter clarity. "Peace is the only true direction of human progress—and not the tensions caused by ambitious nationalisms, nor conquests by violence, nor repressions which serve as mainstay for a false civil order." He warned of "the danger of believing that international controversies cannot be resolved by the ways of reason, that is, by negotiations founded on law, justice, and equity, but only by means of deterrent and murderous forces." Instead, citing the encyclical *Pacem in Terris* of his predecessor Saint John XXIII, he extolled "the sense and love of peace founded upon truth, justice, freedom, and love." In the intervening fifty years, these words have lost none of their significance or urgency.

On this occasion, I would like to reflect on *nonviolence* as a style of politics for peace. I ask God to help all of us to cultivate nonviolence in our most personal thoughts

---

[20] Ken Butigan, "Pope Calls for Nonviolence in 2017 World Day of Peace Message: U.S. Religious Readers Respond," Catholic Nonviolence Initiative, December 12, 2016, http://www.bridgefolk.net.

and values. May charity and nonviolence govern how we treat each other as individuals, within society and in international life. When victims of violence are able to resist the temptation to retaliate, they become the most credible promoters of nonviolent peacemaking. In the most local and ordinary situations and in the international order, may nonviolence become the hallmark of our decisions, our relationships and our actions, and indeed of political life in all its forms.

A Broken World

2. While the last century knew the devastation of two deadly World Wars, the threat of nuclear war and a great number of other conflicts, today, sadly, we find ourselves engaged in a horrifying *world war fought piecemeal*. It is not easy to know if our world is presently more or less violent than in the past, or to know whether modern means of communications and greater mobility have made us more aware of violence, or, on the other hand, increasingly inured to it.

In any case, we know that this "piecemeal" violence, of different kinds and levels, causes great suffering: wars in different countries and continents; terrorism, organized crime, and unforeseen acts of violence; the abuses suffered by migrants and victims of human trafficking; and the devastation of the environment. Where does this lead? Can violence achieve any goal of lasting value? Or does it merely lead to retaliation and a cycle of deadly conflicts that benefit only a few "warlords"?

Violence is not the cure for our broken world. Countering violence with violence leads at best to forced migrations and enormous suffering, because vast amounts of resources are diverted to military ends and away from the everyday needs of young people, families experiencing hardship, the elderly, the infirm, and the great majority of people in our world. At worst, it can lead to the death, physical and spiritual, of many people, if not of all.

The Good News

3. Jesus himself lived in violent times. Yet he taught that the true battlefield, where violence and peace meet, is the human heart: for "it is from within, from the human heart, that evil intentions come" (*Mt* 7:21). But Christ's message in this regard offers a radically positive approach. He unfailingly preached God's unconditional love, which welcomes and forgives. He taught his disciples to love their enemies (see *Mt* 5:44) and to turn the other cheek (see *Mt* 5:39). When he stopped her accusers from stoning the woman caught in adultery (see *Jn* 8:1–11), and when, on the night before he died, he told Peter to put away his sword (see *Mt* 26:52), Jesus marked out the path of nonviolence. He walked that path to the very end, to the cross, whereby he became our peace and put an end to hostility (see *Eph* 2:14–16). Whoever accepts the Good News of Jesus is able to acknowledge the violence within and be healed by God's mercy, becoming in turn an instrument of reconciliation. In the words of Saint Francis of Assisi: "As you announce peace with your mouth, make sure that you have greater peace in your hearts."

To be true followers of Jesus today also includes embracing his teaching about nonviolence. As my predecessor Benedict XVI observed, that teaching "is realistic because it takes into account that in the world there is *too much* violence, *too much* injustice, and therefore that this situation cannot be overcome except by countering it with *more* love, with *more* goodness. This '*more*' comes from God." He went on to stress that: "For Christians, nonviolence is not merely tactical behavior but a person's way of being, the attitude of one who is *so convinced of God's love and power* that he or she is not afraid to tackle evil with the weapons of love and truth alone. Love of one's enemy constitutes the nucleus of the 'Christian revolution.'" The Gospel command to *love your enemies* (see *Lk* 6:27) "is rightly considered the *magna carta* of Christian nonviolence. It does not consist in succumbing to evil . . . , but in responding to evil with good (see *Rom* 12:17–21), and thereby breaking the chain of injustice."

More Powerful Than Violence

4. Nonviolence is sometimes taken to mean surrender, lack of involvement and passivity, but this is not the case. . . . The decisive and consistent practice of nonviolence has produced impressive results. The achievements of Mahatma Gandhi and Khan Abdul Ghaffar Khan in the liberation of India, and of Dr. Martin Luther King Jr. in combating racial discrimination will never be forgotten. Women in particular are often leaders of nonviolence, as for example, was Leymah Gbowee and the thousands of Liberian women, who organized pray-ins and nonviolent protest that resulted in high-level peace talks to end the second civil war in Liberia. . . .

Such efforts on behalf of the victims of injustice and violence are not the legacy of the Catholic Church alone, but are typical of many religious traditions, for which "compassion and nonviolence are essential elements pointing to the way of life." I emphatically reaffirm that "no religion is terrorist." Violence profanes the name of God. Let us never tire of repeating: "The name of God cannot be used to justify violence. Peace alone is holy. Peace alone is holy, not war!"

The Domestic Roots of a Politics of Nonviolence

5. If violence has its source in the human heart, then it is fundamental that nonviolence be practiced before all else within families. . . . From within families, the joy of love spills out into the world and radiates to the whole of society. An ethics of fraternity and peaceful coexistence between individuals and among peoples cannot be based on the logic of fear, violence, and closed-mindedness, but on responsibility, respect, and sincere dialogue. Hence, I plead for disarmament and for the prohibition and abolition of nuclear weap-

ons: nuclear deterrence and the threat of mutual assured destruction are incapable of grounding such an ethics. I plead with equal urgency for an end to domestic violence and to the abuse of women and children.

My Invitation

6. Peacebuilding through active nonviolence is the natural and necessary complement to the Church's continuing efforts to limit the use of force by the application of moral norms; she does so by her participation in the work of international institutions and through the competent contribution made by so many Christians to the drafting of legislation at all levels. Jesus himself offers a "manual" for this strategy of peacemaking in the Sermon on the Mount. The eight Beatitudes (see *Mt* 5:3–10) provide a portrait of the person we could describe as blessed, good, and authentic. Blessed are the meek, Jesus tells us, the merciful and the peacemakers, those who are pure in heart, and those who hunger and thirst for justice.

This is also a program and a challenge for political and religious leaders, the heads of international institutions, and business and media executives: to apply the Beatitudes in the exercise of their respective responsibilities. It is a challenge to build up society, communities, and businesses by acting as peacemakers. It is to show mercy by refusing to discard people, harm the environment, or seek to win at any cost. To do so requires "the willingness to face conflict head on, to resolve it and to make it a link in the chain of a new process." To act in this way means to choose solidarity as a way of making history and building friendship in society. Active nonviolence is a way of showing that unity is truly more powerful and more fruitful than conflict. Everything in the world is inter-connected. Certainly differences can cause frictions. But let us face them constructively and non-violently, so that "tensions and oppositions can achieve a diversified and life-giving unity," preserving "what is valid and useful on both sides." . . .

May we dedicate ourselves prayerfully and actively to banishing violence from our hearts, words, and deeds, and to becoming nonviolent people and to building nonviolent communities that care for our common home. "Nothing is impossible if we turn to God in prayer. Everyone can be an artisan of peace."[21]

John Paul II (1920–2005)

Like Pope Francis, John Paul II was a trailblazer who transformed the role of the Catholic Church in the modern world and helped to inspire the historic nonviolent resistance movement that led to the fall of communism in Poland and contributed to the ending of the Cold War. The first non-Italian pontiff in more than 450 years and the first from a Slavic country, John Paul II reigned for 26 years and was the most peripatetic pope in history, meeting millions of people all over the world in his frequent travels. He sought to improve relations between Catholics and other believers and openly apologized for past Catholic calumny against Jews and Muslims.

John Paul II was strongly anticommunist and was critical of liberation theology for what he considered its Marxist materialist tendencies. Among those he criticized on these grounds was Leonardo Boff of Brazil. But John Paul II was firmly committed to the church's ministry on behalf of the poor, and he was critical of capitalism's exploitive tendencies. He condemned war and armed violence and emphasized the messages of love and nonviolence. He sought to rekindle the church's traditional commitment to economic and social justice and the rights of labor,

---

[21] The Vatican, *Message of His Holiness Pope Francis for the Celebration of the Fiftieth World Day of Peace; Nonviolence: a Style of Politics for Peace*. Reprinted in Dennis, ed., *Choosing Peace*. January 1, 2017, https://w2.vatican.va.

as expressed in the very first papal encyclical, *Rerum Novarum*, issued by Pope Leo XIII in 1891. He chose the hundredth anniversary of that historic teaching to issue a new letter, *Centesimus Annus*, reiterating the church's support for workers and the poor and highlighting the recent heroic role of workers in his native country, inspired by a religious zeal he helped to create.

> New forms of democracy have emerged which offer a hope for change in fragile political and social structures weighed down by a painful series of injustices and resentments, as well as by a heavily damaged economy and serious social conflicts . . . showing that the complex problems faced by those peoples can be resolved through dialogue and solidarity, rather than by a struggle to destroy the enemy through war. . . .
>
> It cannot be forgotten that the fundamental crisis of systems claiming to express the rule and indeed the dictatorship of the working class began with the great upheavals which took place in Poland in the name of solidarity. It was the throngs of working people which foreswore the ideology which presumed to speak in their name. On the basis of a hard, lived experience of work and of oppression, it was they who recovered and, in a sense, rediscovered the content and principles of the Church's social doctrine.
>
> Also worthy of emphasis is the fact that the fall of this kind of "bloc" or empire was accomplished almost everywhere by means of peaceful protest, using only the weapons of truth and justice. While Marxism held that only by exacerbating social conflicts was it possible to resolve them through violent confrontation, the protests which led to the collapse of Marxism tenaciously insisted on trying every avenue of negotiation, dialogue, and witness to the truth, appealing to the conscience of the adversary and seeking to reawaken in him a sense of shared human dignity.
>
> It seemed that the European order resulting from the Second World War . . . could only be overturned by another

war. Instead, it has been overcome by the non-violent commitment of people who, while always refusing to yield to the force of power, succeeded time after time in finding effective ways of bearing witness to the truth. This disarmed the adversary, since violence always needs to justify itself through deceit, and to appear, however falsely, to be defending a right or responding to a threat posed by others. . . . I pray that this example will prevail in other places and other circumstances. May people learn to fight for justice without violence, renouncing class struggle in their internal disputes, and war in international ones. . . .

Sacred Scripture continually speaks to us of an active commitment to our neighbor and demands of us a shared responsibility for all of humanity.

This duty is not limited to one's own family, nation, or State, but extends progressively to all mankind, since no one can consider himself extraneous or indifferent to the lot of another member of the human family. No one can say that he is not responsible for the well-being of his brother or sister (cf. Gen 4:9; Lk 10:29–37; Mt 25:31–46). Attentive and pressing concern for one's neighbor in a moment of need—made easier today because of the new means of communication which have brought people closer together—is especially important with regard to the search for ways to resolve international conflicts other than by war. . . .

I myself, on the occasion of the recent tragic war in the Persian Gulf, repeated the cry: "Never again war!" No, never again war, which destroys the lives of innocent people, teaches how to kill, throws into upheaval even the lives of those who do the killing and leaves behind a trail of resentment and hatred, thus making it all the more difficult to find a just solution of the very problems which provoked the war. Just as the time has finally come when in individual States a system of private vendetta and reprisal has given way to the rule of law, so too a similar step forward is now urgently needed in the international community. Furthermore, it must not be forgotten that at the root of war there are usually real and serious grievances: injustices suffered, legitimate aspirations frustrated, poverty, and the exploitation of multitudes of desperate people who see no real possibility of improving their lot by peaceful means.

For this reason, another name for peace is *development*. Just as there is a collective responsibility for avoiding war, so too there is a collective responsibility for promoting development. Just as within individual societies it is possible and right to organize a solid economy which will direct the functioning of the market to the common good, so too there is a similar need for adequate interventions on the international level .... But to accomplish this, the poor—be they individuals or nations—need to be provided with realistic opportunities. Creating such conditions calls for a *concerted worldwide effort to promote development*, an effort which also involves sacrificing the positions of income and of power enjoyed by the more developed economies.

This may mean making important changes in established life-styles, in order to limit the waste of environmental and human resources, thus enabling every individual and all the peoples of the earth to have a sufficient share of those resources. In addition, the new material and spiritual resources must be utilized which are the result of the work and culture of peoples who today are on the margins of the international community, so as to obtain an overall human enrichment of the family of nations.[22]

Maulana Wahiduddin Khan

An internationally known Islamic religious scholar from northern India, Maulana Wahiduddin Khan has authored more than a hundred books, originally written in Urdu, many of them

---

[22] John Paul II, Holy Father, *Centesimus Annus*, Encyclical Letter ... on the Hundredth Anniversary of *Rerum Novarum* (1991), paras. 22, 23, 25, 51, 52, http://w2.vatican.va.

translated into Arabic, English, Hindi, and other languages used in the Islamic world. His easy-to-read interpretations of Scripture and translations of the Qur'an have made Islamic teachings more understandable to modern audiences. In 1970 he established the Islamic Centre in Delhi, which later became the publishing house for his monthly magazine *al-Risiila*, named for the Arabic word for "message." His writings and televised lectures have reached wide audiences in multiple languages around the world.

Wahiduddin Khan strongly emphasizes the message of peace at the heart of Islam. One of God's names in the Qur'an is *al-Salam* or Peace. The Prophet teaches believers to follow the pathways of compassion, mercy, and peace if they wish to please God. Khan espouses a theology of nonviolence and peaceful coexistence based on inner spiritual discipline and the cultivation of peaceful relations with others. These virtues are rooted in the practice of patience, which Khan defines as one of the cardinal virtues of Islam. Patience is clearly preferred in the Qur'an because it implies a peaceful response, whereas impatience implies a violent response.

Wahiduddin Khan has been criticized for his quietist belief that one should not engage in social action or exert political pressures. His position is close to that of absolute pacifists who withdraw from the world of politics and social contestation and focus on personal piety. On the fraught question of communal relations within India, he has chastised Muslims for their hostility and mistrust of Hindus and urged them to avoid actions that might spark Hindu violence, a position that has won him support among Hindu nationalists but criticism from Islamic teachers who believe he unfairly blames Muslims for sparking communal violence. Wahiduddin Khan has expressed great admiration for Gandhi, but on matters of social engagement the two are far apart. Gandhi believed in the need to resist rather than accept social injustice, and he campaigned vigorously for greater communal harmony between Hindus and Muslims.[23] Wahiduddin Khan rejects protest and political action.

---

[23] Ifran A. Omar, "Towards an Islamic Theology of Nonviolence: A Critical Appraisal of Maulana Wahiduddin Khan's View of Jihad," *Vidy-*

Notwithstanding these concerns, Wahiduddin Khan remains an indispensable and highly influential voice on the core teachings of nonviolence and peace within Islam. In the excerpts below, he identifies some of the core irenic principles within the Qur'anic tradition and helps to correct widely propagated distortions of Islam that are prevalent in the world today.

Islam Is Peace

The literal meaning of jihad is "effort" or "struggle." The Quran speaks about a "great jihad" . . . (25:52).[24] According to a *hadith*, a *mujahid*, one who engages in jihad, is one who, for the sake of obedience to God, combats his own lower self, or *nafs*. According to another *hadith*, when the Prophet returned from the Tabuk campaign,[25] he said, "We have returned from lesser jihad to greater jihad." The "lesser jihad" is military struggle, while the "greater jihad" is the struggle against one's own lower self, that is to say, the struggle to control one's negative and undesirable feelings and to persevere in the life of God's choice in all circumstances.

Jihad, if understood correctly, is an entirely peaceful action. At the individual level, to engage in jihad is to refuse to deviate from God's path in the face of the desires and inclinations of one's *nafs*. . . . It is to face the difficulties and challenges that stand in one's path and remain steadfast on the path of the Truth. At the collective level, jihad may be defined as a peaceful struggle.[26] . . .

Peace is integral to the meaning of the very word "Islam" itself. The root of the word "Islam" is *s-l-m*, which is related

---

ajyoti Journal of Theological Reflection 72, no. 9 (September 2008): 671–80.

[24] All citations from Maulana Wahiduddin, *Islam and World Peace* (Chennai, India: Goodword Books, 2015).

[25] One of the major military campaigns of the Prophet described in chapter 53 of the Qur'an.

[26] Wahiduddin, *Islam and World Peace*, 5.

to the Arabic word for "peace." And so, Islam means a religion of peace. . . . The Prophet is reported to have declared that a Muslim is one from whose tongue and hands people live safely. In other words, a Muslim, in the true sense of the word, is a person who does not harm anyone by his or her words or deeds.

Of the various names or attributes of God mentioned in the Quran one is *As-Salam*, or "The Source of Peace." That is to say, God is Peace. Similarly, in a *hadith* recorded in the *Sahih al Bukhari*,[27] the Prophet observed that God Himself is Peace. Moreover, God's guidance is referred to in the Quran (5:16) as the ideal abode for Man, and the Quran (10:25) refers to heaven as *daar us-salaam* or the "home of peace." . . .

We are told by the Quran (4:128) that "reconciliation is best." This means that, in terms of consequences, reconciliation is the better option. According to the law of nature that God has devised, reconciliation leads to successes and achievements that would simply be impossible by having recourse to violence.[28]

War and Peace

Followers of Islam do not have the right to unleash war against whomsoever they consider to be the enemies. The only thing they can do is engage their enemies in peaceful *dawah*, that is, to invite them to God's path, not wage war on them. In this regard, the Quran clearly states:

> Who speaks better than one who calls to God and does good works and says, "I am surely of those who submit." Good and evil deeds are not equal. Repel evil with what is better; then you will see that one who was once your enemy has become your dearest friend. (41:33, 34)

---

[27] One of the six collections of *hadith* or prophetic traditions in Sunni Islam.
[28] Wahiduddin, *Islam and World Peace*, 8.

This Quranic verse clearly tells us that we should engage in peaceful efforts and thereby make our opponent our friend, rather than branding him as an incorrigible enemy and declaring war against him.

It is true that Islam does give permission to engage in war in some situations, but this is only when all efforts to avoid war have failed and the opposing force launches an attack, creating a situation that necessitates defensive measures....

War, it must be understood, is completely undesirable as far as Islam is concerned. Just as trade can prosper only in a climate of peace and moderation, so is the case with Islam. In this regard, a *hadith* contained in the *Sahih al Bukhari* advises believers not to desire confrontation with their enemies. Rather, they should seek peace from God....

There are some verses in the Quran about which there is considerable misunderstanding. For instance, the verse which says, "Slay them wherever you find them" (2:191). On the basis of such verses, the impression has been formed that Islam is a religion of war. This, however, is a baseless view....

All the verses of the Quran are, directly or indirectly, based on peace. There are more than 6000 verses in the Quran. Of these, hardly 40 are about commandments of *qital* or war—in other words, less than 1 percent....

... The Quran was not revealed all at once, in the form of a book. Rather, it was revealed in installments, over a period of 23 years, in accordance with prevailing conditions. If this period of 23 years is divided on the basis of peace and war, then some 20 years of this period were years of peace, while only around three years were a time of war. The Quranic verses about war were revealed in this three-year period. Besides these verses, the other verses ... were all related to peaceful teachings—to matters such as intuitive knowledge of God, worship, morals, justice, and so on....

When the Prophet Mohammed migrated from Mecca to Medina, the polytheists launched aggressive attacks on him.

But he repeatedly staved off these attacks through patient steadfastness and the avoidance of fighting. However, there were occasions when there was no option left but to reply to these attacks. That is why, on such occasions the Prophet responded in the form of defensive fighting. It was in these circumstances that the exceptional Quranic commandments about fighting were revealed. These commandments were related to a temporary situation, and were not meant to be universally applied.

According to Islam, terrorism is not permissible or legitimate under any circumstances.

Terrorism is a form of violence undertaken by non-state actors. Using violence to attain a certain objective, if the need so arises, is the prerogative only of a duly established government. No matter what the conditions, it is improper and impermissible for non-state actors, including both individuals and groups, to adopt violent methods.[29]

Climate of Peace

A *hadith* in the *Sahih Muslim*[30] tells us that God gives in response to gentleness what He does not in response to harshness. From this we learn that peaceful activism is clearly superior to violent activism.

What this *hadith* relates is not something mysterious. Rather, it is an obvious, well-known, and natural fact. War and violence only further exacerbate hatred and enmity between opponents. They cause much destruction of resources, besides taking precious lives. They lead entire societies to fall prey to negative thinking. Obviously, in a climate of war there is no possibility left for positive and constructive activities. . . .

On the other hand, in a climate of peace, people can establish propitious and balanced relations with each other.

---

[29] Ibid., 13–15, 21–23, 36.
[30] A collection of sayings and deeds by the Prophet also known as the *sunnah*.

Friendship and love can flourish. As a result of this sort of a favorable atmosphere, positive and constructive activities and the use of resources for progress are possible. Such an atmosphere is conducive to positive thinking, which promotes progress in terms of thought and action. . . .

According to the Prophet's *sunnat*, or practice, when peaceful methods are practically available, these methods alone must be used and violent struggle should be avoided. One can very well say, without fear of exaggeration, that today, violent methods have not only become difficult, but that they are also, in practical terms, completely counterproductive. In contrast, peaceful methods are easier to adopt and also much more likely to be successful. No longer is the use of peaceful methods a question of choosing between two possible options—peaceful versus violent. Rather, the peaceful method is now simply the only possible and viable existing option. . . .

The Quran tells us:
Whenever they kindled a fire of war, God puts it out.
(5:64)

From this Quranic verse we learn something about God's creation plan. We learn that this plan is based on the principle of peace. We learn that if someone is bent on kindling the fires of violence, we should try to put out the flames through peaceful measures so that the fire does not spread.[31]

Abdul Ghaffar Khan (1890–1988)

One of the most important Muslim practitioners of nonviolent action was Abdul Ghaffar Khan, a Pashtun from the Northwest Territories of modern-day Pakistan. A prominent ally of Gandhi in the struggle against British rule, he led a significant movement of nonviolent resistance among a people known for

---
[31] Wahiduddin, *Islam and World Peace*, 20, 30, 43.

their fierce warrior ethic. Ghaffar Khan developed his unique organization and nonviolent method before he met Gandhi, basing his movement entirely on Islamic teachings from the Qur'an and *hadith*. He integrated the Islamic teachings of compassion and justice with an emphasis on endurance and patience. Ghaffar Khan said,

> I am going to give you such a weapon that the police and the army will not be able to stand against it. It is the weapon of the Prophet, but you are not aware of it. That weapon is patience and righteousness. No power on earth can stand against it. . . . Tell your brethren that there is an army of God, and its weapon is patience.[32]

Ghaffar Khan created the *Khudai Khidmatgar*, the "Servants of God," and molded it into a nonviolent army of determined opposition to British rule. With as many as one hundred thousand members, his nonviolent "army" wore uniforms, engaged in physical training, and employed strict discipline like a regular army, but it carried no weapons, and its duties consisted of humanitarian service and political resistance to the British.[33] Ghaffar Khan turned the fighting spirit of the Pashtun people into an effective force for nonviolent revolution. The *Khudai Khidmatgar* played an important role in the freedom struggle and was an embodiment of Gandhi's vision of creating a peace army that would combine support for economic and social development with nonviolent struggle for justice and political self-determination.

Below are excerpts from Ghaffar Khan's writings and sayings:

---

[32] Quoted in Robert C. Johansen, "Radical Islam and Nonviolence: A Case Study of Religious Empowerment and Constraint among Pashtuns," *Journal of Peace Research* 34, no. 1 (February 1997): 38.

[33] Makulika Banerjee, *The Pathan Unarmed: Opposition and Memory in the North West Frontier* (Karachi: Oxford University Press, 2000).

Violence or Nonviolence

There were two freedom movements in our province, one believed in violence and the other in nonviolence. The violent movement had been founded first. It was not until 40 or 50 years later, in 1929 that the nonviolent movement was started.

The British had been able to deal with the violent movement by taking violent counter measures. But they had not been able to suppress the nonviolent movement in spite of all their unspeakable cruelty and innumerable arrests and imprisonments.

The violent movement had created fear and cowardice in the people's minds, it had weakened people's courage and morale. But the nonviolent movement had made people fearless and brave, and inspired them with a high sense of morality.

The violent movement had preached hatred, but the nonviolent movement preached love and brotherhood. It spoke of a new life for the Pathans,[34] a life of dedication to their nation and to their brethren. It spoke of a great and splendid revolution in art, in culture, in poetry, in their whole social life.

The truth is, of course, that violence is born of hatred, and nonviolence is born of love.

One reason for the hatred was the injustice on the part of the British. Suppose someone had killed an Englishman, and he was caught—the British would then not only punish the culprit, but they would make his whole village and his whole district suffer. Heavy fines would be imposed, arrests would be made, many people would be imprisoned.

People would naturally look upon the culprit and upon his whole violent movement as the sole cause of all the cruelty and oppression they had to suffer.

---

[34] Also known as Pashtuns, the Pashto-speaking population of northwest Pakistan and southern Afghanistan.

On the other hand they saw that in the nonviolent movement everyone tried to avoid trouble, everyone tried to prevent harm being done to the innocent people. They saw that our movement was only concerned with the welfare of the country, and that made them sympathetic towards our movement.

These were the reasons why the violent movement failed and the nonviolent movement was successful. It was through nonviolence that the country would be freed, through nonviolence that the British would be driven out.

But the *Khudai Khidmatgar* movement was not just a political movement. Apart from being the political party of the Pathans, it was also a spiritual movement. It was the movement that taught the Pathans love and brotherhood, that inspired them with a new sense of unity, patriotism, and the desire to serve.

The Pathans used to quarrel amongst themselves; antagonism and feuds ruined their homes and their families. Through the nonviolent movement all that was changed. The British used to say, "A nonviolent Pathan is more dangerous than a violent Pathan."[35]

The Servants of God

In 1929 we were able to found the kind of organization we wanted. We decided to call it the *Khudai Khidmatgar* movement. . . . Our motive for choosing that name was that we wanted to awaken in the Pathans the idea of service and the desire to serve their country and their people in the name of God, an idea and a desire which was sadly lacking among them.

Another thing was that the Pathans were inclined to be violent and their violence was directed against their own

---

[35] An autobiography of Badshah Kahn as narrated to K. B. Narang, *My Life and Struggle* (Delhi: Hind Pocket Books/Orient Paperbacks, 1969), 143–45.

countrymen, against their own kith and kin, against their closest relations. They were like the smoldering embers, always ready to flare up and inflict harm and injury on their own brethren.

One of their worst characteristics was their habit of taking revenge. They badly needed to change their anti-social customs, to check their violent outbursts, and to practice good behavior. And this was what we thought the *Khudai Khidmatgar* movement could and would do.

Anyone aspiring to become a *Khudai Khidmatgar* had to take this solemn vow:

I am a *Khudai Khidmatgar*, and as God needs no service, but serving His creation is serving Him, I promise to serve humanity in the name of God.

I promise to refrain from violence and from taking revenge. I promise to forgive those who oppress me or treat me with cruelty.

I promise to treat every Pathan as my brother and friend.

I promise to refrain from anti-social customs and practices.

I promise to live a simple life, to practice virtue and to refrain from evil.

I promise to practice good manners and good behavior, and not to lead a life of idleness. I promise to devote at least two hours a day to social work.[36]

With Gandhi

When we were chatting one day, the subject of nonviolence came up, and I said to Gandhiji:

"Gandhiji, you have been preaching nonviolence in India for a long time now, but I started teaching the Pathans nonviolence only a short time ago. Yet, in comparison, the Pathans seem to have learned this lesson and grasped the

---

[36] Ibid., 96–97.

idea of nonviolence much quicker and much better than the Indians. Just think how much violence there was in India during the war, in 1942. Yet in the North West Frontier Province,[37] in spite of all the cruelty and the oppression the British inflicted upon them, not one Pathan resorted to violence, though they, too, possess the instruments of violence. How do you explain that?"

Gandhiji replied:

> Nonviolence is not for cowards. It is for the brave, the courageous. And the Pathans are more brave and courageous than the Hindus. That is the reason why the Pathans were able to remain nonviolent.

Whenever I am at a prayer meeting in a Harijan[38] Colony, or in Sevagram,[39] or anywhere else, I always read from the Holy Quran. At Sevagram, a Japanese Buddhist youth used to chant from his holy scriptures. Then the Hindu prayers would begin. Gandhiji had the same respect for all religions, and he believed that they were all based on the same Truth. And that has always been my firm belief, too. I have studied both the Holy Quran and the *Bhagavat Gita* profoundly and reverently. . . .

My religion is truth, love, and service to God and humanity.

Every religion that has come into the world has brought the message of love and brotherhood. And those who are indifferent to the welfare of their fellowmen, those whose hearts are empty of love, those who do not know the meaning of brotherhood, those who harbor hatred and resentment in their hearts, they do not know the meaning of Religion.[40]

---

[37] A region of Pakistan.

[38] A word meaning "child of God" that Gandhi used to describe the Dalits, formerly referred to as untouchables.

[39] The village in Maharashtra where Gandhi's ashram was located in the latter years of his life.

[40] Narang, *My Life and Struggle*, 193–95.

On Revolution

A revolution is like a flood, it can bring blessings, but it can also bring devastation; it can bring fertility and prosperity, but it can also bring ruin. Only a nation that is wide awake, whose people are aware of themselves as a nation, where all live together as brothers, in harmony and love, only that nation, I tell you, will benefit by the revolution.

A revolution is like a flood. If the people are vigilant they will be ready for the flood and when it comes the whole nation will move along with it. And like the flood, when it subsides, it leaves fertile fields behind, so the revolution, when it is over, leaves the ground clear for the reconstruction of the nation. But if the people are asleep, indifferent to each other and indifferent to the country, the whole nation will be swept away by the flood, by the revolution when it comes. . . .

Therefore I want to impress this upon your minds: If you want your country and your people to prosper you must stop living for yourselves alone, you must start living for the community. That is the only way to prosperity and progress.[41]

---

[41] Ibid., 94–95.

Conclusion

The search for truth is essential to human experience and is a central concern of religion and philosophy. It is also the basis for social contestation and lies at the heart of law and politics. The quest is eternal and continues today with urgency as political leaders show contempt for the facts and ignore the findings of science even as the perils of doing so increase.

Globally people today are better educated and more informed than in the past, and they are demanding justice and respect for their rights as never before. The world has become a more contentious place, as indicated by the many civil society movements and resistance campaigns that have emerged in recent decades to challenge oppression and injustice. New social actors have entered the political stage, and they are challenging traditional power structures and interpretations of truth.[1] They are mobilizing to change policy and shape new norms and principles of behavior.[2]

Most of these political and social struggles are waged nonviolently, and many are settled to the mutual satisfaction of the parties. Conflict always exists and is a normal pattern in society as groups compete over rights and interests. Indeed conflict may be necessary at times and if waged nonviolently can be a constructive

---

[1] Moisés Naím, *The End of Power: From Boardrooms to Battlefields and Churches to States, Why Being in Charge Isn't What It Used to Be* (New York: Basic Books, 2013).

[2] Margaret Keck and Kathryn Sikkink, *Activists beyond Borders: Advocacy Networks in International Politics* (Ithaca, NY: Cornell University Press, 1998).

step toward challenging exploitive hierarchies. Social protest is often a catalyst for conflict transformation, a way of addressing social and political grievances and achieving a higher synthesis of truth through struggle and dialogue.[3] At times a veritable uprising of civil resistance may be necessary.[4] Disciplined strategic nonviolence has demonstrated enormous potential for settling social and political differences and transforming relationships to achieve progress, as the authors of this volume attest.

Nonetheless, many cling to the belief that violence and physical force are necessary to overcome injustice. In political science and the affairs of state, military might is still regarded as the ultimate arbiter, the foundation of political power. For many policy makers and scholars, the threat or use of armed force is considered the most important instrument of international policy. These beliefs persist despite empirical evidence and recent cases showing that war and the use of force often fail to achieve their intended political purposes or are counterproductive.[5] Nonmilitary tools of diplomacy and incentives-based bargaining can be effective means of resolving political disputes. Sustainable peace depends upon good governance, economic development, human rights, and citizen inclusion and participation, especially of women.[6] Around the world peacebuilding and development programs are proving the worth of these approaches, but they receive far less attention and support than military interventions.

---

[3] John Paul Lederach, *The Little Book of Conflict Transformation* (Intercourse, PA: Good Books, 2003).

[4] Mark Engler and Paul Engler, *This Is an Uprising: How Nonviolent Revolt Is Shaping the Twenty-First Century* (New York: Nation Books, 2016).

[5] Micah Zenko, *Between Threats and War: Discrete Military Operations in the Post-Cold War World*, Stanford Security Series (Stanford, CA: Stanford University Press, 2010); Christopher A. Preble, "Learning the Limits of American Military Power," *National Interest* May 20, 2016, https://nationalinterest.org.

[6] United Nations Development Programme, *Governance for Peace: Securing the Social Contract* (New York: United Nations Development Programme and Bureau for Crisis Prevention and Recovery, 2012).

Even in social movements, some activists think that violent methods are necessary. Antifa groups employ "physical confrontation" in the struggle against white supremacy. They come to demonstrations masked and wearing black, often looking for a fight. They clash not only with right-wing thugs but at times with the police. These militant protesters believe they are being tough and effective in countering neo-fascism, but their actions can have negative consequences.[7] Fighting and violence create images of mob mayhem and divert attention from the central concern for justice. They allow rightist groups to portray themselves as victims and peddle a false narrative of violence on the left. Destructive protest methods turn away people who otherwise agree with the goal of opposing white supremacy but do not want to endanger themselves or their families. As Deming, Chenoweth and Stephan, and many others have taught, movements for justice win when they attract a mass following and use effective means to seize and hold the moral high ground against their opponents.

The passages presented in this volume argue decisively against the use of violence. The authors show through courageous example, eloquent analysis, moral and religious teaching, and social science evidence that nonviolence is the preferable choice. In social struggles and in disputes between and within states, nonviolent approaches offer creative and effective options for overcoming injustice and oppression. Peaceful means are not only morally superior. They are the most effective way of creating positive change and striving for truth.

---

[7] Molly Wallace, "'Violent Flank Effects' and the Strategic Naiveté of Antifa," *Waging Nonviolence*, November 11, 2017, https://wagingnonviolence.org.

Index

Africa. *See* Ghana; South Africa
African National Congress (ANC), 147–49, 150, 157–58, 192
al Assad, Bashar, 144
Amos, Prophet, 42, 214
Amro, Issa, 181–82
Annan, Kofi, 90
Antifa groups, 245
apartheid
  global movement against, 148
  Mandela, embodying resistance to, 149, 150, 153, 155, 156
  Netanyahu, learning lessons from, 192–93
  Tutu, opposing apartheid regime, 154, 157–59
Appleby, Scott, 198
Augustine, Saint, 40, 199
Awad, Mubarak, 174–76, 177–81

Barber, William J., II, 216–17, 217–19
Barnett, Ross, 43
Baruch, Ilan, 186, 191–94
Ben Ali, Zine el Abidine, 141
Benedict XVI, Pope, 223
Bernhardt, Michael, 103–104
Bhatt, Shamal, 20
Boff, Leonardo
  background, 207–208
  on active nonviolence, 209–10, 212
  on cosmic democracy, 212–13
  Francis, inspired by, 220
  John Paul II, as criticized by, 226
  on love as subversive and transforming, 210–11
boycotts

Chavez on, 61–62
economic boycotts, 130
Gandhi, calling for, 56, 59–60
in Ghana, 147
Huerta, organizing boycott of table grapes, 63
Intifada, as a tactic used during, 174
King, advocating, 36, 138
moral shame, awakening in an opponent, 32
as nonviolent weapons, 59, 64
types of, 126
YAS, urging boycott of Israeli settlements, 182
British Raj, 1, 56
Buber, Martin, 40
Bunyan, John, 43
Butcher, Charles, 144

Câmara, Hélder, 209, 210
Camus, Albert, 82, 83–84, 85–88
Catholic Worker (newspaper), 66, 71, 73
Catholic Worker movement, 56, 69, 71–72
Catonsville Nine and DC 9 as aggressive groups, 106–107
Chaitin, Julia, 186–88, 188–91
Chavez, Cesar
  Catholic background, 57, 66
  fasts, holding for nonviolence, 65
  Gandhi, impressions of, 57–60
  King, homage to, 60–63
  male machismo, helping to overcome, 64
  nonviolent action, on the strange chemistry of, 93

247

Chavez, Cesar *(continued)*
  United Farm Workers, as co-leader, 56, 63
Chenoweth, Erica
  Major Episodes of Contention project, as head of, 140
  on movements for justice, 245
  nonviolent action, revolutionizing the study of, 122
  original research, updating, 138
  violence, on the limited use of, 142
  "Why Civil Resistance Works" essay, 134–36, 136–38
civil disobedience
  in Birmingham, 36
  civil resistance, necessity of, 244
  of Gandhi, 1, 59–60, 149
  Intifada, during, 174
  nonviolent action, as a tool of, 126
  satyagraha, civil resistance as an offshoot of
  "Why Civil Resistance Works" essay, 134–36, 136–38
  of Youth Against Settlements, 182
civil rights movement
  desegregation efforts in Birmingham, 36
  Emmett Till murder as generating support for, 145
  Heschel as a part of, 220–21
  labor activists, joining with civil rights leaders, 218
  legal and non-violent pressure, utilizing, 38
  nonviolent methods, employing, 64
  in Palestine, 177
  success of, 23, 47
  training of civil rights activists, points used for, 31–34
  Vietnam War as hindering efforts of, 48
communism
  Anti-Imperialist League, 68
  Camus, membership in Communist Party, 85
  Dorothy Day and, 69–70, 71
  John Paul II as anticommunist, 226
  King on, 34–35

Day, Dorothy, 66, 68–69, 69–71, 71–74
de Klerk, F. W., 154, 155, 193
Deming, Barbara
  background, 91–93
  changing minds and gaining supporters, 101–107
  moral high ground, on seizing, 245
  on revolution and equilibrium, 93–101
  on societal change through nonviolence, 120
Douglass, Frederick, 3–4, 217
Du Bois, W. E. B., 22

Erasmus, Desiderius, 199
Esquivel, Adolfo Pérez, 210
Evangelii Gaudium (Joy of the Gospel), 219–20

Fanon, Franz, 92, 93–95
Fellowship of Reconciliation, 75, 121, 204
feminist struggle to end oppression, 108–14
Fischer, Louis, 2, 57
Francis, Pope, 208, 219–20, 220–26
Francis of Assisi, Saint, 57, 72, 223
Frazier, E. Franklin, 29
Freire, Paolo, 113, 211
Friends. *See* Quakers

Gandhi, Mohandas K.
  as an inspiration
    African nations, admiring, 147, 148–50
    Castro as influenced by, 92–93
    Chavez, emulating, 56–57, 65
    Gandhi movement, 79–82
    King, as applying Gandhian methods, 22–24
  British officials, meeting with, 57–58

on converting the oppressor, 151
core of philosophy as *ahimsa*,
  10–12
on fighting as preferable to
  cowardice, 31–32
Gandhism, no such thing as, 21
home rule, goal of, 116
loyalty, prizing, 58
New Testament, as shaped by,
  19–20
nonviolence and
  boycotts as instruments of
    nonviolent change, 62
  compassion, on being moved
    to, 211
  nonviolence, defining, 4–7
  nonviolent resistance, 1, 33, 138
  Pathans, on their path of
    nonviolence, 239–40
  peace army, envisioning, 236
  Sharp, as codifying the
    Gandhian methods of
    nonviolence, 120–21
political change, spiritual stance
  toward, 17–18
religious beliefs, 2
salt march, 59
satyagraha, defining, 12–16, 96
social injustice, on the need to
  resist, 230
war, on the efforts to outlaw,
  7–10
Gaza Strip, 173, 174, 185, 186–90,
  192, 194, 196
Gbowee, Leymah, 224
Ghaffar, Abdul, 235–36, 237–40,
  241
Ghana, achieving independence
  with nonviolence, 146–47
Gottlieb, Lynn, 203–207, 231–32
Green Belt movement, 163, 164, 167
The Green Line, 184, 193, 196
Guardini, Romano, 68–69

Hamas (fundamentalist movement),
  188, 193–94
Hanh, Thich Nhat, 101
Harris, Terri, 200, 204
Hebron, occupation of, 181
Heschel, Abraham Joshua, 200–
  201, 201–202, 202–203
Hillel the elder, 206
Hinduism
  Gandhi, as influenced by, 18, 19,
    59, 240
  non-attachment concept in, 2, 85
  nonviolence as the root of
    Hinduism, 6
  Wahiduddin Khan on Hindu-
    Muslim relations, 230
hooks, bell, 107–108, 108–14
Hourton, Jorge, 212
Huerta, Dolores, 55–56, 63,
  64–66
Hugo, John, 72

India
  cow-slaughter, objection to, 7
  nonviolence, Gandhi on
    liberation for India through,
    17, 22, 56, 57–58, 120, 224,
    239–40
  political independence movement
    in, 1, 5–6, 23, 80, 82
  satyagrahis in India and South
    Africa, 150
  Wahiduddin on communal
    relations within, 230
  worship of arms as a cultural
    factor, 14
  See also Hinduism
Islam
  Catholic apology for calumny
    against Muslims, 226
  on dawah as the path of God,
    232
  jihad, correct understanding of,
    199, 231
  Khudai Khidmatgar as servants
    of God, 236
  patience as a cardinal virtue of,
    230
  Peace Primer, Muslim teachings
    in, 204
  peaceful activism, *hadith*
    inspiring, 234
  salaam, similarity to Jewish
    shalom, 198–99

Islam *(continued)*
  war, limited permission to engage in, 233
  See also Mohammed, Prophet
Israel
  Arab violence, fear of, 175
  Awad, deporting for civil disobedience, 174
  Gaza, bombing of, 187
  illegal settlements, YAS seeking to end, 181–83
  international community, disregarding, 176
  Israel-Gaza war, 186
  Israeli-Palestinian conflict, 190–91
  militarized society of, 168
  Netanyahu as Prime Minister, 192–94
  nonviolent resistance to Israeli policy, 194
  as a nuclear power, 173
  occupation of Palestinian land, 171, 172, 177–79
  Oslo accord, reneging on, 185
  Other Voice, Israeli citizens as members of, 189–90
  Palestinian national movement, repressing, 143
  two-state solution, not in favor of, 180
Israeli Defense Force (IDF), 177, 182, 184, 195–197

Jain tradition, 2
Jefferson, Thomas, 43, 44
Jesus Christ
  Christians, emulation of Jesus expected of, 159–60
  extremism and, 42–43
  love ethic of, 23, 29
  love of the enemy, encouraging, 2, 24–25, 199, 218
  nonviolence, teachings on, 28, 30, 78, 223
  as a peacemaker, 211
  peacemaking strategy of, 225
  the poor, on caring for, 214–15
  Sermon on the Mount, influence on Gandhi, 19–20

jihad, 199, 231
John Paul II, Pope, 226, 227–29
John XXIII, Saint, 221
Johnson, Lyndon, 47
Johnson, Mordecai, 23
Jubilee tradition, 214
Judaism
  calumny against Jews, John Paul II apologizing for, 226
  Heschel, building on Jewish tradition of piety, 200
  kavod ha-adam teaching on human dignity, 205
  mitzvot, performing to restore peace, 204
  rabbinic Judaism, preference for nonviolence, 206–207
  shalom, defining, 159, 198–99
just war doctrine, 199

Kennedy, John F., 50
Kennedy, Robert, 91
Khayyam, Omar, 53
Khudai Khidmatgar movement, 236, 238–39
King, Martin Luther, Jr.
  active nonviolence, demonstrating its viability, 210
  alliance between labor and social activists, calling for, 217, 218
  Arabic, works translated into, 174
  assassination of, 91
  Chavez and, 56–57
  "eye for an eye" retaliation, as against, 162
  Gandhian methods, applying, 22–24
  Ghana independence, celebrating, 147
  Heschel, joining forces with, 201, 202–203
  homage to, 60–63, 154
  just ends, achieving by just means, 34–35
  "Letter from a Birmingham Jail," 36–45
  "Loving Your Enemies" excerpts, 25–31

nonviolence, on the six elements of, 31–34
nonviolent resistance, engaging in, 137
Palestine, applying techniques in, 179
Poor People's Campaign, continuing King's work, 216
as proven right, 138–45, 156–57
as a realistic pacifist, 54
Riverside Church address, 47–53
"Where Do We Go From Here?" speech, 45–47

Laudato Si' (Praise to thee), 208, 220
Lebanon, occupation of, 177, 185, 186, 194, 195
Leo XIII, Pope, 227
Levy, Jacques, 57
liberation theology, 207, 211–12, 226
Lincoln, Abraham, 43
love for the enemy, 25, 28–29, 30, 42, 72, 199, 223–24
Luther, Martin, 43
Luthuli, Albert, 154

Maathai, Wangari, 162–65, 165–67
Magnificat (Song of Mary), 214
Mandela, Nelson
  Africa Peace Award, receiving, 152–53
  ANC, founding, 147–49
  on global peace, 151–52
  Long March to Freedom excerpts, 149–50
  Nobel Peace Prize, accepting, 154–57
  release from prison, 193
  as a role model, 162, 179
  Satyagraha Centenary Conference, message to, 150–51
March for Our Lives anti-gun movement, xii–xiii
Marxism, 86, 226, 227
Maurin, Peter, 66, 69
Meredith, James, 44
#MeToo movement, 91
mística of nonviolence, 210, 212

Mohammed, Prophet
  on defensive fighting, 233–24
  on God as peace, 232
  jihad, teachings on, 199, 231
  patience as the weapon of, 236
  peaceful methods, using over violent struggle, 235
  on pleasing God, 230
Moral Mondays movement, 216
Muste, Abraham Johannes (A.J.)
  air raid drills, publicly disobeying, 71
  Camus, citing essay of, 56, 82, 83–84
  on the Gandhi Movement, 79–82
  Nonviolence in an Aggressive World, 75–79
  Sharp, as personal secretary to, 121

NAVCO Data Project on nonviolent resistance, 140
Nehru, Jawaharlal, 120
Netanyahu, Benjamin, 192–93
Niebuhr, Reinhold, 38, 45
Nietzsche, Friedrich, 25, 46–47
Nkrumah, Kwame, 147
Nobel Peace Prize, 147, 154–57, 163, 165
nonviolence
  active nonviolence, 170, 173, 209–12, 221, 225
  adversaries, winning as friends, 217–18
  Boff, on resisting various forms of violence, 208–209
  creative options for, 245
  Deming on the power of, 92–93, 94–101
  ends and means of nonviolent resistance, 34–35
  farmworkers, nonviolent stance of, 63–65
  Francis on the cultivation of, 221–22
  Gandhi, teachings on, 1, 4–7, 57, 59, 62, 79–82, 120
  injustice, on breaking the chain of, 223–24

nonviolence *(continued)*
  Intifada, practicing nonviolence during, 174–76, 177–81
  King, advocating for, 22–24, 36–38, 42, 49, 53, 60
  in Latin America, 208–13
  lessons learned from employing, 141
  maternal nonviolence, cultivation of, 115–19
  moral authority and, 161
  Muste, as influence on nonviolent activism, 75
  noncooperation as assertive and constructive, 97
  nonviolent peace stewardship, 204–205, 206
  Palestine, nonviolent strategies employed in, 168
  the poor, nonviolent struggle of, 61, 62
  religious motivation for engaging in, 2, 56–57, 66, 172, 198
  satyagraha as, 96
  Sharp, codifying strategic principles of, 121–22, 126, 130
  six elements of, 31–34
  women as peacemakers, 90–91, 169–74
  after World War I, 7–10
  See also nonviolent resistance; pacifism
Nonviolence and Just Peace Conference, 220
nonviolent resistance
  ANC, adopting methods of, 149
  brutal repression, effect on, 143–44
  civil resistance, effectiveness of, 136–38
  cowards, not a method for, 31–32
  critics of, 138–39
  Deming as analyzing, 92–93
  fall of communism in Poland and, 226
  internal violence of the spirit, avoiding, 33
  to Israeli policy, 194
  Issa Amro, urging campaigns of, 181–82
  "Letter from a Birmingham Jail" on the power of, 36
  Major Episodes of Contention project, analyzing, 140
  Nehru, accepting the method of, 120
  nonviolent anti-colonial resistance as positive action, 147
  in Palestine, 173, 174–76
  Pashtuns, nonviolent resistance of, 235–40
  suffering, accepting without retaliation, 34

Ofir, Adi, 195–96
Other Voice group, 188–90

Pacem in Terris encyclical, 211
pacifism
  absolute pacifists, as withdrawing from the world, 230
  Awad, pacifist upbringing of, 174
  Dorothy Day and pacifism against war, 71–74
  early Christians as strict pacifists, 199
  Gandhi, pacifists learning from, 80, 82
  justice, on achieving through nonviolence, 79
  King as a realistic pacifist, 54
  misconceptions, 137
  religious pacifists, 2, 55, 169
  of Sharp, 121
  See also peace
Palestine
  first and second Intifada, 144, 174, 177, 180, 185, 186
  Israelis, common future with, 171–72
  Lebanon war, effect on, 177, 185, 186, 194–95
  Negrev region, attacks on, 186–88
  Palestinian suffering, 175–76
  peace, convincing Israeli public on the benefits of, 178–79

principled nonviolence *vs.* strategic nonviolence, distinguishing between, 179–80
Quaker presence in, 169
West Bank occupation, 168, 173, 174, 184, 190, 192, 194, 196
YAS, nonviolent direct action of, 181–86
Palestine Liberation Organization (PLO), 182–83
Palestinian Centre for the Study of Nonviolence, 174
passive resistance, 12–13, 16, 18–19, 32
Paul VI, Pope, 221
peace
  2017 World Day of Peace message, 220–26
  Africa Peace Award, 152–53
  Christians as peacemakers, 159–60
  development as another name for peace, 229
  Francis on social equality and peace, 219–20
  Jesus Christ as a peacemaker, 199, 211, 223, 225
  JFK on peaceful revolution, 50
  justice and, 91, 149, 158–59, 162, 168, 169–70, 173, 212, 219–20, 225
  King, speaking for peace in Vietnam, 53
  Mandela on global peace, 151–52
  mística of gospel-based peace, 212
  Nobel Peace Prize, 147, 154–57, 163, 165
  patience as a peaceful response, 230
  Peace Now organization, 184–85
  peaceful means as morally superior, 245
  shalom as a Jewish practice of peace, 159, 198–99, 204–206, 207
  ubuntu as an African term for peace, 146
  Wahiduddin on peace in Islamic teachings, 231–35
  women, as contributing to peacemaking, 89–90
Pearlman, Wendy, 143
Persian Gulf War, 228
the poor
  biblical references to, 213–16
  Dorothy Day as affiliated with, 68–69
  houses of hospitality, making available to, 66, 74
  nonviolent efforts of, 61, 62
  realistic opportunities, providing with, 229
  war as the enemy of the poor, 48–50
Poor People's Campaign, 216

Quakers, 55, 81, 169, 199

Rabin, Yitzhak, letters to, 195–197
racial justice, 23, 29, 30, 32, 42, 55, 75, 204
Rawls, John, 55
Rerum Novarum encyclical, 227
Reuther, Walter, 46
revolutionary violence, 208, 209
Ruddick, Sara, 114–15, 115–19

Sabeel theology center, 169
Sandino, Augusto César, 68
satyagraha, 2–3, 5, 12–16, 16–17, 96, 150–51
Schock, Kurt, 142
Sehested, Ken, 204
Sermon on the Mount, 2, 19–20, 59, 72, 215, 225
Sevagram ashram, 240
Shahid, Waleed, 177
shalom (peace), 159, 198–99, 204–207
Sharp, Gene
  Arabic, works translated into, 174
  creative potential of nonviolent resistance, 139
  nonviolent action, codifying, 120–21
  peace studies, as a classic author on, 89

Sharp, Gene *(continued)*
  pillars of power, undermining, 130–31
  on power and obedience, 127–29
  on pre-Gandhi examples of nonviolence, 1
  repression, how to deal with, 131–34
  strategy, on the key principles of, 122–25
  tactics and methods, utilizing, 125–27
Sharpeville massacre, 148
Shutte, Augustine, 146
Smuts, Jan Christian, 19
social justice, 24, 55–57, 63, 66, 82, 146, 149, 158, 162–63, 213, 217, 226
South Africa
  apartheid regime, 148, 153, 156, 158, 192–94
  Gandhi in, 120, 148, 150, 152
  Mandela as head of, 149, 154–57
  racial restrictions on Asians, 1, 22
  satyagraha in, 2, 12–13, 19
  Tutu, on joining the struggle for a new South Africa, 160–61
South African Council of Churches (SACC), 157, 158
Spellman, Francis Cardinal, 73, 74
Stephan, Maria J., 122, 134–36, 136–38, 138–45
suffering
  collective punishment and, 196, 237
  endurance of, 30–31, 174
  freedom, suffering as the price of, 17
  humiliation as causing, 150
  non-retaliation for, 33, 34
  nonviolent action method, as a reality of, 3–4, 5
  of nonviolent volunteers, 132–33
  pacifists, sacrificial suffering of, 79
  of the Palestinian people, 176
  of piecemeal violence, 222
  retribution, demanding in the midst of war, 187
  of South African *satyagrahis,* 13
Sutton, Jonathan, 144
Svensson, Isak, 144

Tambo, Oliver, 149
Thomas Aquinas, Saint, 40
Till, Emmett, 145
Tillich, Paul, 40
Tolstoy, Leo, 20
Toynbee, Arnold, 52–53
Tutu, Desmond, 154, 157–58, 158–62

United Farm Workers of America (UFW), 56, 63

Vietnam War
  "Beyond Vietnam" essay by King, 47–53
  Clergy and Laymen Concerned About Vietnam, 48, 201
  Dorothy Day, opposing, 56, 71, 73–74
  Heschel, moral revulsion for, 202–203
  My Lai massacre, insights received from, 103
  National Mobilization Committee to End the Vietnam War, 75
  Tet Offensive, as a turning point for political opposition to, 92

Wahiduddin, Maulana, 229–31, 232–34, 234–35
Wallace, George, 43
Wallis, Jim, 213–16
Women's March movement, 90–91
The Wretched of the Earth (Fanon), 92, 94–95

Yesh G'vul movement, 186, 194–97
Young, Andrew, 54–55
Youth Against Settlements (YAS), 181–83

Zaru, Jean, 169–74